Toward a Critical Politics
of Teacher Thinking

Critical Studies in Education and Culture Series

Education under Siege: The Conservative, Liberal and Radical Debate over Schooling
Stanley Aronowitz and Henry A. Giroux

Literacy: Reading the Word and the World
Paulo Freire and Donaldo Macedo

The Moral and Spiritual Crisis in Education: A Curriculum for Justice and Compassion
David Purpel

The Politics of Education: Culture, Power and Liberation
Paulo Freire

Popular Culture, Schooling and the Language of Everyday Life
Henry A. Giroux and Roger I. Simon

Teachers As Intellectuals: Toward a Critical Pedagogy of Learning
Henry A. Giroux

Women Teaching for Change: Gender, Class and Power
Kathleen Weiler

Between Capitalism and Democracy: Educational Policy and the Crisis of the
Welfare State
Svi Shapiro

Critical Psychology and Pedagogy: Interpretation of the Personal World
Edmund Sullivan

Pedagogy and the Struggle for Voice: Issues of Language, Power, and Schooling for
Puerto Ricans
Catherine E. Walsh

Learning Work: A Critical Pedagogy of Work Education
Roger I. Simon, Don Dippo, and Arleen Schenke

Cultural Pedagogy: Art/Education/Politics
David Trend

Raising Curtains on Education: Drama as a Site for Critical Pedagogy
Clar Doyle

Toward a Critical Politics of Teacher Thinking

MAPPING THE POSTMODERN

Joe L. Kincheloe

Critical Studies in Education & Culture Series
Edited by Henry A. Giroux and Paulo Freire

BERGIN & GARVEY
Westport, Connecticut • London

Library of Congress Cataloging-in-Publication Data

Kincheloe, Joe L.
    Toward a critical politics of teacher thinking : mapping the
Postmodern / Joe L. Kincheloe.
        p.   cm.—(Critical studies in education & culture series,
ISSN 1064–8615)
    Includes bibliographical references and index.
    ISBN 0–89789–270–4.—ISBN 0–89789–271–2 (pbk. ; alk. paper)
    1. Critical pedagogy. 2. Thought and thinking. 3. Teachers—
Training of. 4. Educational change. I. Title.   II. Series:
Critical studies in education and culture series.
LC196.K56   1993
370.11′5—dc20   92–32181

British Library Cataloguing in Publication Data is available.

Library of Congress Catalog Card Number: 92–32181
ISBN: hb 0–89789–270–4; pbk 0–89789–271–2
ISSN: 1064–8615

First published in 1993

Bergin & Garvey, 88 Post Road West, Westport, Connecticut 06881
An imprint of Greenwood Publishing Group, Inc.

Printed in the United States of America

The paper used in this book complies with the
Permanent Paper Standard issued by the National
Information Standards Organization (Z39.48–1984).

10 9 8 7 6 5 4 3 2 1

To Henry Giroux and Peter McLaren

Contents

Series Foreword   ix

Acknowledgments   xiii

Chapter 1   Modernism and the Cognitive Passivity of Technical Teacher Education   1

Chapter 2   Rumblings of Empowerment   17

Chapter 3   The Politics of Thinking   39

Chapter 4   The Escape from the Politics of Modernist Thinking   59

Chapter 5   Mr. Huxley's Neighborhood: Can You Spell Postmodernism?   83

Chapter 6   Critical Constructivism   107

Chapter 7   Contextualizing Cognitive Development   125

Chapter 8   The Nature of Post-Formal Thinking   145

Chapter 9   Action Research, Educational Reform, and Teacher Thinking   175

Chapter 10   Reframing the Debate about Teacher Education   195

Chapter 11   Preparing the Post-Formal Practitioner   213

Bibliography   233

Name Index   247

Subject Index   251

Series Foreword

Within the last decade the debate over defining the meaning and purpose of education has occupied the center of political and social life in the United States. Dominated largely by an aggressive and ongoing attempt by various sectors of the political Right, including "fundamentalists," nationalists, and political conservatives, the debate over educational policy has been organized around a set of values and practices that take as their paradigmatic model the laws and ideology of the marketplace and the imperatives of a newly emerging cultural traditionalism. In the first instance, schooling is being redefined through a corporate ideology which stresses the primacy of choice over community, competition over cooperation, and excellence over equity. At stake here is the imperative to organize public schooling around the related practices of competition, reprivatization, standardization, and individualism.

In the second instance, the New Right has waged a cultural war against schools as part of a wider attempt to contest the emergence of new public cultures and social movements that have begun to demand that schools take seriously the imperatives of living in a multiracial and multicultural democracy. The contours of this cultural offensive are evident in the call by the Right for standardized testing, the rejection of multiculturalism, and the development of curricula around what is called, euphemistically, a "common culture." In this perspective, the notion of a common culture serves as a referent to denounce any attempt by subordinate groups to challenge the narrow ideological and political parameters by which such a culture both defines and expresses itself. It is not too surprising that the theoretical and political distance between defining schools around a common culture and denouncing cultural difference as the enemy of democratic life is relatively short indeed.

This debate is important not simply because it makes visible the role that schools play as sites of political and cultural contestation, but because it is within this debate that the notion of the United States as an open and democratic society is being questioned and redefined. Moreover, this debate provides a challenge to progressive educators both in and outside of the United States to address a number of conditions central to a postmodern world. First, public schools cannot be seen as either objective or neutral. As institutions actively involved in constructing political subjects and presupposing a vision of the future, they must be dealt with in terms that are simultaneously historical, critical, and transformative. Second, the relationship between knowledge and power in schools places undue emphasis on disciplinary structures and on individual achievement as the primary unit of value. Critical educators need a language that emphasizes how social identities are constructed within unequal relations of power in the schools and how schooling can be organized through interdisciplinary approaches to learning and cultural differences that address the dialectical and multifaceted experiences of everyday life. Third, the existing cultural transformation of the United States into a multiracial and multicultural society structured in multiple relations of domination demands that we address how schooling can become sites for cultural democracy rather than channeling colonies reproducing new forms of nativism and racism. Finally, critical educators need a new language that takes seriously the relationship between democracy and the establishment of those teaching and learning conditions that enable forms of self and social determination in students and teachers. This suggests not only new forms of self-definition for human agency, it also points to redistributing power within the school and between the school and the larger society.

Critical Studies in Education and Culture is intended as both a critique and a positive response to these concerns and the debates from which they emerge. Each volume is intended to address the meaning of schooling as a form of cultural politics, and cultural work as a pedagogical practice that serves to deepen and extend the possibilities of democratic public life. Broadly conceived, some central considerations present themselves as defining concerns of the series. Within the last decade, a number of new theoretical discourses and vocabularies have emerged which challenge the narrow disciplinary boundaries and theoretical parameters that construct the traditional relationship among knowledge, power, and schooling. The emerging discourses of feminism, post-colonialism, literary studies, cultural studies, and post-modernism have broadened our understanding of how schools work as sites of containment and possibility. No longer content to view schools as objective institutions engaged in the transmission of an unproblematic cultural heritage, the new discourses illuminate how schools function as cultural sites actively engaged in the production of not only knowledge but also social identities. This series attempts to encourage this type of analysis by emphasizing how schools might be addressed as border institutions or sites of crossing actively involved in exploring, reworking, and translating the ways in which culture is produced, negotiated, and rewritten.

Emphasizing the centrality of politics, culture, and power, *Critical Studies in Education and Culture* deals with pedagogical issues that contribute in novel ways to our understanding of how critical knowledge, democratic values, and social practices can provide a basis for teachers, students, and other cultural workers to redefine their role as engaged and public intellectuals.

As part of a broader attempt to rewrite and refigure the relationship between education and culture, *Critical Studies in Education and Culture* is interested in work that is interdisciplinary, critical, and addresses the emergent discourses on gender, race, sexual preference, class, ethnicity, and technology. In this respect, the series is dedicated to opening inventive discursive and public spaces for critical interventions into schools and other pedagogical sites. To accomplish this, each volume attempts to rethink the relationship between language and experience, pedagogy and human agency, and ethics and social responsibility as part of a larger project for engaging and deepening the prospects of democratic schooling in a multiracial and multicultural society. Concerns central to this series include addressing the political economy and deconstruction of visual, aural, and printed texts, issues of difference and multiculturalism, relationships between language and power, pedagogy as a form of cultural politics, and historical memory and the construction of identity and subjectivity.

Critical Studies in Education and Culture is dedicated to publishing studies that move beyond the boundaries of traditional and existing critical discourses. It is concerned with making public schooling a central expression of democratic culture. In doing so it emphasizes works that combine cultural politics, pedagogical criticism, and social analyses with self-reflective tactics that challenge and transform those configurations of power that characterize the existing system of education and other public cultures.

Henry A. Giroux

Acknowledgments

I would like to thank Ian for his intellectual encouragement, Meghann for her athletic support, Chaim for the male bonding, and Bronwyn for her waggish post-formality. Special thanks are in order for Kudra (who was with me throughout the process) and Juno. Justice would dictate that Shirley Steinberg be listed as a coauthor; not only did she rewrite, inspire, criticize, comfort, and chastise, but she typed most of the book. Her love is the foundation.

Toward a Critical Politics
of Teacher Thinking

Chapter 1

Modernism and the Cognitive Passivity of Technical Teacher Education

This book is about teacher thinking. To consider this topic, however, we must set the stage on the terrain of culture, the history of ideas. Thus, the analysis of teacher thinking is a study of cultural context, of power relations—in other words, politics. Too often, studies of teacher thinking offer little more than abstract taxonomies or stage theories to be learned by students in teacher education programs. My attempt in this work is to contextualize teacher thinking, to examine the social and historical forces that have shaped it, and to understand who benefits and who is punished when it is defined in particular ways. Such historicization will provide a grounding for the effort to break free from these constraints. The freedom achieved will allow teachers the perspectives to reconceptualize their profession in a manner consistent with the ideals of democracy and the dignity of the profession itself. Such a reconceptualization will be both nurtured and extended by new forms of practitioner thinking that transcend the blinders of traditional scientific "ways of seeing."

THE ADVENT OF MODERNISM

During the Middle Ages science was grounded on a Thomist–Aristotelian synthesis of faith and reason. The main goal of the synthesis was to understand the nature of natural phenomena. But when the Black Death swept across Europe, killing about one-fourth of the population, many realized that the medieval way of seeing was inadequate. Under the pressure of such catastrophic sickness, Western scholars began contemplating a new way of perceiving the natural world—a way that would enable them to understand and control the outside world (Fosnot 1988, 2; Kincheloe, Steinberg, and Tippins 1992; Leshan and Margenau 1982, 30–31).

With the coming of the Scientific Revolution, or the Age of Reason, in the sixteenth and seventeenth centuries, nature was to be controlled, "bound into service and made a slave" (Capra 1982, 56). The basis of this control was founded on the epistemological separation of knower and known. This bifurcation legitimates the assumption that the human perceiver occupies no space in the known cosmos; existing outside of history, the knower knows the world objectively. Thus, knowers are untainted by the world of opinions, perspectives, or values. Operating objectively (without bias), the knower sets out on the neutral mission of science—the application of abstract reasoning to the understanding of the natural environment. Reason told the pioneers of science that complex phenomena of the world can be best understood by reducing them to their constituent parts and then piecing these elements back together according to laws of cause–effect (Kincheloe 1991, 27; Mahoney and Lyddon 1988, 192).

All of this took place within René Decartes' separation of mind and matter, his *"cognito, ergo sum."* This view led to a conception of the world as a mechanical system divided into two distinct realms: (1) an internal world of sensation; and (2) an objective world composed of natural phenomena. Building on the Cartesian dualism, scientists argued that laws of physical and social systems could be uncovered objectively by researchers operating in isolation from human perception with no connection to the act of perceiving. The internal world of mind and the physical world, Decartes theorized, were forever separate and one could never be shown to be a form of the other (Lavine 1984, 125; Lowe 1982, 163; Kincheloe 1991, 27). We understand now, but could not have understood then, that this division of mind and matter had profound and unfortunate consequences. The culture's ability to address problems like the Plague undoubtedly improved, as our power to control the "outside" world advanced. At the same time, however, Western society accomplished very little in the attempt to comprehend our own consciousness, our "inner experience" (Leshan and Margenau 1982, 31).

Sir Isaac Newton extended Decartes's theories with his description of space and time as absolute regardless of context. Clarifying the concept of cause and effect, Newton established modernism's tenet that the future of any aspect of a system could be predicted with absolute certainty if its condition was understood in precise detail and the appropriate tools of measurement were employed. Thus, the Cartesian–Newtonian concept of scientific modernism was established with its centralization, concentration, accumulation, efficiency, and fragmentation. Bigger became better as the dualistic way of seeing reinforced a rationalistic patriarchal expansionist social and political order welded to the desire for power and conquest. Such a way of seeing served to despiritualize and dehumanize, as it focused attention on concerns other than the sanctity of humanity (Fosnot 1988, 3).

Along with Sir Francis Bacon, who established the supremacy of reason over imagination, Descartes and Newton laid a foundation that allowed science and technology to change the world. Commerce increased, nationalism grew, human labor was measured in terms of productivity, nature was dominated, and European civilization gained the power to conquer in a way previously unimagined. The rise of modernist science was closely followed by a decline in the importance of religion and spirituality. An obsession with progress supplied new objectives and values to fill the vacuum left by the loss of religious faith. Even familial ties were severed as the new order shifted its allegiance to the impersonal concerns of commerce, industry, and bureaucracy (Aronowitz and Giroux 1991, 57; Bohm and Peat 1987, 109–10). Rationality was deified, and around the scientific pantheon the credo of modernity was developed: The world is rational (logocentric) and there is only one meaning of the term. All natural phenomena can be painted within the frame of this monolithic rationality whether we are studying gunpowder, engines, dreams, or learning (Kincheloe, Steinberg, and Tippins 1992).

ONE-TRUTH EPISTEMOLOGY AND EDUCATION

This modernist view of knowledge, this one-truth epistemology affected all aspects of Western life, all institutions. Education was no exception. Since knowledge (like a child's conception of pre-Columbian North America) is predefined waiting to be discovered "out there," what use is it to teach speculative and interpretive strategies? Schools of the post-Enlightenment era emphasized not the *production* of knowledge but the learning of that which had already been defined as knowledge. Students of modernism's one-truth epistemology are treated like one-trick ponies, rewarded only for short-term retention of certified truths. Teachers learn in their "educational science" courses that knowledge is acquired in a linear skill or subskill process. Preidentified in the context of adult logic, the linear process is imposed on children in a manner that focuses teacher/parent attention away from the child's constructions of reality, away from the child's point of view. Thus, children's answers are often "wrong," when actually, given their point of view, the wrong answer may indicate ingenuity (Brooks 1984, 24).

Even though it may blind us to various aspects of the social world, this one-truth epistemology of modernism has held and still holds great appeal. Seduced by its claim to neutrality, scientists and educators employ Cartesian–Newtonian epistemology in their quest for the "higher ground" of unbiased truth. The ideal modernist educator becomes the detached practitioner, an independent operator who rises above the values of "special interests." The detached practitioner occupies a secure position immune from critique—he or she has, after all, employed the correct methodology in reaching his or her position. If pursued "correctly," there is no questioning the authority of the scientific method. Thus, the educational status quo is protected from critics, such as John Dewey, Paulo Freire, or Maxine Greene, with their "agenda" and value judgments. Their critiques are not scientific; they are "mere opinions" (Codd 1984, 10; Harris 1984, 43).

The Reagan–Bush era witnessed a reconfirmation of modernism's one-truth epistemology. Reacting to the threats of social change and the critique of those concerned with the underside of modernism, mainstream conservatives and liberal educators sought educational solutions within Cartesian–Newtonian boundaries. Spurred by the Reagan–Bush reforms, state after state adopted technocratic reform packages emphasizing modernist scientific testing and evaluation procedures and standardized curricula.

There seems to be a consistency to the state reforms that revolves around the assumption that teaching, learning, and thinking are generic—that, like polyester stretch pants, one style, one size fits all. Teaching practices that are not teacher-directed or do not hold knowledge transference as a primary goal do not fit into the reform schemes. Teachers who are concerned with improving student thinking skills, who attempt to connect schooling with life, who value the knowledge that students bring with them to school, or who take seriously the cultivation of civic courage and citizenship cannot be evaluated until they conform to the vision of teaching tacitly embedded in the reform proposals. Only learning outcomes that can be measured by standardized tests or teachers behaviors that lend themselves to quantification, such as time-on-task measurements, count in the assessment of a teacher. Pedagogical dimensions such as a teacher's knowledge of content or a teacher's understanding of the knowledge that is produced when student experience collides with the concerns of the subject matter disciplines are irrelevant—inadmissable evidence in the teacher's attempt to prove self-worth as a professional.

The reforms require not only direct instruction by the teacher but a narrow academic focus, drill and recitation, little student choice of activities and materials, large group as opposed to small group instruction, truncated exploration of conceptual knowledge, and an emphasis on convergent questions with short *correct* answers. Such strategies privilege a fragmented, unconnected form of thinking that tends to match Piaget's description of concrete cognition. Undoubtedly, it is easy to measure whether students have "mastered" this type of thinking and it is hard for school leaders to resist the facile, commonsense justifications that play so well in the media and the political arena. The only problem with such a pedagogy is that it does not challenge students with anything significant; it trivializes education, rendering it a meaningless game, a fatuous rite of passage into adulthood (Jones and Cooper 1987, 1–4).

A GNAWING DISCOMFORT WITH MODERNISM

Individuals and groups from all segments of the culture have expressed discomfort with modernism. From fundamentalist Christians to advocates of a postmodern critique, the continuum of antimodernists takes in a variety of assumptions and perspectives. Fundamentalists attack modernism from a premodernist perspective, asserting that the one-truth epistemology of science has excluded God and religious ways of knowing. Postmodern analysts question the modernist view of what knowledge is, where it comes from, and the human role in its production.

Postmodern thought subjects to analysis social and education forms previously shielded by the modernist ethos. It admits to the cultural conversation previously forbidden evidence derived from new questions asked by previously excluded voices. Postmodern thinkers challenge hierarchical structures of knowledge and power which promote "experts" above the "masses," as they seek new ways of knowing that transcend empirically verified facts and "reasonable," linear arguments deployed in the quest for certainty (Greene 1988, 126; Hebridge 1989, 226). When postmodernism is grounded on a critical system of meaning that is concerned with questioning knowledge for the purpose of understanding more critically oneself and one's relation to society, naming and then changing social situations that impede the development of egalitarian, democratic communities marked by a commitment to economic and social justice, and contextualizing historically how world views and self-concepts come to be constructed, postmodernism becomes a powerful tool for progressive social change (Kincheloe, Steinberg, and Tippins 1992; Kincheloe 1991; Giroux 1988a, 1991).

Please do not confuse what I have just described, postmodernism as critique, with postmodernism as social condition. Though the two are intimately connected, this is the point where many individuals become lost on the postmodern linguistic landscape. Jean-François Lyotard uses postmodernism to refer to the general condition of contemporary Western civilization. The "grand narratives of legitimation" (i.e., all-encompassing explanations of history like the Enlightenment story of the inevitable victory of reason and freedom) in the postmodern world are no longer believable. They fail to understand their own construction by social and historical forces. Reason is undermined because of its co-option by those in power who speak with the authority of a science not subjected to introspection, to self-analysis (Giroux 1991, 19–20). Thus, the postmodern condition has arisen from a world created by modernism; the postmodern critique attempts to take us beyond the nihilism of the modern world, the deadening routine of the traditional school.

A critical postmodern analysis will be applied to education and teacher thinking throughout this book. Part of my task will be to employ postmodern modes of deconstruction to expose the caricature of certainty offered by modernist institutions, education in particular. Contemporary visions of education and educational reform often employ a Cartesian–Newtonian conception of linear, cause–effect logic. Thinking and the teaching act are viewed as an English sentence, subject acting on object. Postmodernism denies this simplistic view of reality, contending that often in a classroom (and in life) numerous events act on one another simultaneously. For example, consider a fight between two fourth-grade students. Teachers know that it is often impossible to determine who instigated the fight, that is, to determine linear cause–effect. Another common experience of nonlinearity is dreaming. Our dreams may consist of a plethora of images appearing to us simultaneously, but in our telling we transform them into lines of narrative sequence. Such a sequence represents a *distortion* of the "truth" of the dream. The tendency is common in our lived worlds.

Here we confront a significant aspect of the postmodern critique in language as a reservoir of unexamined cultural and political assumptions. Indo-European languages, for example, confine us to particular ways of thinking. They often fragment experience by devaluing *relationship*. Because of their subject-predicate matrix, these languages induce us to consider the world in terms of linear cause–effect. Trapped in the view of language as a neutral medium of communication, modernist thinkers have found it hard to talk (or think) about subjects such as quantum physics, the nature of consciousness, higher orders of cognition, or any other concept without identifiable boundaries, specified beginnings and ends, and a clear delineation of then and now. Postmodern critique attempts to denaturalize the modernist universalization of Indo-European linquistics. Pointing to the fact that events in nature often have simultaneous multiple causes, postmodernists argue that not all human languages have difficulty with nonlinearity. Hopi and Chinese, for example, speak "nonlinearity." Westerners from ancient Greece to modern America say *"the lightflashed"* even if the light and the flash are inseparable. If we spoke Hopi, we would simply say, *"Reh-pi,"* meaning "flash" (Ferguson 1980, 106, 149). No linearity, no cause nor effect is implied. Postmodernism offers an alternative to modernism, a starting place in our attempt to formulate new forms of teacher thinking—forms that allow us to see what is now eclipsed by the modernist moon.

MODERNIST BARRICADES: THE TAMING OF THE PEDAGOGICAL IMAGINATION

Before we can consider the postmodern critique in detail, we must study the etymology of educational modernism. Undoubedly modernist concerns with the development of a rational and controlled social order influenced the common school crusade of the 1840s and the subsequent development of public schools and normal schools for teacher training in the rest of the nineteenth century. Still, modernism's greatest assault on the institution of schooling came with the infusion of hyper-rational management strategies into conceptions of pedagogy around the turn of the twentieth century.

Scientific management influenced schooling to such an extent that power relations between administrators, teachers, and students were profoundly affected. When behavioral psychology was added to the pedagogical recipe, teachers began to be seen more and more as entities to be controlled and manipulated. In the spirit of the times Edward Thorndike announced that the human mind is an exacting instrument given to precise measurement. Teachers, he concluded, are not capable of such measurement, and therefore the formulation of instructional strategies and curriculum development should be left to experienced psychologists. It is no surprise that the behaviorists soon won the battle for the soul of the school, shaping its ambience with their control of instructional design (Popkewitz 1987, 498).

Though subsequent decades have witnessed an evolving sophistication of their strategies, the forces of efficiency, productivity, and scientific management unleashed by Taylor and Thorndike have helped shape the twentieth century. Efficiency, productivity, science, and technology have achieved almost godlike status on the twentieth-century modernist landscape. The daily lives of educators attest to the power of the forces, as teachers teach subject matter that has been broken into an ordered sequence of separate tasks and "factoids." Trained to follow a pretest, drill work, posttest instructional model, teachers efficiently follow a scientific pedagogy that has insidiously embedded itself as part of their "cultural logic"—a logic which serves to tame their pedagogical imagination. No thought is necessary, it's just common sense to assume that if one wants to teach somebody something, you simply break the information into separate pieces, go over the pieces until the learner has mastered them, then test him or her to make sure the pieces have been "learned" (Goodman 1986, 22).

In other words, teachers have internalized as common sense a professional approach that breaks the complex task of teaching into a series of simple steps that even unskilled laborers can perform—that is, they have been *deskilled*. As Taylor put it to one of his workers: "[You're] not supposed to think; there are other people paid for thinking around here" (Wirth 1983, 12). The need for the judgment of the worker would be eliminated in Taylor's system. The deskilling of teaching was thus rationalized; the conception of the pedagogical act was separated from its execution. Teachers did not need to learn the intricacies of subject matter, nor did they need to understand the sociohistorical context in which the knowledge to be taught was produced. All they needed to do was to identify the subject matter to be transferred to the learner, break it into components, present it to the student, and test him or her on it. It was a strategy as right as rain, so commonsensical it defied the need for justification.

A brief examination of the teacher manuals that accompany reading textbooks documents the progressive deskilling of teachers. In the 1920s small manuals contained brief professional discussions and bibliographies for students. The pamphlets emphasized the teaching of reading. Fifty years later the manuals had added scores of pages which included complete scripts (about four pages per day) specifying exactly what teachers were to say, where to stand as they said it, and how to test and evaluate their students. The manuals of the 1970s were not as concerned with the teaching of reading as they were with the teaching of specific skills needed on standardized tests (Popkewitz 1987, 498).

It seems obvious what has happened here. The scientific management of teaching with its accompanying deskilling has initiated a vicious circle of harm to the profession. As teachers were deskilled they lost more and more autonomy. As they became accustomed to the loss of autonomy, it was argued that they were incapable of self-direction. While in no way romanticizing work conditions for nineteenth- and early twentieth-century teachers, contemporary teachers are subjected to forms of control unimagined by older teachers. Teacher education often serves to enculturate teachers into their deskilled role. Prospective teachers learn to be supervised in courses that teach them to meticulously write behavioral objectives and lesson plans in the "correct" format.

Enculturated into an academic culture of passivity, teachers find themselves in workplaces that impose both teaching objectives and testing and evaluation procedures. As a result, teachers have little input into what to teach, how to teach it, or how to judge the outcome. Such a system is an insult to teacher dignity, as it assumes that teachers are too ignorant, dumb, and/or lazy to be permitted to decide such matters. Teachers become the pawns in a cult of expertise—just as Thorndike envisioned it—taking orders from experts conversant with the language of efficiency and scientific management. In such a system some teachers do grow lazy and apathetic. But are we surprised, when they have suckled at the breast of passivity and grown up professionally in a bureaucratic system that discourages initiative? Critical and responsible teachers find themselves too often as pariahs, outsiders who are banished because of their "bad attitudes" and their reluctance to become "team players" (Kamii 1981, 5–6).

Underlying these barricades to autonomous, freethinking educational professionals is a functionalist social theory that views schooling as the organ of society responsible for the transmission of culture in a manner that perpetuates the social system's equilibrium, in other words, that upholds the status quo. Despite protestations to the contrary—protestations issued in the language of democracy promising important decision-making roles for teachers—teachers are relegated to the role of spectators who receive the directives of their superiors (Britzman 1991, 48). Students will continue to suffer from their contact with teachers whose intellect and autonomy are not respected. Students who struggle to survive within the existing school framework will especially suffer. So often they need a nurturing teacher with a creative approach to learning to release them from a cycle of failure. In the schools envisioned by the Reagan–Bush era reformers, however, these students find themselves with constrained teachers who exercise little control over the curriculum, are vulnerable to harassment for their creative approaches, and are chained to the conventional instruction demanded by standardized tests. Unfortunately, these students slip through the cracks of the system uneducated. Indeed, most students find the school to be more of a sorting and labeling machine and less of a vehicle for intellectual and personal growth (Bullough and Gitlin 1991, 36–37).

Students will continue to find school intellectually irrelevant as long as teachers succumb to the barricades of the implicit functionalism and the deadening mechanical routines of the school workplace. The standardization, the dull uniformity of the modernist school becomes a cognitive anaesthetic, a psychotropic hidden curriculum that numbs teacher and student curiosity. Critical postmodern critique issues a call for pedagogical audacity, a manner of teacher thinking that refuses to swallow the anaesthetic of modernism, that goes "cold turkey" in a postmodern context.

TECHNICAL TRAINING AS TEACHER EDUCATION

Behavioristic teacher education has been the most influential position within colleges of education over the last three decades. Indeed, state legislatures have mandated teacher education programs that rely on behavioristic assumptions. Because of such legal action, behavioristic professional programs continue to grow in importance (Garrison 1988, 495; Pumroy 1984, 5–6). Representing possibly the quintessential expression of the hyper-rationality of modernism, behavioral training of teachers traces its roots back to Thorndike and Taylor but finds its modern expression in the work of Ralph Tyler in the late 1940s.

Tyler saw education as a process of modifying behavior patterns in individuals. To accomplish this objective, he maintained that teachers had both to specify the behaviors to be changed (expressed as behavioral objectives) and to develop a scientific approach to determine if the objective had been attained. In the process learning was reduced simply to a technical problem of management. Break knowledge into discrete parts so its acquisition by the learner can be accurately measured. Use standardized materials that carefully specify objectives and delineate exactly what knowledge is to be committed to memory. Train the teacher to oversee the process. The effect of the procedure was to remove the teacher as an active agent in the educational process. The curriculum guides, the standardized materials determined the action of the class, not the teacher (Bowers and Flinders 1990, 7–8; Britzman 1991, 30).

Robert Bullough and Andrew Gitlin help us discern the effects of behavioristic teacher training. A technical ethos is created which eventuates in, first, a constricted view of teacher cognition, which reduces the intellectual act of teaching to merely a technique. Teachers become rule followers, guidebook readers who are discouraged from engaging in interpretative acts. Next, a radical individualism is created that pits teacher education students against one another in competition for grades, praise from supervisors, instructional resources and ideas, and, of course, positions in the schools. Most importantly, this individualist ethic masks the common interests of teachers and obscures the necessity of collective teacher action in the struggle for educational change. Third, the resulting teacher reliance upon experts leads to disparate power and status relations—relations that invariably position teachers on the bottom rung of the status ladder. Fourth, a banking view of teaching and learning will develop, which positions the teacher as a banker storing and dispensing knowledge and students as customers taking out loans of facts for tests. Fifth, teachers will act as consumers, not producers of knowledge. As consumers, the life histories and experiences of teacher education students are irrelevant. They are shapeless blobs of clay waiting to be molded into teachers. Finally, there will be an exaggeration of the importance of that which is measurable in schools. The spotlight is directed to only explicit forms of knowledge that can be observed. Such an emphasis fits with the view of teaching as a managerial act. Learning is trivialized and the student is transformed from spirit to product, an entity that can be shaped and packaged to meet the demands of the employers who will hire him or her (Bullough and Gitlin 1991, 37–38).

Within the behaviorist–technicist model of teacher education, ideas such as Henry Giroux's vision of "teachers as intellectuals" are alien monsters that befuddle the technicist professors of education. The emphasis in the behavioral tradition has little to do with the production of scholarly, reflective practitioners—its raison d'être revolves around technical *competence*, mastery of the predefined skills of teaching. This emphasis on training for technical competence results in a tendency toward conformity. Experience is monosemic, open to only one interpretation, and the task of the neophyte is to adapt to existing institutions by imitating the behaviors of those serving in them. This culture of conformity often creates an atmosphere of hostility toward those who are in some way different. Social relations often become defensive and devoid of honest criticism, as specialists trained for specific tasks perform narrowly defined jobs. Counselors advise; janitors clean; administrators discipline; math teachers teach math; reading teachers teach reading (Bullough and Gitlin 1991, 37; Britzman 1991, 29–30; Lesko 1989, 12). Boundaries are drawn with permanent ink; "No Trespassing" signs abound.

Nothing illustrates the perversity of technical forms of teacher education as explicitly as the way good teaching is defined in such contexts. Simply put, a teacher is good if he or she produces students who on average answer more questions correctly on multiple-choice standardized achievement tests than expected, based on their performance on the pretest. Under such conditions the technicist evaluator will proclaim that students in the effective teacher's class have learned more than expected. Such a definition *demands* that teachers utilize methods of direct instruction, assumes that there is nothing problematic about the knowledge covered by the tests, and covertly imposes, in the name of neutrality, a particular vision of educational purpose, which assumes that schools exist to transmit culture without comment. The proper way to accomplish this task, it concludes, is to fragment the knowledge of that culture into components that can be inserted into student consciousness (Ashburn 1987, 3; Jones and Cooper 1987, 14). What we label "good teaching" carries with it some heavy baggage.

TECHNICAL TEACHER EDUCATION

A crude practicality characterizes technically-oriented teacher education programs. Course work that does not impart "how to" information is deemed impractical, superfluous, or too theoretical. Schools-as-they-are are taken as natural—the role of teacher education is simply to fit the neophytes to them. Questions of the nature and purpose of schooling, the connection between school and society, the relationship between power and teaching, schools as social organizations, or curricular questions of what is worth teaching or the nature of school knowledge are infrequently asked. Rarely considered are the implicit meanings of commonly used terms such as educational excellence or quality education. Upon interrogation, for example, we often find that such terms have definite class and race dimensions, as poor or minority-dominated schools are rarely deemed "excellent." Without such forms of analysis, teachers too often are taught to simply follow orders, to unquestioningly take a predetermined body of information and transfer it to students via a variety of strategies (Ross 1988, 1; Britzman 1991, 49–50; Greene 1986, 70).

It is particularly disturbing that many teacher education programs maintain a virtual silence on the influence of the sociocultural patterns that shape the thinking of teachers. Because Cartesian–Newtonian lenses focus only on the explicit level of school life, that which can be observed and measured, the less obvious cultural dimensions are ignored (Bowers and Flinders 1990, 14). What is interesting in this context is the unabashed rejection by some technical educators of the importance of studying the cultural dynamics of education. Daniel Duke argues, for example, that cultural contextualization is not simply superfluous to the education of teachers, it is actually dangerous. When we attempt to explain social behavior in terms of cultural influences, he contends, we depersonalize blame. Individual students guilty of misbehavior are released from responsibility for their actions by those who value culturally grounded analysis. Duke concludes that teacher professionalism would be better protected by dismissing context and recognizing the supremacy of individualism (Duke 1979, 356–59).

Such a naive view ignores the ways individual identity is structured. Our subjectivities are formed by the cultural forces of race, class, gender, and place; such factors are beyond our power to reverse as they construct boundaries and possibilities in our various relations. They help shape the kind of friends we have, the work we do, and the mates we choose. Our interactions with our families, churches, peer groups, workplaces, and, of course, schools help shape our identities. If these forces were not enough, our consciousness is constructed by our involvement with changing technologies and the mass media and popular culture they help produce (Aronowitz and Giroux 1991, 160–61).

Embedded within the naive notion of individualism is a historical amnesia, an atemporality. Duke's individuals, for example, have no connections with the past; they live in a freeze frame of the present. The school in this conception is jerked out of history. What exists always has been, as school cannot be seen as an evolving institution that grows and falters through the years. We have no way of understanding the motivations of individuals or the purposes of school. We are incapable of self-analysis, for we have no grounding that empowers us to see where we originated. In the same way we are incapable of critical analysis of school purpose, for we have no idea why schools do the things that they do. This is the condition under which much teacher education takes place.

Peter McLaren extends this theme arguing that since teacher education has been mired in the language of efficiency and the logic of management techniques and accountability schemes, it is not surprising that cultural questions have been ignored. Technically oriented teacher education programs don't study the power dimensions of tracking students into college bound or vocationally bound curricula. Higher status is accorded the college-bound track. This track teaches a knowledge more abstract and theoretical than the vocational track. A white middle-class student from an affluent home has less trouble with such material than a minority student from an economically disadvantaged home, because in the affluent home such knowledge is common in the linguistic and social dimensions of everyday life. When teachers fail to study such sociopolitical aspects of schooling, they tend to blame the victims of power inequities for their failings. Without empathy the vicious cycle of economic disadvantage and educational disenfranchisement continues uninterrupted (McLaren 1991a, 233–36).

Teacher education, both pre-service and in-service, is saturated with cognitive experiences that encourage conservative, individualistic, competitive, and decontextualized tendencies in the thinking of teachers. Prospective teachers encounter few experiences that challenge the status quo in schools. Given the way research is conducted in education, the "knowledge-base" produced perpetuates that "which is" (Zeuli and Bachmann 1986, 6; Floden and Klinzing 1990, 16). As long as teacher educators believe that novice survival is a cardinal goal of professional education and that teachers learn to teach best by engaging in apprenticelike experiences, little substantive change will occur. Teacher education as apprenticeship induces neophytes to model the master teacher, rendering the study of teaching less essential than "correct" performance based on the master teacher's opinion and local standards within a particular school. The conformity encouraged results in a uniformity of thought, a mechanistic approach to the profession, and an inability to critically intervene in the world of school practice (Cruickshank 1987, 5; Britzman 1991, 29).

Students often enter the college of education with a set of conservative expectations and predispositions. They want to become teachers like the ones they've had or known and they expect to teach students just like the ones who were their friends and associates in school. More often than students in other fields, they attend colleges close to their homes and desire to teach in their home states. Because of these and other factors, their acculturation into the profession marks little break with their pasts, their childhood values. Thus, teacher education students tend not to be seekers of alternative ways of seeing; they often are not especially interested in finding new lenses through which to conceptualize knowledge and pedagogy. Instead they walk into classes searching for recipes for information delivery and classroom discipline. Questions of purpose, context, and power are alien, irrelevant. What does such information have to do with teaching?, they ask (Zeuli and Bachmann 1986, 7).

At least moderately successful in schools, prospective teachers are hard-pressed to forget the conventional educational practices that worked well for them. Thus, they feel that schools are alright as they are; with a few practice attempts out in the field and a few strategies to help with discipline, everything will be fine. The culture of passivity works at all levels: It certainly worked for the prospective teachers when they were elementary and secondary students; there is no reason to believe that listening well and following directions literally won't work now.

Questioning, interpretation, and intellectual flexibility rest at the core of what university faculty term essential cognitive acts. Technicist-oriented teacher educators tend not to appreciate these traditional academic values. Indeed, it is too often the case that teacher educators who work the closest to schools and to student and practicing teachers find themselves isolated from the more traditional culture of academia. Theirs is often a terrain of eight-to-five, punch-clock hours, little professional reading, ideological naiveté, limited interpretative practice, and minimal analysis of the professional world. The logic of such working conditions emphasizes something quite unlike interpretive thinking. There is an undertow in such an environment—an unseen tendency to surrender to the given, to view existing institutional arrangements as objective realities. Without the catalyst of interpretation, of an intellectually active analytical community, pronouncements tend to speak at a literal level—they speak "for themselves." Without an analytical view of the everyday and of institutional requirements and activities, thought is fragmented and conceptual synthesis is blocked. Indeed, our relationship to knowledge is severed. As a result, our role as participants in social and institutional life is unexamined and our power to anticipate the consequences of social actions is devoured (Zeuli and Bachmann 1986, 29; Greene 1988, 6–7; Britzman 1991, 36).

Jesse Goodman has studied the effects of this modernist teacher education culture on student teachers. Even those students who entered practice teaching with beliefs in teacher's responsibility to help determine curriculum, the inadvisability of emphasizing fragmented skills over the interpretation of social content, the value of curricular integration, the obligation to use learning activities to promote critical thinking, and the sanctity of creativity found themselves far more concerned with technicist school objectives by the end of their experience. One of the students Goodman observed, Karen, created an original, progressive unit on occupations at the beginning of her student teaching. After a few weeks of immersion in the schools, she discarded the unit. Almost all of her lessons, Goodman tells us, came point by point from the teacher's guides. Karen became more and more concerned with using the textbooks effectively—indeed this concern became far more important to her conception of good teaching than the ability to make curricular and instructional decisions. Her concerns with teacher power were virtually silenced and she worked to win the approval of her student teaching supervisor, her practicing teachers, and her other personnel in the school (Goodman 1986, 20–22).

The power of the modernist institution had again triumphed, subduing the zeal of youthful reform. But hope exists, possibility lives. In the following chapters we will explore the variety of challenges that may upset the passivity of the educational process.

Chapter 2

Rumblings of Empowerment

Despite recent rumblings for teacher empowerment within teacher organizations and colleges of education, too many teacher education programs still fail to interrogate the meaning of, much less teach, sophisticated forms of practitioner thinking. The professional educational research community too often has been guilty of viewing research in a manner that inhibits teachers from becoming critical reflective practitioners. This is the problem with modernist social and educational science: What is the benefit of the knowledge it produces? By the very techniques it employs, the very questions it is limited to legitimately ask (see Kincheloe 1991 for an expanded analysis of those research techniques), educational research creates trivial information. The response of practitioners is often, "So what?"

MODERNIST EDUCATIONAL RESEARCH: FROM EXALTED EXPERT TO LOWLY PRACTITIONER

Undoubtedly, the most powerful form of knowledge during the modernist era is scientific knowledge. The last quarter of a century has witnessed a dramatic expansion of the scientific basis of teaching—a virtual knowledge explosion. Yet, as James Garrison and many others have argued, there is virtually no indication that this new body of information has contributed to the improvement of teaching or the empowerment of teachers (Garrison 1988, 488). One reason for this revolves around the discursive features of education research. Power regulates discourses. Discursive practices are defined as a set of tacit rules that regulate what can and cannot be said, who can speak with the blessing of authority and who must listen, whose socioeducational constructions are scientific and valid and whose are unlearned and unimportant (McLaren 1989, 167–82).

Consider the power relations in the existing mechanisms for producing and distributing scientific knowledge about teaching. In this discourse teachers are deprived of power, as they are effectively eliminated from the *active* process of uncovering and disseminating knowledge. They are delegated instead to the passive role of knowledge consumers of the predigested products of educational science (Garrison 1988, 488). Typically, this predigested scientific knowledge is grounded on a simplistic input–output vision of educational experience. Like the factory production on which it is metaphorically bolted, there must be certain forms of output that can be measured in order to discern failure or success (Koetting 1988, 3). In the case of education, standardized test scores serve as the output to be measured. Many do not believe that such scores present a realistic measurement of teacher effectiveness. Since standardized tests measure that which is easy to measure—short answer-based concrete level cognition—they tend to focus attention on the trivial while neglecting the profound. Thus, teachers "learn" from research that teaching is a technology with an identifiable outcome lending itself to short-term teaching goals. Of course, this identifiable outcome is the improvement of standardized test scores. The power of discourse overwhelms the intuition of teachers that something is amiss with this system. But before these intuitions can be formulated into words of dissent, the discourse's conspiracy of silence disallows the naming of the discomfort.

The purpose of much of the empirical research produced is the generation of generalizations about teaching. Again the dynamics of discourse analysis aid our attempt to discern the consequences of such inquiry. Positivistic research produces generalizations that are used by curriculum designers and supervisors as justifications for suppressing teacher ingenuity in their own classrooms. General rules come to substitute for the actual experiences of teachers. What constitutes an appropriate teacher action is preordained by a remote expert. In case after case educational research produces generalizations that often serve to delegitimize the experiences of teachers (Elliot 1989a, 1; Lincoln and Guba 1985, 181). The researchers themselves view this process very differently, as one would expect. They feel that they are making a valuable contribution to teacher knowledge by reducing practitioner uncertainty. They don't seem to realize that teaching is inherently an uncertain act and any attempt to deny this characteristic can only result in problems.

Such denial, in the first place, creates the problematic belief that there is a direct mechanistic connection between research generalizations and what should be taught in teacher education and what teachers should do in the classroom. Second, this denial of uncertainty results in attempts to cultivate teacher confidence in the certainty of the classroom applicability of generalizations about teaching. Third, it seems to induce everyone involved to ignore the fact that teaching and thinking about teaching are dependent upon time, context, and outcome desired. What is true about teacher thinking in one time or place may not be true in another. What may be true about teaching thinking when one particular goal is sought may not be true for another goal. Fourth, it promotes the tendency for research generalizations to be turned into technical prescriptions, which are employed to evaluate what constitutes good teaching. Such an orientation discourages teachers from adjusting their teaching to the particular goals they embrace and the particular topics and students they are teaching (Zeuli and Bachmann 1986, 2; Floden and Klinzing 1990, 16–17).

The technicist process is really quite simple: Since all teachers operate in the same way, rationally planning their learning objectives, generating a variety of alternatives, and then choosing the optional alternative, all we have to do is let them know what the research tells us is the best way to plan and what constitutes the proper objectives. Then we simply train supervisors to assess whether or not teachers follow the research-generated programs. Of course, *no* teacher operates in this hyper-rationalistic manner—the nature of the teaching act won't allow it. Still, technicist teacher education operates as if this were all true, as if reality were this simple. This top-down, researcher to practitioner discursive model chugs along on a daily basis turning out young teachers befuddled by the irrelevance of their professional education. In this context of teacher thinking the technicist education professors work to teach their students the knowledge they need to run their classes efficiently, all the while writing recipe books possibly entitled "39 Steps to High Test Scores" or "How to Think as a Teacher." As Christopher Clark argues, these teacher trainers are waiting for the second phase of thinking research which lays out even more specifically the step-by-step process of "teacher thinking in effective schools" complete with detailed lists of "steps to thinking about planning," "steps to methods of decision making," and "steps to thinking about critical thinking." I can imagine teacher education students copying these lists from overhead projectors in classrooms around the world (Clark 1987, 1–2; Glickman 1985, 4).

Because of this top-down technicist approach, student and practicing teachers find it hard to tolerate education courses that dish out "theory." Educational theory is threatening to teachers because it is generated by a cadre of status-superior outside experts who use a set of certified procedures to inquire into the practice of teaching (Torney-Purta 1985, 73). Delivered in a language abstracted from the teachers's reality, theory is viewed by teachers as a finished product, an accomplished fact beyond negotiation. Regardless of the teacher's own experience, theory remains above it, an unchanging entity. Educational theory in its separation from teacher experience represents an excellent example of modernism's fragmentation of reality.

If theory in education is ever to mean anything to teachers, it must be conceived as merely one dimension of a lived relationship—always enmeshed in the everyday world of teaching and ever-prepared for reinterpretation when confronted with changing conditions. Theorizing is a tentative process of reflection about one's experience for the purpose of becoming an author of that experience (Britzman 1991, 49–50). William Pinar and Madeleine Grumet have written of a reconceptualized notion of theorizing, viewing it as a contemplative activity that doesn't seek an immediate translation into practice. Reconceptualized theory, they argue, interrupts taken-for-granted understandings of teaching, it allows the demands of the lived world of the classroom to assume a depth and complexity that respects the human condition (Pinar and Grumet 1988, 98–99).

DOES THINKING HAVE A ROLE IN TEACHER EDUCATION?

The implicit message of technicist teacher education, the positivistic research that often grounds it, and the state reform movements that share the same epistemological assumptions is that teachers must do what they are told, they must be careful about thinking for themselves. Such caution eventually turns into apathy as teachers lose interest in the creative aspects of teaching which originally attracted them to the profession. Teacher thinking is profoundly affected by the top-down flow, the teacher-proof curricula that assume practitioner incompetence. As they are rewarded in teacher training for their passive acceptance of expert-generated knowledge, prospective teachers gain little experience in contextually grounded interpretive thinking about the purpose of teaching in a democratic society. Management science is geared to the control of human beings in line with visions of institutional efficiency and standardization. Teacher education often contributes to such management orientations by conveying the belief that the laws of social and educational life are well known and devoid of ambiguity (Glickman 1985, 4; Baldwin 1987, 17; Popkewitz 1981, 310).

In this context consider Madeline Hunter's quite popular teaching/supervision model used in thousands of teaching education programs and school districts. Hunter's model assumes a predetermined, prescribed version of teaching based on "seven essential steps." Teachers guided by Hunter follow these specific (and measurable) steps in every lesson regardless of the subject matter. Supervisor evaluation is simplified, standardized, and streamlined as administrators come to define good teaching as that which conforms to Hunter's model. Accountability is ensured, Hunter and the technicists argue, as teachers come to understand what is expected of them so they can perform appropriately.

The range of teaching behaviors that may be considered appropriate is narrowed under Hunter's model. Supervisors and teacher educators admit that innovative lessons that fail to follow the model must be evaluated as unsatisfactory. Thus, rewards for teaching are not based on reasoned notions of competence and creativity but on adherence to format, that is teacher compliance. Teacher education becomes a conformity mill, an adjustment procedure where novices are fine-tuned to the Hunter channel. Like workers in Frederick W. Taylor's scientifically managed factories of efficiency, the technicist system à la Hunter strips teachers of their role in the conceptualization of the teaching act. Teachers become executors of managerial plans. The moral and ethical dimensions, not to mention the cognitive aspects of the teaching act, are submerged in a pool of standardization and conventionalism (Garman and Hazi 1988, 680–72).

When thinking is taught in technicist colleges of education, it is rarely conceived in the context of the unique cognitive demands of the practitioner. Cognitive theories are typically presented one after another without any attempt to critically assess or relate them to actual classroom practice. Such information is presented at a concrete cognitive level, as students commit to memory what B. F. Skinner, Kurt Lewin, Freud, or Piaget said. Because of a particular emotional attachment, particular students latch on to certain cognitive theories. Many theories are useless and have little to do with the everyday life of teachers. Consistent with the technicist assumptions about neutrality and objectivity, many education professors believe that students should learn a little about every major cognitive theory so they can make their own choices. Such an approach is in many ways an abrogation of pedagogical responsibility, as it ignores each theory's significance, its explanatory power, its epistemological dimensions, and, especially important for this work, its political implications. If teachers were empowered to understand the relationships between

Piagetian constructivism and, say, Skinnerian behaviorism from pedagogical, epistemological, and political perspectives, they would not allow the simple-minded imposition of lesson plan *formats*, behavioral objective writing, or bulletin board making to dominate their pre-service and in-service teacher education (Kamii 1981, 12–13).

Teachers agree that it is important to induce students to think critically, but few are sure how such a goal might be achieved. It seems obvious, but overlooked: Teachers must learn to think in a sophisticated way before they can teach students to do so. A central theme of this work is the development of a post-Piagetian form of teacher thinking. This post-Piagetian or post-formal thinking is a self-reflective form of thought that attempts to move beyond the logical base of Piagetian formalism by employing women's ways of knowing, critical theory, and postmodernist critique. Practitioner ways of knowing are unique, quite different from the technical, scientific ways of knowing traditionally associated with professional expertise. Professional expertise, as Donald Schon maintains, is an uncertain enterprise as it confronts constantly changing, unique, and unstable conditions. Teachers never see the same classroom twice, as teaching conditions change from day to day. The students who reacted positively to a set of pedagogical strategies yesterday, respond differently today (despite William Bennett's assurances of "what works"). Schon's practitioners relinquish the certainty that attends to professional expertise conceived as the repetitive administration of techniques to similar types of problems. In the post-formal reconceptualization of practitioner thinking the ability of practitioners to develop research strategies that explore the genesis and efficacy of comfortable assumptions and implicit objectives is extremely important (Schon 1983, 299, 345).

In education, post-formal teachers become teachers-as-researchers who question the nature of their own thinking as they attempt to teach higher order thinking to their students. What are the limits of human ways of knowing? Where do we begin conceptualizing post-formal modes of teacher thinking that lead to a metaperspective, to empowerment? Drawing upon our critical postmodern system of meaning, we cannot help but anticipate ways of knowing and levels of cognition that move beyond Piagetian formalism. Adults do not reach a final cognitive equilibrium beyond which no new levels of thought can emerge; there have to be modes of thinking that transcend the formal operational ability to formulate abstract conclusions, understand cause-effect relationships, and employ the traditional scientific method to explain reality. We know too much to define formality as the zenith of human cognitive ability (Arlin 1975, 602–3).

It is the issue of critical empowerment, the ability of individuals to disengage themselves from the tacit assumptions of discursive practices and power relations in order to exert more conscious control over their everyday lives, that psychological models of cognition fail to address. Rational, accurate thinking emerging from modernism's one-truth epistemology produces not only a congregation of nervous right-answer givers and timid rule followers, but a rather mediocre level of education unrelated to any ethical effort to constructively use our ability to reason. The technicist efforts to cultivate higher order or critical thinking among teachers too often involve removing prospective practitioners from their lived worlds in order to control the variables of the situation. As a result, thinking is sequestered in artificial laboratory settings where passion and authentic feelings of love, hate, fear, and commitment are scientifically removed. Cartesian–Newtonian models of the rational process are always culturally neutral, always removed from the body and its passions. These modernist models assume that a practitioner can be removed from his or her embeddedness in a physical context without affecting cognition (Hultgren 1987, 28; Bobbitt 1987, 67; Bowers and Flinders 1990, 9–10).

BUT HASN'T SCIENCE PROVEN THAT WE NOW KNOW HOW TO TEACH?

But this separation of context from cognition is exactly what's wrong with teacher education. Whether we are teaching high school math, elementary language arts, or teacher education, the approach is the same: break down the information to be learned into discrete parts that can be easily memorized. Thus, cognitive theories, grammatical rules, vocabulary, math computation skills, the "causes" of the Civil War, can all be "learned" in this way. As long as the curriculum is conceived in a technical way with prespecified facts to be learned, with improvement of standardized tests the goal of instruction, with little concern granted to connecting school and life, with no debate over the role of learning in a democratic society, then maybe science has proven that we know how to teach (Jones and Cooper 1987, 4).

Take the way science has taught us to teach reading. Mastery learning programs break reading skills into subskills such as beginning consonant sounds, vowel sounds, ending consonant sounds, consonant blends, and vowel diagrams. Teachers learn to teach these in a structured, sequenced manner until students pass the mastery test on each subskill. Again, the commonsense, linear methodology seems to satisfy everyone's demands.

Upon deeper examination, however, problems begin to materialize—even on the superficial level on which such programs are assessed.

Researchers have found that in the first few years of the program, reading skill *scores* among early elementary students actually increased. By the time the children were in the sixth grade, reading levels not only decreased, but students were not reading. Although students were scoring high on achievement tests, the examinations only measured what early grade teachers had taught—the subskills. Reading or language arts classes had revolved mainly around worksheets or dittos on the subskills. Very little actual reading was taking place. Students had learned the fragmented curriculum well. They had indeed learned the isolated subskills and had reflected that knowledge on the standardized tests. Even so, they were not reading for knowledge, enjoyment, or meaning—they were not even reading. The reading program had committed a fatal modernist error: It had assumed that the parts add up to the whole. As with most human endeavors the whole was far greater than the parts (Fosnot 1988, 7–9; Shannon 1989, 62–66).

REFORM IMPULSES

Throughout the post-Enlightenment history of schooling, a tradition of dissent has questioned the application of Cartesian–Newtonian science to education. The tradition that finds its early expression in Rousseau embraces a form of romantic maturationism. Romantic maturationists have argued that the most important element of education involves the protection of the innate development of the child. The child is the center of the educational universe and his or her cognitive, social, and emotional development is simply a process of biological programming.

Rousseau compared Emile to a flower, implying that the child is innately good and needs only a nurturing, gentle environment in order to reach his or her full potential. Arnold Gesell extended Rousseau's metaphor by numerous observations and subsequent delineations of child development stages. His work raised a red flag to educators: Do not tamper with the child's divinely ordained maturation process. When romantic maturationists planned curriculum and instruction, they heeded Gesell's warning, as teaching became a process of assessing the correct developmental level of the child and carefully planning appropriate activities (Fosnot 1988, 9–10; Zigler and Finn-Stevenson 1987, 11–13).

Though the attempt to confront the power of modernist science was noble, the romantic maturationists were doomed to failure. Teaching collapsed into endless assessments and attempts to match activities with them. Usually implemented in early childhood programs and in "free schools" of another era, teachers played the role of therapists, unobtrusive guides whose role was to help students experience personal growth. After teachers constructed the environment, they withdrew, allowing play activities and experience to naturally foster learning. Teachers were not the deskilled laborers of the efficient technicist schools, but there was little need for higher order practitioner thought (Ashburn 1987, 4; Fosnot 1988, 10).

In the last couple of decades, however, educational thinkers have begun to realize the need for both teacher and students to transcend the rote-based, fragmented thinking that has degraded modernist schools. Many of the attempts to foster such cognition—referred to as critical thinking— found themselves trapped within a modernist logic. In such a condition, thinking was hyperrationalized, reduced to a set of micrological skills that promote a form of procedural knowledge. In its reductionism this "uncritical critical thinking" removed the political and ethical dimensions of thinking. Students and teachers were not encouraged to confront why they tended to think as they did about themselves, the world around them, and their relationship to that world. In other words, these uncritical critical thinkers gained little insight into the focus that had shaped them, that is, their consciousness construction. In addition, the critical thinking movement was virtually unconcerned with the consequences of thinking, viewing cognition as a process that takes place in a vacuum. Thinking in a new way always necessitates personal transformation; indeed if enough people think in new ways, social transformation is inevitable. The nature of this social and personal change was not important to uncritical critical thinking advocates.

Uncritical critical thinking advocates were unable to transcend the boundaries of formal thinking. As they reduced thinking to the micrological skills, they taught a fragmented version of scientific thinking (the highest expression of formality). Students were taught to differentiate, to group, to identify common properties, to label, to categorize, to distinguish relevant from irrelevant information, to relate points, to infer, and to justify—usually in isolation from any scientific or larger conceptual problem. It can be argued that such an approach to critical thinking actually obscured more than it exposed by hiding its hyperrationality behind its scientific appearance. Though its intentions were well founded, the movement never realized that critical thinking is more than a cognitive skill to be mastered, that it is not the province of only the gifted, that teacher education must teach critical thinking in the context of reflective practice. Uncritical critical thinking always saw higher order thinking as a process separate from the environment of the school. Proponents never saw the critical, emancipating dimensions of thinking that are inseparable from the democratic way students, teachers, and administrators interact with one another (Hultgren 1987, 28; Grimmett, Erickson, MacKinnon, and Riecken 1990, 33).

EMPOWERMENT AS A GOAL OF THINKING—THINKING AS A SOCIAL ACTIVITY

So what is "critical critical thinking?" Authentically critical thinking moves in an emancipatory direction with an omnipresent sense of self-awareness. Moving in an emancipatory direction implies a concern with the development of a liberated mind, a critical consciousness, and a free society. Teachers as critical thinkers are aware of the construction of their own consciousness and the ways that social and institutional forces work to undermine their autonomy as professionals (Ashburn 1987, 4; Hultgren 1987, 28). Drawing upon our critical postmodern system of meaning, emancipatory teacher thinking sets the self "in question." Self-images, inherited dogmas, and absolute beliefs are interrogated, teachers begin to see themselves in relation to the world around them, to perceive the school as a piece of a larger mosaic. Teachers begin to see an inseparable relationship between thinking and acting, as the boundary between feeling and logic begins to fade from the cognitive map—a map redrawn by feminist cartographers.

Indeed, as the main theme of this book maintains, cognitive style holds specific and ideological consequences. We cannot think about thinking without considering the power dimensions of the act—the em*power*ment of higher orders of thinking. For teachers to think in an emancipatory manner involves empowered actions—activities that contribute to the best interests of students, community members, and other teachers and conduct that enables those affected to employ their intelligence and ethics. Thus, the move to "critical critical teacher thinking" involves the transcendence of the notion that thinking is merely a cognitive psychological activity. This may be the key to understanding the static flatness of uncritical critical thinking. As both a psychological and social activity, teacher thinking is perceived as "in process," ever in a state of being constructed. For example, teachers cannot think about the curriculum outside of a social context. If they do, they are deceived by the political innocence of a body of agreed-upon knowledge being systematically passed on to students by an ever-evolving, but always neutral, instructional process. We know too much to be seduced by the never-aging sirens of political neutrality. As a deliberate process, the curriculum is always a formal transmission of *particular* aspects of the culture's knowledge. Do we teach women's and African Americans' history in eleventh-grade social studies? Do we read Toni Morrison and Alice Walker in twelfth-grade literature? These are sociopolitical questions—that is, they involve power.

Thinking affects social practice; it is never detached. How we think about teaching works to change or maintain the status quo. Descriptions of the world do not rest, they do not retreat to a sociological easy chair. They are part of the commerce of the world; as they define it, they change it. Thinking is always a major strategy in the cultural battle. If such is so, then conceptual matters can never be sequestered in the psychological domain. Cognition in a critical postmodern context becomes sociocognition (Codd 1984, 13–14; Harris 1984, 44; Hultgren 1987, 28).

In this book we will discuss a form of higher order teacher thinking that we will label post-formal thinking. The attempt will not be to concretely define post-formal thinking but to "uncover" it. To define it would imply that it was a discrete stage with universal features. Such definition would fall back to the totalizing inclination of modernism, its tendency to capture meaning. The postmodern uncovering of post-formal thinking induces us to "do" post-formal thinking, to dive into the post-formal waters. As such, it will remain elusive, a prisoner-at-large resistant to the trap of consistent meaning. The way it is defined will always involve the interaction between our general conceptions of it and its interactions with its ever-changing experiences, the new contexts in which it finds itself. As Heidegger once put it, thinking is not so much a cognitive action as it is a "way of life." Thinking, he concluded, is how human beings remember who they are and where they belong (Hultgren 1987, 28–33; Bobbitt 1987, 67).

Remembering who we are and where we belong involves the ability to make critical preferences. Post-formal teachers, following the concerns of Heidegger, employ a critical postmodern system of meaning to choose between competing theories and curricular and instructional strategies. Without the ability to make critical preference, teachers are disinclined to teach their students critical critical thinking. Students are cognitively and ethically deskilled, as they find themselves unable to distinguish work of quality from drivel. Finding themselves in this situation students consider schooling normal when it immerses them in busy work and mindless rote-based, test-driven exercises. Of course, they lose interest in learning (Harris 1984, 44; Bobbitt 1987, 67). Who wouldn't?

THE POSTMODERN PARADIGM SHIFT:
MODERNISM AND THE COGNITIVE ILLNESS

The word paradigm, comes from the Greek word for pattern. Paradigm, as most academics know by now, is a pattern, a scheme for understanding the nature of the world. Although Thomas Kuhn (1962) was thinking about science when he popularized the term, people now employ the word in medical, political, and educational contexts. The technical teacher education we have referred to over the last two chapters is the product of the old modernist paradigm. In many ways it corresponds to the Cartesian–Newtonian pattern for viewing the world. Just as Issac Newton saw the physical world in terms of predictable mechanical forces in a clockwork universe, technicist teacher educators perceive the educational world in terms of predictable generalizations that could be derived by isolating teaching and controlling its variables in laboratory settings. The clockwork universe extended from Newton's apple falling out of the tree to the apple sitting on the teacher's desk in front of the classroom.

In the physical sciences, researchers who hoped to solve the questions emerging from Newton's pattern of the universe were frustrated, as data from Einstein's, Niels Bohr's, Werner Heisenberg's, and David Bohm's research in physics refused to fit the pattern. As the Cartesian–Newtonian paradigm was strained, new patterns began to emerge and new questions arose. The linear, cause–effect Cartesian–Newtonian paradigm began to crumble. In much the same way, the old educational patterns have begun to disintegrate in the minds of many over the past decade or so. Still a minority in the colleges of education and especially in the public schools, these thinkers have used the term "paradigm shift" to describe their questioning of modernism's cause–effect linearity in the social and educational world (Ferguson 1980, 26–27).

An awareness of the paradigm shift in the realm of education carries with it a recognition of the postmodern condition described in Chapter 1 and the educational manifestation of that condition—the *cognitive illness*. This pathology of thinking threatens the very survival of the human species. While we have developed important ways for the study of the "world out there," we have failed in the modernist era in the attempt to study the "me in here." Caught in this mode of thinking, this Cartesian dualism, we find ourselves able to gather copious data about matter and energy but unable to increase our insight into the minds that put such information to use. Indeed, over the past 2,000 years we have increased our capacity to wage war, while at the same time learning little about the causes of war (Leshan and Margenau 1982, xiii).

Modernism has encouraged a competitive impulse that has moved humans to experience themselves and their consciousnesses as separate from one another. Such an orientation is a part of the cognitive illness which holds destructive implications. It becomes a mental prison, replete with teachers as thought police, that refuses to release us on our own cognitive recognizance. Our social imagination is restricted, as we are bound to simple personal desires. Our affection is limited to the family unit, to a few individuals close to us. Part of our therapy, our emancipation from the cognitive illness involves freeing ourselves from its confines by expanding our realm of concern to all living creatures and the whole of nature in its interrelated complexity. Our private experience of empathy must be transferred into public policy. In empathetic social orders with their empathetic schools, natural time takes precedence over the artificial rhythm of the industrial modernist order with its time clock and processed time. The empathic social order rejects the modernist cognitive illness's tendency to decontextualize temporality, that is, to rob women and men in their pasts and futures. An emancipatory postmodern education is grounded on this understanding and seeks to contextualize both information and the lives of students accordingly (Resnick 1980, 862; Rifkin 1987, 226).

Thus, post-formal thinking is a vaccine against modernism's cognitive illness. Bringing hidden cultural infrastructures—such as time—to consciousness, post-formal thinking attempts to empower teachers and other individuals to make conscious choices concerning their lives. Reflecting the cognitive illness, educators move through sixteen to twenty years of schooling without ever being induced to think about their own thinking and the infrastructures and discourses that have shaped it (Bohm and Peat 1987, 11). The discourse of modernist science with its obsession with measurement, for example, has shaped the nature of teacher education and the form that schools have taken. Educational science has devoted much attention to the development of more precise systems of measurement and the application of such measurement to the mind of the learner. As a result, many educators and lay people cannot think of intelligence in any terms other than quantitative.

This same modernist science has fragmented the world to the point that individuals are blinded to certain forms of human experience. Attempting to study the world in isolation, bit by bit, educational scientists have separated the study of schools from society. For the purpose of simplifying the process of analysis, disciplines of study are divided arbitrarily without regard for larger context. Educational reforms of recent years have been formulated outside of the wider cultural and political concerns for empathy. As the politicians mandate test-driven curricula, they create a new form of the cognitive illness. Finding its roots in modernist fragmentation, recent "excellence" reform has produced a "factoid syndrome" where students learn isolated bits and pieces of information for tests without concern for relationships between the facts or their application to the problems of the world.

This modernist fragmentation and the "infected" education it produces has weakened our ability to see the relationships between our actions and the cosmos. As we come to value autonomy over participation, isolation over communion, we begin to view natural phenomena as objects for exploitation and manipulation. Science thus mutates into a device for prediction and control that is comfortable when in the name of progress and short-term profits it leads to a rape of the natural world (Rifkin 1989, 259).

Many scientists have argued that their attempt to isolate and analyze the various components of the physical world would result in an absolute understanding of nature. Students of human and social science have labored under the same banner, contending that we will eventually produce mechanical models of the human mind and human societies. Such perspectives are based on the assumption that everyone possesses a common frame of reference. The idea that they reflect a particular world view or dominant ideology emerging from a particular time and place is rarely considered in the world of schooling. Thus, this quest for absolute knowledge, in its refusal to examine the assumptions that guide it, obscures more than it uncovers (Gordon, Miller, and Rollock 1990, 15).

Our unquestioned educational trek for absolutism and certainty results in a twelve- to sixteen-year training program for Cartesian–Newtonian modernity. Modernist schools emphasize quantities, distance, and location, not qualities, relationships, or context. Modernist assumptions are deeply embedded in various aspects of school life. The tests typically given in North American schools, for example, prepare students to think in terms of linear causality and quantification—the foundation of modernism. Because we are not taught to think in critical terms, in terms of exposing the tacit assumptions in our conventions and everyday practices, disempowered teachers are oblivious to the fact that they are propagating a specific ideology when they design their tests and teach their classes.

Modernist education is chained to a bed covered with a crazy quilt of unexamined assumptions. These hidden assumptions dictate the questions asked about schooling in the public conversation and the tenets of the reform proposals offered by politicians. Modernists attempt to piece Humpty Dumpty back together again by employing more and more of the king's horses and men—they attempt to reform schools with only our existing tools. They think of schools in the context of the old paradigmatic assumptions, refusing to realize that the educational crisis is symptomatic of the larger enigmas of modernism (Ferguson 1980, 28).

Presidents Reagan and Bush did not even commit many "horses and men" in the educational reforms of the 1980s and 1990s. Operating exclusively in a modernist paradigm, Reagan and Bush turned to increased standardized testing, increasingly strict accountability procedures for teachers, and more business and school partnerships in their programs for educational reform. The goals of reform did not embrace much of a concern for critical thinking, either of the noncritical or the "critical critical" varieties described previously. For example, the goals of George Bush's educational goals for the year 2000 focused on the economic purposes of education, the training of competitive and productive workers. Instead of educating courageous citizens dedicated to justice and the life of the mind, the Bush proposals attempted to produce workers who were compliant and loyal to their companies, that is, disempowered. These "team players" do not pose any significant challenge to the injustices and myopia of the modernist paradigm. If such proposals are left unchallenged, the status quo will grind along into the next millennium (Spring 1991, 25–27).

Confronted with such an undesirable future, we must acquaint ourselves with the nature of change in a postmodern era. How does transformation occur? Postmodernism in a sense, marks the change of change. Contrary to traditional modernist beliefs, change is a nonrational, often an irrational, process. Change viewed in paradigmatic terms, forces us to reexamine the concept of self and social transformation from new perspectives. Because the self is not viewed as an entity which is shaped in a rational, linear, and predictable way, the postmodern paradigm shift allows us to see the multidimensional forces that often interact with our desires to create erratic personal and thus erratic social development.

For example, sexual impulses guided by identifications with popular cultural imagery move us in directions unimagined by our ancestors in their pre-electronic folk culture. The way individuals construct categories of meaning within the competing *Zeitgeists* of the postmodern culture shape how they respond to sociopolitical events. Teachers negotiate their professional roles around the interrelationship among their categories of meaning, the postmodern culture, and the discourse of teaching. When empowered, these teachers come to understand their students' response to school knowledge in the same process that they come to understand their own response to the role of teacher. This process involves an appreciation of the dynamics of change in a postmodern cosmos; it involves understanding the sites and social practices that shape experiences and through which individuals construct their identities. The sites and social practices may vary—they might include the church, gospel music, boy scouts, and Disneyland; or anarchist youth culture, skateboarding, and industrial music; or more commonly the combination of some of the above (White 1978, 135–49; Giroux and Simon 1989, 3; Giroux 1991, 232).

THE POSTMODERN TURN AND THE RECONCEPTUALIZATION OF TEACHER KNOWLEDGE

The possibility of teacher empowerment necessitates a reconceptualization of teacher knowledge, that is, what teachers need to know to perform their jobs successfully. Teachers develop what many have called "practitioner knowledge," in a variety of ways—experience being one of the most important means of acquisition. This practitioner knowledge alerts teachers to the fact that the classroom is a complex and chaotic place with significant and peripheral variables. Such an understanding alerts teachers to the innate problems with modernist attempts to produce empirical generalizations about the best way to teach. Even though they intuitively understand the limitations of these empirical generalizations, teachers are unable to escape the shadow of their scientific power. In their seemingly perpetual vulnerability to the vicissitudes of public opinion, teachers are unable to prove their competence through their practitioner knowledge. Because it has not been scientifically validated, it holds no legitimacy in the court of public opinion. Thus, state legislatures demand scientific validation of teaching practice. As a result, teachers are forced to abandon practitioner knowledge in favor of practices the research base has scientifically endorsed—practices that may directly contradict subtle practitioner understandings (Altrichter and Posch 1989, 25–26; Madaus 1985, 615; Garrison 1988, 488–89).

Knowledge about teaching produced by modernist science smashes the experience of teaching into discrete fragments that are one generation removed from the subtle interplay of focus which made experience what it was originally. As educational science issues its injunction to keep experience away from verified knowledge, a chasm develops between the official discourse required by modernist science and the compelling discourse that teachers develop in action. Teachers come to be personally excluded from the process of producing knowledge about their profession. The concept of teachers as virtuosos who create brilliant pieces of pedagogical performance is alien to the modernist conception of educational knowledge. In a modernist context teachers are expected to follow imperatives that are scientifically derived, not to produce teaching masterpieces (Britzman 1991, 35; Clark 1987, 19).

The forms of teacher education that emerge from these perspectives on practitioner knowledge involve transmitting the forms of teacher thinking that researchers have connected to improved student standardized test performance to prospective teachers. These forms of teacher thinking or teacher cognitive schematas are not transportable from the teacher education classroom to the elementary or secondary classroom. A critical postmodern teacher education would attempt to expose the assumptions about knowledge (the epistemology) and the nature of modernist research which are buried in the officially approved cognitive schematas. As it deconstructed the cognitive schematas, a critical postmodern teacher education would reconceptualize the ways that practitioner knowledge is analyzed and shared with teacher education students. The attempt to extract generalized schemata would be replaced by an analysis of the way practitioners in all fields including teaching think in action (Lampert and Clark 1990, 21; Haroutunian-Gordon 1988, 237).

Teachers in action acquire and employ knowledge in context, in interaction. With this in mind, critical postmodern teacher education engages novices in the analysis of the context in which teaching takes place. Assuming that teachers' knowledge cannot be separated from the socioeducational and the classroom context in which it is generated, students study the process of teacher thinking. What conditions contributed to the cognitive processes employed? What subliminal signals did the teacher pick up and how did such codes and signs help shape the cognitive schemata adopted? What implicit social and cultural assumptions were at work and how did they affect the teacher's thoughts and actions? Thus, students of teaching begin to recognize that practitioner knowledge is elusive, so elusive in fact it cannot be transferred like the knowledge of multiplication tables or parts of speech. The contextual contingency, the uniqueness of particular teaching situations can no longer be ignored—the elusiveness, the postmodern uncertainty of the practitioner's cognition and knowledge must be addressed (Schon 1987, 6, 11–12; Lampert and Clark, 1990, 22).

Here is where the concept of teachers as researchers becomes so important in the reconceptualization of teacher education. If teachers are to be empowered to move beyond the static modernist views of teacher cognition and practitioner knowledge, they must become researchers of educational contexts. As prospective teachers study the interaction between context and teacher cognition, they employ the tools of qualitative research. Ethnography (the study of events as they evolve in natural settings) and semiotics (the study of the codes and signs that enable humans to derive meaning from their surroundings) become important subjects of study. Learning such research strategies in pre-service education allows novices to become meta-analysts of teacher knowledge and thinking. This means that they are empowered to reveal the deep structures that determine the professional activities of teachers. In the process they develop a reflexive awareness that allows them to discern the ways that teacher perception is shaped by the socioeducational context with its accompanying linguistic codes, cultural signs, and tacit views of the world.

This reflexive awareness, this stepping back from the world as we are accustomed to seeing it, requires that the prospective teachers construct their perceptions of the world anew. This reconstruction of their perceptions is not conducted in a random way but in a manner that undermines the forms of teacher thinking that appear natural, that opens to question expert knowledge that has been officially verified. Reflexively aware action researchers ask where their own cognitive forms come from, in the process clarifying their own critical postmodern system of meaning as they reconstruct the role of practitioner. The ultimate justification for such research activity is practitioner empowerment—an empowerment that provides teachers the skill to overcome the modernist tendency to discredit their integrity as capable, reflexively aware professionals (Slaughter 1989, 264; Carr and Kemmis 1986, 39, 56).

Indeed, there is more to teaching than meets the modernist eye, more than is included in technicist teacher education programs. The purpose of a postmodern teacher education is not to learn the right answers, the hand-me-down knowledge of the research experts; on the contrary, critical postmodern teacher education consists of making the most of the unanticipated complications of the classroom. Technicist methods courses and student teaching do not address the innate uncertainty of teaching—they attempt to deny it. Thus, postmodern teacher educators refuse to promise the provision of a generic form of teacher thinking applicable to all students in all contexts. Neither do they promise to reduce the uncertainty of the profession by the application of quick technical fixes. The postmodern turn implies a humility, an admission that teacher educators also agonize over the confusing uncertainties of everyday practice. To do otherwise would be to revert to the dishonesty of modernism's veil of certainty (Clark 1987, 19–20).

Thus, as postmodern teacher education students eschew right answers, they learn to produce their own knowledge. In modernist teacher education programs, teachers don't produce knowledge. James Garrison finds such a situation strange and remarkable. No wonder teachers are disempowered. Garrison argues; they are not even viewed as professionals. The knowledge they convey to students is on loan from the experts, it is not the property of the teachers (Garrison 1988, 488). Teachers as researchers audaciously claim the right to participate in the production of knowledge, while at the same time retaining their humility concerning the tentative, provisional nature of the knowledge. The production of new knowledge gleaned from the lived world of the students and the members of the community surrounding the school is very much a part of a critical postmodern effort to reconstruct culture and reconceive the role of education around a democratic system of meaning. As long as officially certified experts retain the power to determine what counts as knowledge, little reform is possible. If we hold the power to produce our own knowledge, then we are empowered to reconstruct our own consciousnesses. The tyranny of expert-produced interpretations of traditions can be subverted and our futures can be reinvented along the lines of a critical postmodern system of meaning.

This issue of knowledge control moves us into a direct confrontation with teacher power. We cannot maintain a view of students as democratic participants and teachers as disempowered technicians. Over sixty years ago, John Dewey argued that teachers must assume the power to assert their perspectives on matters of educational importance with the assurance that this judgment will affect what happens in schools. Present technicist models of teacher education do not accept this argument, often teaching novices not to seek empowerment, not to think in an independent manner. Indeed, the hidden curriculum of technicist teacher education promotes a passive view of teachers, they are seen as rule followers who are rendered more "supervisable" with their standardized lesson plan formats and their adaptation to technical evaluation plans.

Advocates of critical democratic teacher empowerment are offended by technicist teacher educators and technicist school administrators who dismiss the role of teachers as active participants in policy making on the grounds that they lack competence. As Dewey argued decades ago, if teachers are incapable of such a role, how can they execute the dictates of their superiors in any other way than an incompetent manner? The argument that we must wait until men and women are prepared to assume the responsibilities of participation has been deployed as an attempt to thwart every democratic impulse in history. In the discourse of Reagan–Bush educational reform, the concept of teacher empowerment is lost as democracy is reduced to a set of inherited principles that teach teachers (and students) to adapt to rather than to question the social and institutional arrangement they encounter. The teacher education that accompanies these reforms disregards any analysis of the nature of the democratic impulse and avoids the cultivation of the skills necessary to a critical examination of the social and educational institutions in which they live and work (Aronowitz and Giroux 1991, 187; Brown 1982, 11).

THE CONSTRUCTIVIST DANCE: FROM COGNITIVE TO POLITICAL EMPOWERMENT

Constructivism builds a cognitive path to a political door in teacher education. If teacher education was to view teacher learning and thinking from a constructivist perspective, the technicist effort to adapt teachers to undemocratic, hyperrational schools would appear inappropriate—as out of place as Jim Nabors in a Woody Allen movie. When teacher educators act on the constructivist notion that the learner and the environment comprise a dynamic system in which cognitive growth is constrained and extended by sociopolitical infrastructures, the content of teacher education will change. Intelligence itself has something to do with this interaction, with the capacity to act upon the world in particular ways (Codd 1984, 14). Thus, if cognition always involves the interaction of learner and environment, why do schools in general and teacher education in particular neglect the study of the environment, the social context in which learning takes place?

Here is where constructivism moves to critical constructivism. Critical constructivists perceive a socially constructed world and ask what are the forces that shape our constructions. Our constructions of reality are not freely made but are shaped by power interests in the larger society. We construct our consciousness within the boundaries of discursive practices and regimes of truth molded by power. In order to understand our constructions, we must familiarize ourselves with these power interests. Without this sociopolitical grounding, constructivism often falls prey to psychologism—an emphasis of the cognitive features of consciousness construction to the neglect of the sociological. Without our critical grounding we are helpless to answer Peter McLaren's quintessential critical question: Why are some constructions of educational reality embraced and officially legitimated by the dominant culture while others are repressed (McLaren 1989, 169)?

Our critical constructivist politicization of cognition empowers our ability to critique teacher education in ways that expose not only hidden assumptions but also hidden outcomes. For example, the technicist emphasis on research on teaching that compares instructional methods of teachers ignores the most important aspect of the instructional process—the way students cognitively process what and how the teachers teach. The study of this processing would move far beyond quantitative analysis of student test scores vis-à-vis particular categories of instructional methods. It would involve the analysis of student consciousness, student constructions of particular disciplinary areas, and the social forces that have helped shape these constructions both before and after the formal instructional process occurred.

In this way teacher educators could begin to make far more sense of the sociocognitive impact of various instructional processes. Contextualized in this manner, such studies would be far more useful to prospective teachers but would involve them in the analysis of the instructional process, the contextual dynamics of consciousness construction. Thus, novices would become action researchers who explored the phenomenology of the teaching process, uncovering semiotic codes and discursive practices which granted insight into the deep structures moving classroom events. In such a professional education, student teaching becomes a period of experimentation where novices explore the socioeducational dynamics of the school and community, while at the same time, researching themselves in their own teaching.

Constructivism assumes that human behavior cannot be properly studied when isolated from social and psychological variables—for example, race, class, gender, place, repressed desires, intentions, and emotional states. Individuals will always reorganize incoming information on the basis of prior constructions, ideologies, and value orientations (Jones and Cooper 1987, 9). If we accept such constructivist assertions, how then is it possible for us to perpetuate forms of teacher education that take no account of prospective teachers' constructions of reality and, at the same time, fail to teach prospective teachers a battery of research methods to uncover their future students' constructions? Thus, the meanings of student answers, of classroom events in general depend on these prior constructions of ideology, values, and school purpose: How have classroom meanings, codes, and conventions been negotiated; how have individual students "made meaning"? Without such knowledge or the ability to uncover it, teachers never become insiders to the lived world of the classroom. They never bridge the chasm between teaching and learning, as they remain an ethereal presence that haunts the periphery of student experience.

Critical constructivist teacher education is grounded on an understanding of instruction as an intricate dance involving the teacher, the child, and the child's environment. Contrary to the beliefs of maturationists, the development of the learner is not an automatic process. Critical constructivists maintain that the process of development must be nurtured. As a result, critical constructivists advocate a teacher education that provides prospective teachers experiences helping students construct knowledge by way of hypothesizing, posing questions, researching answers, developing systems of meaning, imagining, and inventing (Fosnot 1988, 12–20). Prospective teachers study the etymology of their own constructions which, in turn, enable them to facilitate such a process with their students.

This etymological study is complex, involving a critical study of the ways power manifests itself in both social convention and individual consciousness. Prospective teachers would need to study the race, class, gender, and place dimensions of identity formation and how such a process takes place on the terrain of popular culture and youth subculture. Novices would explore the historical purposes of schooling and how these purposes were manifested in their own school lives and their own consciousness construction. In other words, a critical constructivist teacher education would transform colleges of education into serious academic institutions dedicated to an intense sociopsychological analysis of the effects of schooling. The ways that women and men construct their consciousnesses and the role that education plays in that process would become a guiding concern of teacher education—a concern that would necessitate interdisciplinary connections and research alliances across the university.

Admittedly, such a vision of a critical constructivist teacher education is radical—especially in the political ambience of the 1990s. Teacher thinking has become politicized in this vision of education, as questions of power and its impact on how we construct our belief systems and subjectivities become cardinal concerns. Such a vision of teaching cannot claim political neutrality, for it identifies itself with a critical system of meaning—a source of authority that aligns itself with the disempowered, those who suffer as a result of existing social and educational arrangements. Let us now delve more deeply into the politics of thinking and its relationship to the empowerment of teachers.

Chapter 3

The Politics of Thinking

Education is an inherently political process. Whether we are making decisions about who gets to attend school (in 1965 southerners were debating whether or not to admit black students to their state colleges) or what information to include in the curriculum (do we teach what it was like to be poor and female in New York City in 1820?), questions of power arise. We may privilege whites over blacks, males over females. Critical postmodern teachers are not politically neutral, as they identify with a critical system of meaning and all of its allegiances. The difference between critical postmodern teachers and teachers who see themselves as neutral is that critical postmodern practitioners admit to their political preference. Claims of neutrality ring rather hollow when one examines the work of teaching. On a daily basis teachers choose to include some forms of knowledge while excluding others from the curriculum, they legitimate particular beliefs while delegitimating others.

Michel Foucault extends our understanding of the political nature of education. Discursive practices—the tacit rules that define what can and cannot be said, who speaks and who must listen, and whose constructions of reality are valid and scientific and whose are unlearned and unimportant—will always reflect political relationships in the society, in the classroom. Fields of knowledge, Foucault concludes, will take their forms as a result of the power relations of discursive practices (Bowers and Flinders 1990, 157–61). Thus, the courses of action teachers take will reflect forms of pedagogical knowledge that have been officially legitimated by publishers, colleges of education, and school districts. As time passes such knowledge comes to be viewed not as a political discourse but as unquestioned common sense. Ethical or moral concerns with the assumptions embedded within the knowledge are dismissed and debates about policy are removed from the moral and ethical arena and transferred to technical questions of what constitutes efficient instruction.

For example, questions concerning teaching strategies that make use of the knowledge brought to school by traditional Appalachian Mountain children are ethical in nature. They are ethical in that such strategies are based on an ethic of cultural inclusivity that attempts to avoid the privileging of dominant cultural ways of being over subordinate or economically disadvantaged cultures. After a state-mandated educational reform required teacher-directed inculcation of facts for the purpose of improving standardized test scores, supervisors informed teachers that class research projects on Appalachian culture simply do not fit into the teacher evaluation techniques. "We are evaluating a teacher's ability to present a body of information to a group. How would we evaluate a teacher on a day that students were putting together interviews into a booklet on their Appalachian heritage? On that day the teacher wouldn't really be teaching, providing information to the students." Thus, the ethical issue, the issue of power and politics would be relegated to the realm of the technical. The political dimension of teacher thinking, of the teaching process—the recognition of the dignity of the Appalachian subculture and its role in the curriculum—cannot even be discussed.

COGNITIVE PASSIVITY UNDERMINES POLITICAL FREEDOM

Not only does modernist education inadvertently dismiss the political dimensions of teaching, it fails to connect questions of intellectual passivity to political freedom. If instruction involves simply providing information that is intended to improve standardized test scores or even designed to facilitate participation in practical activities that are always prescribed, the thinking that results from the intent of such instruction will hold little meaning for the student or the teacher. Indeed, such instruction may be viewed by some educational critics as ineffective but at least politically neutral, as it passes along the truths of earlier generations, to contemporary students. Again, the political dimension is hidden. As students are subjected to such instruction, they are tied to the whipping post of tradition.

Rewarded for uncritical acceptance of the values of the past, students remain victims of the restraints of earlier generations. Critical thought is not the province of the school—it takes place in the students' own time, on a very different terrain of culture. Ironically, it is not the school that encourages such analysis but the world of music, TV, and film. Unfortunately, the two worlds often remain unconnected, as students come to see the cold, concrete, disembodied school experience as no place for critical, analytical thought. Thinking in the modernist school for both student and teacher often is rewarded for the degree to which it reflects the dominant ideology of mainstream courtesy marked by a conception of dissent as distasteful and the status quo power relations implied by an acceptance of laissez-faire capitalism. Thus, a form of politically passive conformity is cultivated that views good students and teachers as obedient to externally imposed ways of thinking and rules that possess little personal meaning. In such a context neither students nor teachers are encouraged to construct new ways of seeing when beset with an unanticipated contradictory situation. Piaget labeled this process accommodation, the reshaping of cognitive structures to accommodate unique aspects of what is being perceived in new contexts. In other words, through our knowledge of a variety of comparable contexts we begin to understand their similarities and differences, we learn from our comparison of the different contexts.

Employing critical theory to push Piaget one more cognitive step, a more critical notion of accommodation is offered. Understanding the socially constructed nature of our comprehension of reality, critical accommodation involves the attempt to disembed ourselves from the pictures of the world painted by power. For example, a teacher's construction of intelligence would typically be molded (assimilated) by a powerful scientific discourse that equated intelligence with scores on intelligence tests. The teacher would critically accommodate the concept as she or he began to examine students who had been labeled by the scientific discourse as unintelligent but upon a second look exhibited characteristics that in an unconventional way seemed sophisticated. The teacher would then critically accommodate (or integrate) this recognition of exception into a definition of intelligence that challenged the dominant discourse. Thus empowered to move beyond the confines of the socially constructed ways of seeing intelligence, the teacher could discover unique forms of intelligence among his or her students—students who under the domination of the scientific discourse of intelligence testing would have been overlooked and relegated to the junk heap of the school. In a sense, this process of critical accommodation is what Howard Gardner employed when he conceived his theory of multiple intelligences (Gardner 1983). This is the kind of thinking that allows us to escape the gravitational pull of modernist passivity with its cognitively deadening, uninterpreted inculcation of tradition.

In a postmodern reality saturated as it is by media imagery, critical educators are faced with a difficult but not impossible task in their attempt to unmask the hidden political dimensions of thinking. Critical postmodern educators must "capture the image" of what it means to be a teacher, to be a thoughtful, educated person. We must become a part of the struggle to name popular culture, as we induce our students to question the basic assumptions grounding the society's political ideology; indeed, the questioning of society's political ideology is a basic act of critical thinking. And a dangerous act it is. Whenever we talk of challenging the tacit political dimensions of mainstream thinking, of advocating a pedagogy that admits to its political allegiances, we open ourselves to attack on our alleged attempt to indoctrinate our students. Even in these days of qualitative meta-analysis of educational research and educational policy that has exposed the pseudo-objectivity of so-called value-free and politically neutral positions, many technicist educators continue to charge indoctrination when analyzing critical pedagogy.

We must keep politics out of education, many mainstream educators argue, not understanding the inseparability of political and educational questions. Critical educators such as Henry Giroux and Peter McLaren suggest, as I do here, that educators should be made more political—that we expose the hidden politics of neutrality. Our calls are equated with advocacy of a pedagogy of indoctrination. Henry Giroux responds to such changes, arguing that such criticism is theoretically flawed, as it confuses the development of a political vision with the pedagogy that is used in conjunction with it. He then asks: "How can educators make their own political commitment clear while developing forms of pedagogy consistent with the democratic imperative that students learn to make choices, organize, and act on their own beliefs (Giroux 1988a, 69)?" Drawing upon the work of Paulo Freire, Giroux envisages an ethically grounded, democratically committed answer. Education is never neutral—indeed, when we attempt to remain neutral, like many churches in Nazi Germany, we support the prevailing power structure. Recognition of the political implications of thinking suggest that teachers should take a position and make it understandable to their students. However (and critical pedagogues are very clear about this), teachers' political commitments do not grant them the right to impose these positions on their students.

It is not the critical pedagogues who are guilty of impositional teaching, Giroux contends, but many of the mainstream critics themselves. When mainstream opponents of critical pedagogy promote the reductionist notion that all language and political behavior that oppose the dominant ideology are forms of cultural imposition, they forget how experience is constructed within a social context marked by an inequitable distribution of power. To refuse to name the structural sources of human suffering and exploitation is to take a position that supports oppression and the power relations that sustain it. The mainstream argument that any oppositional way of seeing represents an imposition of one's views on somebody else is similar to the nineteenth-century ruling-class idea that raising one's voice, struggling politically, or engaging in social criticism violated a "gentlemanly" code of civility. Who's indoctrinating whom? In the name of neutrality, the mainstream promotes particular forms of decontextualized thinking—the irony of objectivity.

TRANSCENDING COMMONSENSE NEUTRALITY: OVERCOMING POLITICAL NAIVETÉ

Teacher education does not discuss these issues. Teachers enter schools unaware of the connection between political perspective and school policy. They are blind to the fact that the way their principal "governs" the school in a top-down series of directives holds an implicit political perspective concerning the way power is shared (or not shared) in an institution. They often see language not as medium for codes and signs that signal whose knowledge is legitimate and whose voice may be heard but as a neutral conduit through which unproblematized meaning may pass. Teacher in-service education typically finds such issues outside the concerns of the school and bases its goals on the assumption that teachers are engaged in a process of behavioral management and politically neutral decision making (Goodman 1986, 28–30).

This political naiveté does not emanate only from right-wing school leaders bent on perfecting more effective management techniques of control. Liberals are also guilty even as they recognize that schools are places where political and personal meanings are created. Liberals still buy into the Cartesian–Newtonian belief that discourses can be separated from power. For example, Daniel Liston and Kenneth Zeichner in the name of critical pedagogy argue that the distinction between the teacher as educator and the teacher as political activist must be maintained. In the classroom, they argue, the teacher is first and foremost an educator. In the everyday commonsense conversation this is a powerful argument, implying as it does that teachers should not use the classroom to "shove" their political opinions down their students' throats. Of course, Liston and Zeichner maintain that the world outside the classroom is the venue for political crusading. But like other mainstream educators, Liston and Zeichner miss an important point: The attempt to separate education and politics is not so simple. How is a teacher to choose a textbook or how is he or she to decide what knowledge to teach? These are obvious political decisions that must be made on a daily basis *in* the classroom.

Liston and Zeichner call for educators to help students find their voices and identities, but voices and identities are constructed by incorporating and rejecting a multiplicity of competing ideological constructions. Which ones do teachers encourage? Which ones do they discourage? These are political decisions. Liston and Zeichner contend that teachers should enable students to acquire and critically examine moral beliefs. This must take place before students engage in politically transformative acts. Like weathervanes, such arguments play well to the popular winds with their glorification of neutrality. Political animals who believe that presidents appoint Supreme Court justices who are neutral, who will refrain from letting their political opinions "taint" their judicial rulings, will accept the separation of moral belief from political action. Such a separation reflects a hyperrationalization of politics that represents the political as a very narrow terrain which never overlaps the moral and ethical (Liston and Zeichner 1988, 14). How can the moral and the political be separated? Wasn't the moral commitment to justice the basis of the political work of a Mohandas Gandhi or a Martin Luther King, Jr., or a Susan B. Anthony?

Many teachers who presently are unable to separate themselves from the dominant discourse of neutrality hold a variety of beliefs that can be drawn upon in order for these men and woman to construct a more critical and post-formal mode of practitioner thinking. They are committed to active-intellectual roles for students, a sincere but sometimes vague commitment to human rights, and a budding awareness of the need for gender equality and gender-based constructions of difference. To effectively oppose the forms of teacher disempowerment and student manipulation that too often characterize contemporary schools, they must draw upon these ethical impulses and fuse them with critical political understanding that will help clarify such intuitions and restructure them in a form that can be applied to their everyday practice (Noffke and Brennan 1988, 5).

THE EPISTEMOLOGICAL AND THE POLITICAL: CREATING A CLIMATE OF INQUIRY

The epistemological extension of the modernist revolution initiated by Descartes, Newton, and Bacon is positivism. The assumptions of positivism are drawn from the logic and methods of investigation associated with physical science. In such a context the hermeneutical principles of inter-pretation hold little status. What is important in the positivistic context involves explanation, prediction, and technical control. How we decide what constitutes a desirable state of affairs is of little consequence. Knowledge to the positivist is worthwhile to the extent that it describes objectified data. Critical questions concerning the social construction of knowledge (the codes, media, ideologies, and socioeconomic structures that shape facts and the political interests that direct the selection and evaluation of data) are irrelevant when knowledge is assumed to be objective and value free. Since the hidden values of knowledge are unexamined by the positivistic tradition, the positivistic cult of objectivity suppresses political discussion in the public sphere. Since this knowledge has been arrived upon in what positivists call a value-free manner, it is immune from political questioning. Thus, positivism is silent about its own political nature. It is incapable of gaining insight into how power asym-metries hide in the language of teaching and in everyday life. Since it is incapable of reflecting on the political dimensions of its own thinking, it ultimately offers uncritical support for the status quo (Giroux 1981, 410–53; Scholes 1982).

Patterns of thinking appropriated from the physical sciences simply do not neatly fit in the humanities and education. Focusing on the goals of predication and control, positivistic actions of physical scientific discourse emphasize exactness and precision. In an educational context operating within the orbit of positivist discourse the concern with exactness and precision overrides the latitude and flexibility needed for growth and emancipation. Thus, positivist educators attempt to produce exact forms of empirical proof for concepts that are nonempirical in nature. How might we empirically and precisely measure a student's emancipation or libera-tion from discourses of power? Ever thinking as a positivist, Madeline Hunter extends this point when she admits that the purpose of education may be to develop creative problem solvers and responsible, productive decision makers. But, she says, "I can't cite research to support that statement" (Hunter 1987, 53). Just what kind of research would "support" such a statement? Why would such an nonempirical assertion need to be supported by research even if it were possible to do so?

The inadequacy of the positivist epistemological foundation is well recognized by many students of pedagogy. All too often, however, such ideas have not affected politicians and educational leaders who make policy for public schools. As long as such epistemological assumptions remain unchallenged at the policy-making level, the conversation about teaching and thinking will be stuck in a muddy rut. The creation of a climate of inquiry in which teacher and student can pursue troubling and motivating questions will be delayed by an unquestioned positivism. Behavioral psychology and forms of unrestrained free enterprise capitalism in their decontextualization and disregard of the way social and historical forces shape our consciousness remain important manifestations of a positivist epistemology uncontested by more critical and postmodernist epistemological assumptions.

Obviously positivism, behaviorism, and laissez-faire capitalism are incompatible with critical postmodern epistemology. In positivism's, behaviorism's, and laissez-faire capitalism's acceptance of a decontextualized universe it is assumed that individuals exist outside of history, starting off equally in the meritocratic race for social and economic rewards. Without an appreciation of the socioeconomic forces that help or hinder individuals in their educational and economic pursuits, the concept of social justice is rendered simplistic and unproblematic. Critical constructivism throws a "monkey wrench" into the entire process by forcing us to reconceptualize our notions of social justice and equal opportunity. Social justice involves more than the destruction of legal barriers to economic and educational opportunity. It involves taking into account notions of cultural capital.

Cultural capital involves ways of dressing, acting, thinking, or of representing oneself. For example, the knowledge one would need to deport oneself gracefully in an expensive restaurant is a form of dominant cultural capital. Thus, style, manners, courtesy, language practices, moving, and socializing are all forms of cultural capital. Teachers, Peter McLaren writes, often identify the possession of dominant cultural capital as a natural quality that emanates from a student's "inner essence." However, he cautions, such traits are culturally determined and are inseparable from the socioeconomic class background of the individuals who exhibit them. Students from dominant cultural backgrounds manifest different cultural capital than students from nonwhite or poor homes. Schools will privilege those students who exhibit the dominant cultural capital while punishing those students who possess very different forms of cultural capital. Thus, epistemologies that do not examine contextual factors focus only on hard statistical correlations that dismiss social factors such as cultural capital and its effect on academic performance. Critical postmodern analysts examining educational dimensions that cannot be quantified come to understand that academic performance often does not reflect student ability but represents the school's validation or depreciation of their particular form of cultural capital (McLaren

1989, 190–91; Aronowitz and Giroux 1991, 49–50). A personal anecdote may concretize this concept.

As a young teacher in Tennessee, I taught for a year in an upwardly mobile, suburban middle school. The parents of most of my students were highly educated, successful businesspeople, research scientists, or college professors. As a result, the school was viewed positively in the community. An ethic of academic success was inculcated in most students at home, test scores were high indeed, and most students possessed the dominant cultural capital. And then there was Alvin. Unlike his upper-middle-class schoolmates, Alvin was from a poor family. His father was a greenskeeper at a local public golf course. Coming from such a background, Alvin did not possess the dominant cultural capital. Students and teachers made fun of his thick Tennessee mountain accent with its nonstandard linguistic syntax, his discount-store clothes, his slicked-back hairstyle (before it was "cool"), and his social discomfort (which was interpreted as a lack of good manners). Assessing Alvin's academic performance from a positivistic perspective, he was a failure—his grades were low and his achievement test scores were far below the school average.

But there was much more to Alvin than revealed by statistics. Alvin was very intelligent, intelligent in a variety of interesting ways. Despite his low social status, I watched Alvin exercise sophisticated conflict resolution strategies on the playground, as he several times broke up fights through negotiation. I watched him work for his lunch with the school custodians and the cafeteria workers. Not only was he a good worker but an entertaining social agent as he made them laugh daily. I listened to Alvin's insights into the social and political outcomes of schooling as he talked to me about how hard it was for poor kids to "make it" in a "rich person's school" like ours. I visited Alvin's home—a place devoid of books, magazines, and newspapers—and understood how strange the academic and linguistic dimensions of school must have appeared to a child with Alvin's background. Yet, because of the epistemological infrastructure of school thinking, none of these aspects of Alvin's persona were taken into account; they did not count as knowledge. With his lower socioeconomic class cultural capital some teachers treated him with cruelty, never pausing to see the panoply of fascinating personal qualities, the unique forms of intelligence, and the moral strength that Alvin possessed. Maybe a teacher education that introduced teachers to ways of seeing, to alternate epistemologies that empowered them to disembed themselves from the positivist blinders would prevent the degrading treatment of students like Alvin.

UNDERSTANDING THE SOCIAL
CONSTRUCTION OF KNOWLEDGE:
WAYS OF THINKING, WAYS OF TEACHING

Critical constructivist epistemology reveals the social and power dimensions of knowledge, in the process deconstructing the ways that tradition has shaped both school practice and definitions of "solid" thinking. As critical postmodern practitioners begin to understand these constructions, they realize that the taken-for-granted forms that characterize schools do not find their justification on some "metaphysical truth." Instead, such practitioners find that such forms have discursively won via a long series of historical and political struggles over whose knowledge, whose way of thinking, is the best. Critical postmodern teachers and students thus uncover the socially created hierarchies that travel incognito as Truth. Though known to everyone, the hierarchies mask their "shady" backgrounds of political conflict. As Truth, they are employed as rationales for cultural dominance and asymmetrical power relations (McLaren 1991a, 237).

Thus, schooling as an objective, neutral delivery of the truth—a perspective assumed by all Reagan and Bush reforms—ignores this social construction of knowledge and cognition. It ignores the fact that one of the most important exercises of power in a postmodern world involves the prerogative to define meanings and to specify what knowledge is valuable. Without a critical resistance, knowledge becomes oppression—oppression of nonwhites, the poor, and women. Knowledge that is "totalized" has been unified into a master narrative with the intent of assuming power and seizing control. "Let us wage war on totality," Jean-François Lyotard writes. Lyotard's war is directed toward modernism with its tendency to define an essential human nature, a universal form of intelligence (Aronowitz and Giroux 1991, 67–70; Lyotard 1984, 81–82).

The mainstream educational conversation does not address the power dimensions of schooling, does not concern itself with the way domination is effected in educational contexts. Political and educational leaders' ability to shape the lives and actions of others is often grounded on their ability to employ modes of domination present in mainstream social systems. What often passes as self-policing of behavior is actually a manifestation of this connecting of individual action to the prevailing modes of domination. For example, a male administrator's patriarchal actions toward woman teachers draws upon a long tradition of patriarchal domination. Upper-middle-class students' control of the social life of the school (e.g., cheerleading, dictation of style, student government, proms, homecoming activities, etc.) rests on a tradition of class domination in the larger society. The important point in both examples is that power is validated by its connection to social structure. Its connection to everyday life depends on its relationship to individual consciousness, individual action (Giroux 1988a, 131; Giddens 1986, 91; Britzman 1991, 18).

In this same way, power produces systems of instruction, methods of evaluation, definitions of teacher and student success, and classification and tracking systems that arrange students into advanced, college-bound, general, or vocational tracks. Such divisions provide the knowledge, social practices, cultural capital, and skills required by the class-driven hierarchy of labor in the society's workplaces. The way that power interacts with personal behavior in this case is that school leaders induce students to believe that such class-based divisions of students and workers are natural and necessary. Students from outside the mainstream, the nonwhite and the poor, are convinced that they do not possess the ability to move into upper levels. They are captured by the entanglements of the myths of the cultural and academic inferiority of the outsiders. Black students, for example, who are often very successful in college, report that by the time they were junior high students the culture of the school had convinced them that college was out of the question. Thus, students and their teachers come to accept the myths of inferiority. "How can we expect these students to understand physics?," teachers and guidance counselors ask as they channel the outsiders into nonacademic vocational tracks (McLaren 1991b, 236–37).

ABSTRACT REASONING: THE INVISIBILITY OF THE POLITICAL

Efforts to develop thinking in modern schools, all too often, are under-taken without reference to the political realities inherent in the larger postmodern society. In conceptualizing democratic thinking, many edu-cation scholars expound on the morality of a democratic community. Infrequently, however, do such theorists account for the way power is unjustly distributed in such communities. When such a dramatic political reality is overlooked, schools are at a loss to understand how the quest for democratic educational communities is thwarted by authoritarian impulses which perpetuate and produce oppression and exclusive relationships. These authoritarian impulses take place in the lived world, the everyday lives of students; thus, the experts' view of democratic thinking is removed from the real stories of teachers, students, and administrators (Giroux 1988a, 78). We hear few stories of how particular religious practices, for example, may serve to perpetuate class inequities in the attempt to learn higher orders of thinking.

More traditional, noncritical analyses of thinking would not consider the political dimensions of how fundamentalist religion might influence inequitable power relations expressed in cognitive contexts. Fundamentalism that has exerted tremendous political and educational influence over the past fifteen years is grounded on an absolutist view of religious authority, the literal nature of the Bible as an infallible text, and the centrality of a conversion experience on the road to the solution of the soul. Such perspectives hold serious implications for thinking and teaching and illustrate the often invisible social and political dimensions of cognition. When students with strict fundamentalist backgrounds enter a school dedicated to the idea of teaching post-formal modes of thinking, they find themselves lost and confused. Post-formal thinking requires students to abandon absolutist forms of certainty in their analysis of issues and events. A focus on interpretation devalues the importance of mere rote memorization and recitation. Texts, in a post-formal context, are viewed as code and symbol systems, as deconstruction of hidden or unintended meaning becomes a valued goal of inquiry.

In my own teaching experience I have watched as confused fundamentalist students asked me with fear and a touch of anger before a mid-term exam, *"How can we have a test? We haven't studied anything— everybody has just given their opinions."* From their perspective, the purpose of a classroom is to provide a series of verified facts that are to be committed to memory. The uncertainty of interpretation and analysis is tantamount to "not studying anything." What were these students to memorize for the tests? Metaphorically, what Bible verses were apropos? Fundamentalist students or their friends have told me that upon understanding the "non-Christian" orientation of my class (though the subject of religion specifically had not been addressed), they sought counsel with their ministers. Often the ministers told them to find out how other students made it through the class, to employ those strategies, and to pray during class time to keep any potential negative influences at bay. Other students have stood up in class and "testified" to their love of Jesus Christ and their rejection of the secular humanism that was being promoted in the class. One student announced during a discussion of cognition and women's ways of knowing that as a Christian she was proud to live in subjugation to her husband and to think in the manner he and the Lord saw fit.

As fundamentalist students enter classrooms that promote such post-formal perspectives, they are immediately alienated. Often unable to name their alienation, they find themselves uncomfortable with assignments that might ask students to compare interpretations of different historians on a similar event of the past. Such assignments that tend to point to the socially constructed nature of knowledge are not consistent with home and church perspectives on knowledge. Taught by church leaders the authority of the printed word, the dangerous implications of Biblical interpretation, and the faith-destroying aspects of skepticism, students from fundamentalist backgrounds who find themselves in a post-formal classroom discover that the very same cognitive qualities that are rewarded educationally may send their souls to hell.

Their fundamentalist background has spilled over its religious boundaries into the cognitive sphere. Often the students are unable to reconcile the two worlds. They may be able to escape the cognitive blinders of fundamentalism, finding themselves failures at higher levels of thinking; or they may simply reject the value of such thinking, so they strike out in anger at the secular humanist teachers who attempt to "destroy" their faith; or a few may abandon their religion as they come to understand the inevitable conflict between post-formal thinking and fundamentalism. Add to this that many fundamentalist children come from poor homes with parents who possess minimal formal education and we begin to see not only the social but the economic aspects of the intersection of religion and cognition. This is the lived experience of many students—because of particular social realities they are unable to perform in the ways deemed appropriate by the school. Only through an understanding of the sociopolitical context on which students' lives take shape can we understand the often unseen ways lived sociopolitical reality shapes cognitive ability and thus what dominant educational discourse labels scholastic aptitude.

Another aspect of the invisible political dimension of schooling and cognition involves the attempts of school leaders to use schooling not as much to foster democracy as an ideal but to provide a mechanism for the social control and production of individuals suitable to the needs of the workplace (Kaufman 1978, 20). The recognition of such an intent as it relates to the historic purposes of schooling opens our eyes to a fourth dimension of education, a dimension where the teaching of thinking takes on a meaning quite different than the uncritical orthodoxy would have it. In their attempt to produce "suitable" workers, educational leaders have not questioned the just nature of the existing political order—indeed, they have never embraced an attempt to contextualize cognition by helping students develop a systematic theoretical critique of power inequities and forms of oppression. America is offered to students as a place where a legal equality of opportunity has been achieved in such a context little need exists for forms of thinking that examine the ways that inequality shapes institutions and their impact on individuals (Carlson 1991, 12–13).

Such an absence illustrates the failures of liberal reform to offer alternative ways of seeing—seeing education and cognition in particular. Liberalism has made a fetish of proper process, thus abstracting the lived worlds of individuals and the consequences of particular results from the realm of the political. Complex relations of power and human suffering get lost amidst the celebration of individualism and citizenship. As it focuses on the abstract concept of the fairness of the rules that govern a society, it emphasizes an education for rationality removed from time, place, or the experience of individuals. In other words, as liberalism hyper-rationalizes process, it disregards the social traditions that individuals and groups bring to schools, community organizations, or labor unions. Liberalism's modernist faith that reason and reason alone will lead to a just society, Dennis Carlson carefully argues, squashes its attempt to connect itself with particular political movements and the ways individuals have framed their personal relationships to those movements. Such relationships have relied little on abstract principles and more on our emotional loyalties to those who have suffered alongside us, on our emotional investments in the places we call home. Liberals have assumed that such emotional ties, related as they are to the highly subjective nature of consciousness, are not worthy investments. Thus, to liberals, the modes of thinking that emerge from our subjective lived experience from the perspectives we gain from one particular positions in the web of reality or from the values we develop through experience are too contingent, too tainted by feeling (Carlson 1991, 7–8).

When we examine Carol Gilligan's brilliant feminist critique of Lawrence Kohlberg's abstract, legalistic, and decontextualized theory of moral thinking, we see evidence of the valuing of these subjective forms of knowing. Girls' development of moral reasoning is different from boys, as it involves the consideration of personal experience, caring and connectedness, negotiation over absolute judgments, responsibilities over rights, and contextual and narrative thinking over cognition which is formal and abstract. Despite its gender-based contextualization of thinking about justice, Dennis Carlson argues that Gilligan's critique is still stripped of critical sociopolitical contextualization as illustrated by the fact that her interviewees are largely middle class and all white. Trapped within the confines of "psychologism," Gilligan's critique is stripped of its historical dimensions and, not unlike liberalism in general, is abstracted (or removed) from struggles of power in contemporary society. Individual consciousness comes to be viewed outside the ideological and discursive traditions that construct our ways of understanding ourselves and the world (Carlson 1991, 9–10).

Those of us concerned with a critical postmodern view of schooling grounded upon democratic nations of social justice are troubled by liberalism's inability to recognize the political dimensions of cognition. Compared to liberals, however, conservatives have become the expert magicians of education who can make the political elephant disappear into thin air. The curriculum is viewed by the right wing as a politically neutral repository of static wisdom that is to be uncritically passed down to the present generation. The canon transcends the political, conservatives argue; the great works are timeless and universal and should be employed to teach us the essential of human nature. The mission of the Right, as expressed by William Bennett, is to reclaim a cultural legacy stolen by lightweight liberals. In his eyes the progressive attempt to subject the curriculum—the Western tradition—to a critical examination is illegitimate. Wrapping themselves in the flag of political neutrality, right-wing advocates employ a form of pretzel logic as they hurl charges of educational politicization at their critical adversaries. Listening to the stories of William Bennett, Allan Bloom, Roger Kimball, and Dinesh D'Souza, one gets the impression that schools are ready to wave the scholarly white flag and surrender educational institutions to liberals. Portraying themselves as besieged underdogs, conservatives write of school leaders running from the advancing enemy leaving their intellectual principles and moral grounding behind (Weisberg 1987, 52; Kimball 1990, 33).

Evoking memories of Richard Hofstadter's description of "the paranoid style of American politics," right-wing proponents warn of a grand leftist educational conspiracy. Interest groups pressure schools to revamp their curriculum, conservative Roger Kimball writes, in a way that only ten or twenty years ago would have been disregarded because of its flagrant political bias (Kimball 1990, 3, 14). Questions such as Where are women in the curriculum?, or Where are black people? represent a blatant politicization of the curriculum. Like expert illusionists, however, right-wing analysts frame conservative curricula that exclude the consideration of such questions as politically neutral. Obviously, political assumptions are behind both positions. Education and thinking are political acts, as they inevitably confront questions of power and power distribution.

The conservatives have trouble understanding that reading and our thinking about reading (whether we are reading and thinking about the traditional canon or about student and teacher lives) are sociopolitical acts—our interpretations cannot be separated from where we are standing when we read and think, in other words, our location in the web of reality.

The simplistic right-wing illusion of objectivity will continue to impede a serious analysis of the way modern schools and the modern reform movements of the Reagan–Bush era affect the socially and economically marginalized. In this context teachers often are asked to parrot prearranged and isolated fact bits without attending to their underlying assumptions. Right-wing reform leaders cannot encourage teachers to reflect on the political presuppositions of their lessons (e.g., who is excluded, who is included) because they themselves are blind to the presuppositions of their school reforms in general. Of course, this blindness results from their naiveté to what constitutes a political presupposition. Critical democratic educators need to help teachers learn to think about how knowledge and policy are produced. At this level of deconstruction, teachers will begin to comprehend the "logic" behind the facts, their context and significance, and the difference competing assumptions about knowledge and policy make on the way teachers think and teach and how students think and live their lives.

For example, the difference between the way Allan Bloom views the curriculum and the way John Dewey viewed it in the early part of the century is profound and consequential. Dewey understood that inducting a student into a participatory social role involves the cultivation of a sophisticated form of thinking based on an active engagement with the assumptions and symbols of the culture. Rejecting the argument later made by Bloom that induction into a culture involves the uncritical acquisition of a neutral body of traditional knowledge, Dewey maintained that social symbols should be connected to the understandings that were already present in the students' experience. A democratic public is not a static entity, Dewey concluded, as it is always in the process of defining and redefining itself. When students are simply filled with predigested facts about the society, with unexamined social knowledge, the self-formation process is impeded. What Bloom and the Right fail to understand is that the debate over social meaning is a consummate democratic act; indeed, the public is actually created in the process of the debate, in the struggle to assign meaning to tradition and its impact on the present. The Deweyan vision of the relationship between curriculum and tradition is extended by Mikhail Bahktin's notion of dialogism. In this context tradition becomes a text where the multiple voices and multiple perspectives of the public intersect. Aware of this "heteroglossia," individuals expand their ability to think as citizens—citizens who discover new dimensions in tradition, in the traditional curriculum in particular. Such individuals come to understand the tacit forces of oppression, in the process discovering social possibilities never before considered (Feinberg 1989, 136–37; Greene 1988, 129–30).

COGNITIVE MANIPULATION OR COGNITIVE GROWTH

We have framed the crisis of modernity as a crisis of cognition—the cognitive illness. Marked by an asymmetrical mode of thinking that has become obsessed with the rational management of the lives of individuals, modernist education has found itself trapped within a prison of nihilism, a culture of manipulation. Education in the postmodern world becomes a pawn of powerful groups who attempt to use it as a means of solving social problems in a way that serves their own interests. Pushed and pulled by such groups, schools are not moved by educational and political visions that value the human spirit but by self-serving and often cynical impulses that seek to control that very spirit. Thus, schools, as most teachers would testify, are immersed in a crisis of motivation. Devoid of a meaningful justification for the pursuit of learning, teachers and students wander aimlessly within a maze of fragmented information. Classrooms often become spiritless places where rule-following teachers face a group of students who have no conception of any intrinsic value of the lessons being taught.

Is thinking to be shaped in accord with the perceived demands of economic production or is it to be nurtured by those who are interested in personal and social development? The modernist concern with human development in terms of human capital and productivity allows for mass acceptance of Reagan–Bush educational reform as merely one step in a government-directed economic–technological competitive strategy. Like other aspects of the postmodern landscape, thinking has been commodified—its value measured only in terms of the logic of capital. The moral and ethical dimensions of thinking in this context have grown increasingly irrelevant.

Aware of the need to avoid oversimplification, it can be argued that much of contemporary cognitive education can be divided into one of two classifications: (1) education for cognition manipulation or (2) education for cognitive growth or emancipation. The one-truth epistemology of positivism dovetailed seductively with the scientific management orientations of the proponents of human capital development. Both viewpoints had overcome any moral qualms with the manipulation of human beings for desired ends. The controlled labor of the factory with its "team players" exercising their "democratic" control of the workplace by making decisions about the most trivial dimensions of the operation (e.g., where to locate the water cooler) was similar to types of teachers desired by the "schools of excellence" of the technicist reforms. Such teachers would follow top-down decisions as they taught from their prepackaged, teacher-proof materials and rewarded students for devotion to memory work that studiously avoided the encouragement of questioning attitudes about the entire process (Young 1990, 8–12; Koetting 1988, 3).

Conservatives have sought to employ a cognition of manipulation by appealing to the virtues of the Protestant work ethic to increase productivity in the factories and the schools. In addition to their appeal to traditional values, conservatives have perfected the science of management. Wrapping themselves in the banner of democratic inclusivity, forces of the Right have convinced many that forms of dissent are distasteful, are manifestations of a "bad attitude," or are even unpatriotic. Liberals, on the other hand, have sought to provide a more equitable distribution of wealth, more equal educational opportunities. In this attempt liberals have employed the same modernist forms of thinking, the same modernist bureaucratic mechanisms that led to the cognitive illness and the crisis of motivation in the first place.

In order to accomplish their egalitarian goals, liberals deem it necessary to increase economic productivity. Here is where the tactics of liberals and conservatives converge—both groups focus their attention exclusively on the state and the political economics of labor instead of the individual and his or her community. Liberals have been unable to commit themselves so far to the political and cognitive dimensions of personal development. For example, liberals have been far more sensitive to the concerns of feminism than have conservatives (Young 1990, 12–14). The liberal concern, however, has focused on the political and economic dimensions of feminism—for example, issues of equal representation and equal work for equal pay. As far as the lessons of feminism vis-à-vis cognition are concerned, liberals have expressed little interest. Feminist discomfort with patriarchal thinking, with its hierarchical orientation, its concern with connectedness as opposed to abstract individualism, its interest in the limitations of androcentric logocentrism, and its perspective on the inseparability of the private and public domains, has not altered the masculinist character of mainstream liberalism.

Indeed, the postmodern landscape has been painted by the ethic of manipulation—an ethic unchallenged by the dominant politics of liberalism and conservatism. Modernist science has produced the manipulative strategies of the advertising industry, which in turn has revolutionized the nature of political campaigns. The culture of marketing has dramatically altered the discourse of politics, relegating traditional forms of ethical and political thinking to the cloisters of academia far away from the public sphere. While the intent of the advertising-directed politics of the postmodern is manipulative, progressive impulses are salvaged by a myriad of contradictory readings. No one can predict the outcome of the media capture of campaigning. Many of those who view the ads fall victim to the manipulative intent of the producers; others while recognizing the manipulation become discouraged and turn off any involvement in a corrupt and degraded political system; and still others who recognize the manipulation are inspired to fight it by organizing community groups dedicated by authentic public conversation.

The manipulative intent of the New Right of the late twentieth century is frightening and in no way should be minimized. When considering the politics of thinking, the impact of such an outlook must be carefully examined. The discourse of international competition constructs the framework for the right-wing justification of manipulation. If we are not to be economically surpassed by the developing economics of disciplined and authoritarian Asia, we must cultivate more social obedience and commonness of purpose and less democracy and liberty. As North American economies face more competition from the East with its accompanying diminution of national profits, a disparity grows between the increasing claims made on government and its capacity to provide. The conservatives under Reagan and Bush attempted to reduce claims on government by deflecting them to the "free market" and to volunteerism (Bush's thousand points of light). Also, they attempted to discredit and gain control over voices of dissent such as intellectuals, school teachers, and voices of the mass media. In addition, conservatives—in order to achieve greater steering power for the government—strengthened bureaucratic control of institutions such as education by injecting management strategies like cost-benefit analysis, detailed fiscal management, and quantitative planning strategies.

The most important aspect of the Right's ongoing strategy of manipulation, however, involves a fundamental issue of cognition—the mobilization of consent. This process involves the way in which individuals come to see themselves and their role in society as a result of their identification with meanings produced in popular media and social institutions. For example, the conservatives have been able to draw upon male identification with the view of masculinity promoted by the films of Clint Eastwood or with Sylvester Stallone's *Rambo*. While the identification is often subtle and subliminal, George Bush made the relationship explicit with his famous evocation of Eastwood's "read my lips." What is especially important here for students of the politics of thinking is that the recognition of the way consent is mobilized alerts us to the fact that ideological production and even learning itself are processes that take place outside the boundaries of rational thinking (Giroux and Simon 1989, 15–16). Feeling and desire are often more important in the individual quest for identity than is reason. Conservatives of our era have recognized this reality and have rather cynically used it for their political gain. Ronald Reagan did not attempt, for example, to logically convince the public of the need to return to traditional values; he mobilized the electorate's consent by appeal to the image of traditional values, by connecting them to the pleasure of a romanticized notion of a bygone golden era. We miss a major point when we assume that thinking is a rational process "untainted" by feeling or cultural identification.

It is this aspect of thinking, its emotionality and symbolic identification, that allows the culture of manipulation to operate so effectively. At the same time, however, this aspect of thinking holds emancipatory possibilities as we come to understand the array of moral and ethical identifications that move individuals to perform courageously and heroically. With this understanding individuals can come to think in a manner that connects their logic to an ethical identification with a politics that rejects the manipulation of human beings and the subordination of people to external ends, while supporting an emancipatory politics of self-directed men and women working together in a democratic community. Let us examine in more detail the nature of the critical postmodern thinking that springs from such a politics.

Chapter 4

The Escape from the Politics of Modernist Thinking

When do we make the break from the prison of modernist thinking? When do we release ourselves on our own recognizance to explore the uncharted continents of cognition which are yet to be mapped? A critical politics of egalitarianism values the disclosure of the relationship between social structures shaped by power and our personal identities. Such disclosures form the basis of a radical ethic of agape, a love without strings attached, that is ready to learn from those who are exploited by manipulative social practices. Such a radical love is focused on the fight against inequality, especially those forms of inequality that are rationalized in the name of *equality* and the fight for justice. Radical love is particularly concerned with promoting concrete forms of justice which emerge from specific historical circumstances and involve specific men and women. In these specific circumstances our critical politics creates knowledge as it reclaims and legitimates the voices that power has insidiously silenced—for example, women's voice of caring, Third World voices who speak the doubly conscious poetry of the oppressed, or the student voices struggling to express a sense of self in schools designed to conform them. Thus, our critical cognition values difference and learns from it but always contextualizes it within a larger framework of unity and human solidarity.

THE POLITICS OF DIVERSITY: IT'S ONLY ROCK N' ROLL

As it values difference within the context of human solidarity, our politics of egalitarianism encourages uniqueness and multidimensional standards. Viewing cognition from this vantage point, we are drawn to a position that appreciates a variety of thinking styles, that recognizes multiple forms of intelligence. We do not have to look very far to find different thinking styles—teach any class at any level. Different forms of intelligence are all around us. We read Howard Gardner's *Frames of Mind: The Theory of Multiple Intelligences* (1983) or observe people that schools have labeled as unintelligent. More likely than not, we will discover fascinating and sophisticated forms of intelligence. When we avoid the cognitive reductionism found in many technicist schools, we uncover forms of valuable thinking.

Many of us have observed individuals with little success in formal education display cognitive abilities that far surpass those of far more "successful" students—and I am not referring here simply to categories of intelligence that are commonly attributed to individuals with little formal education, such as mechanical abilities, kinesthetic talents, or primitive (unschooled) musical capabilities. For example, I watched a university custodian who left school after the ninth grade understand long before anyone else that a recognized "scholar" on the faculty was gregarious but intellectually quite shallow. By playing the role of the distinguished intellectual and demanding to be treated as such, the professor wove his colleagues into a tapestry of academic illusion; only the custodian could see that the "emperor was wearing no clothes."

In no way am I attempting to romanticize the unschooled. The point is simple: As our critical politics of egalitarianism embraces unrecognized forms of intelligence, it challenges the reductionism and mechanism of the quantitative measures of thinking that permeate the school. Indeed, our egalitarian politics rejects the evaluation of students against a single standard of cognition. Threatened by the advocacy of multiple standards of evaluation, the technicist forces of the status quo are agitated. Countering what they frame as a breakdown of standards, the vulgarization of society, they attack critical politics. When Allan Bloom (1987) charges that rock music debases our culture or Roger Kimball (1990) asserts that feminism is a threat to all we hold sacred or Dinesh D'Souza (1991) maintains that an emphasis on cultural diversity undermines traditional academic excellence, they are all expressing an ethnocentric fear of losing control of the discourse, losing their right to define quality.

What the conservatives forget again and again is Karl Marx's contention that knowing involves the transformation of reality. Knowing about something does not mean copying it—it means acting upon it. As anti-Cartesians have long maintained, there is no separation between the knower and known. In turn, Piaget argued that there is an unavoidable interaction between a subject and an object. Implicit within our critical constructivist view of knowledge and thinking is the understanding that knowledge is not certified by its status as tradition—it is negotiable. Learning does not entail simply the uncritical accumulation of cultural facts but the dereification of knowledge, that is the removal of social knowledge from its pedestal, its codified status (Benson 1989, 343).

The value of Jacques Derrida's poststructural deconstruction in our political analysis of cognition relates directly to this dereification of knowledge. Western philosophical and educational thought, Derrida contends, has been captured by a logocentrism that arrogantly fastens a signifier to a signified. For example, civilization (the signifier) has been inextricably linked to Western ways of life (the signified)—it is certainly not linked to African modes of living. Thus, the word, civilization, became a tyrant, a wielder of power, as it privileged some ways of living and excluded others. As it privileged or excluded it also justified certain actions. If certain peoples were uncivilized, it became far easier to justify their conquest, their eradication, their banishment from history. The legacy survives in foreign policy, in religion, in education. Thus, deconstruction becomes a political act of cognition as it reveals the nature of the relationship between signified and signifier, as it undermines the stability of traditional meanings. Without this destabilization totalized relations between the signifier and the signified work to oppress alternative readings of the world, readings derived from difference. Without deconstructive destabilization the negotiations over knowledge are ended—traditional meanings prevail, the subjugated return to their humble quarters in silence (Derrida 1976; Gergen 1991, 252).

As we strive for singular truths within a culture, we reduce the number of alternatives we have for relating to others both inside and outside our social context. Just as a ninth chord and a reggae rhythm expand the conceptual vocabulary of a guitar player, so exposing the culture to the impact of alternate ways of thinking magnifies its capacity to develop ethically and politically, to make new forms of social music. Each new language of perception offers another way of framing the world, another vantage point in the fabric of reality. The prison of the "given" forces us to view certain aspects of government or education as problematic while at the same time exonerating other dimensions. Nurtured by modernist assumptions, teachers are expected to assume authoritarian roles in particular subjects. Their appointed task is to systematically fill the minds of their students with a body of approved knowledge.

A critical postmodern educator would reject this role, as she or he framed academic subjects as the conversations of particular communities, for example, historians, sociologists, or anthropologists. Viewed as conversations, disciplines would not be as reluctant to allow new conversationalists into the circle to disrupt the same old jokes, the twice-told stories. We all are experts in the conversations of our own particular subcultures. Based on this recognition critical postmodern educators assume a humility that precludes them from substituting the "truth" for inferior knowledge. Instead, they solicit a dialogue in which everyone benefits from exposure to the conversations of their neighbors. Students become conversationalists, not depersonalized entities to be manipulated—collaborators in the conference of cultural understanding and cognitive development (Gergen 1991, 249–50).

THE AESTHETIC TRANSCENDENCE OF MODERNIST THINKING

Freed from the authoritarian discourse of certainty, students and teachers engaged in the emancipatory conversation come to the postmodern realization that there are always multiple perspectives—indeed, no conversation is over, no discipline totally complete. In the postmodern conversation no one gets the last word. Art teaches this lesson well, as it exposes new dimensions of meaning, new forms of logic never before recognized by the sleepwalking culture of modernism. As a postmodern wake-up call, art challenges what Marcuse called "the prevailing principle of reason" (Marcuse 1955, 185).

Art and imaginative literature provide an alternate epistemology, a way of knowing that transcends declarative forms of knowledge. Literacy texts, drama, music, painting, and dance empower individuals to see and hear beyond the surface level of sight and sound. They can alert the awakened to the one-dimensional profiles of the world promoted by mainstream culture. Herbert Marcuse was acutely aware of this cognitive dimension of art and linked it to the development of a critical politics. Art assumes its emancipatory value, he wrote, when it is viewed in light of specific historical conditions. Thus, for Marcuse aesthetic transcendence of repressive social reality is a deliberate political act that identifies the object of art with the repressive social situation to be transcended. This is not to say that in the quest for aesthetic transcendence art should be reduced to propaganda for a particular political perspective. It is a quite different matter, he maintained, for the critical critic to uncover the utopian demands of artistic productions regardless of historical era and to hold them up to the light of present repression (Bronner 1988, 129–33).

Thus, art illuminates the problematic, as it creates new concepts, new angles from which to view the world (Adler 1991, 79–80). In this way art, through its interpretors, gives birth to meaning, as it breaks through the surface to explore the submerged social and political relationships that shape events (Greene 1988, 131). In effect, Marcuse's aesthetic transcendence becomes a proto-deconstruction, a harbinger of Derrida's poststructural dismantling of modernist reality. While art can be decorative and even frivolous (but deconstructive in its frivolity), it can be transformative when applied to sociopolitical and educational contexts. Consider Matt Groening's "The Simpsons" with its wonderful parodic frivolity. As Bart deconstructs the oppressive self-seriousness of school and its sacred duty to pass the verities of the ages along to the young, Lisa provides a critical feminist vision of an emancipated community where all have voice. Indeed, her blues saxophone situates an aesthetic politics of difference, a knowledge previously excluded by race and class prejudices that will lead us out of the authoritarian maze of modernism. As the aesthetic transcends the take-for-granted, it connects with a critical system of meaning to present its utopian demands.

When it takes such demands seriously, education becomes an act of defamiliarization. Critical postmodern teacher education is grounded on defamiliarization, as teachers learn not only to defamiliarize the common-sense worlds of their students but to create situations where student experience can be used to defamiliarize the world of schooling. As artistic concerns with the "now" defamiliarize the modernist school's tendency to functionalize the role of instruction, teachers and students seek pleasurable ways of rebuilding the institution. Overcoming the tyranny of exclusive reliance on delayed gratification, critical teachers set up a form of thinking that is unbowed by the mystifying power of the given. Emerging from this playful haughtiness is the realization that the arts promote a form of teaching that requires interpretation, a form of thinking that seeks new experiences that facilitate interpretation. Such interpretation, Maxine Greene writes, will help expose the forces that suppress "the spheres of freedom to which education might some day attend" (Greene 1988, 130–33).

THINKING AND THE RESISTANCE TO DOMINANT CULTURAL FICTIONS

Empowered thinkers are aware of these forces that suppress freedom. Indeed, a significant aspect of post-formality involves efforts to expose these forces, to become resistant to the dominant cultural fictions that define and confine us. As empowered, post-formal thinkers we maintain connection to a range of alternative voices that are employed when necessary to protect us from the cultural fictions that promise us material success at the price of relinquishing our critical perspective. Teachers operating in a decontextualized cognitive vacuum are unaware of the cultural fictions and the power relations they entail. Teachers of a variety of stripes, even teachers who march under the banner of Piagetian child-centeredness, ignore these power-grounded cultural fictions. Lisa Delpit describes a culture of power that exists in schools. Middle- and upper-middle-class children gain access to the codes of power before they enter school—such as language forms, attitudes toward the importance of school, and "appropriate" types of responses to teachers. In liberal, child-centered classrooms where teachers attempt to set up an egalitarian environment, Delpit concludes that the cultural fictions and the codes of power can be masked in a manner that makes it even harder for non-middle-class children to recognize the fictions and codes and to learn to deal with them (Delpit 1988, 289–96).

As we move beyond the modernist discourse of developmental psychology into the post-formal netherlands, the attempt to unmask hidden power, to expose the unknown masters becomes vital. The emancipatory impulse with its emphasis on the power to choose and the power to act is intimately tied to post-formality's concern with the demystification of hidden oppression. The taken-for-grantedness, the commonsense nature of the dominant cultural fictions of modernism constitute the essence of their power. The most powerful fictions are not only unquestioned but unarticulated. How often, for example, do school leaders or teachers even speak of the possibility that school teaches anything other than positive academic skills? One can go through an entire career as an educator including pre-service and in-service education and a graduate degree and never even hear an allusion to such a possibility. This is how hegemony operates. A student in a modernist school, for example, most likely will never be exposed to an idea that challenges the conception that achievement is a result of ability plus effort. What a liberating and encouraging notion it would be for a student from a nonmainstream culture to gain a metaeducational understanding of why he or she had experienced trouble with certain aspects of schooling (Greene 1988, 46; Young 1990, 28; Codd 1984, 21).

But from a post-formal perspective, simple awareness of the cultural fictions and the codes of power is not enough. Both Antonio Gramsci and Paulo Freire have argued that only critical understanding can achieve liberation of the mind. Such an awareness must always be coupled with action (praxis) to bring about real social change—indeed, the ultimate manifestation of critical constructivism is social action (Codd 1984, 19). In his insightful critique of Piagetian constructivism, Michael O'Loughlin examines the critical concern with sociopolitical action and cognition. He charges Piagetian developmentalism with privileging mental action over historically grounded active engagement with reality. The abstract mentalism promoted by Piagetian formalism separates thinking and doing—individuals learn to think symbolically, in the process leaving reality as it is. Thus, O'Loughlin concludes that the sociopolitically decontextualized notion of learning extrapolated from Piagetian constructivism can be disempowering. Because of its alienation from an active engagement with the dominant cultural fictions, Piaget's notion of formal thinking with its emphasis on logico-mathematical problem solving and abstract reasoning removed from experience, emphasizes social adaption rather than social action. Here we find a central difference between formality and post-formality: Post-formality insists on an active political resistance to the dominant cultural fictions (O'Loughlin forthcoming, 19–22).

Few offer more helpful insight into this relationship between thinking and political action than does Paulo Freire. His stages of consciousness relate directly to the capacity to act in relation to the dominant cultural fiction. Stage one involves the acceptance of relations of dependency between individuals and the oppressive social structures. In this stage reality appears fixed and given and the dominant cultural fictions seem indistinguishable from the natural order. Individuals in this stage are reduced to silence. In stage two, men and women become aware of the imposition of their dependency. Still, they are unable to act, as their recognitions of oppression are naive in their inability to ascertain the nature of the relationship between sociopolitical power and their lived worlds. Freire terms stage three "conscientization." Political in nature, conscientization cannot exist without overt condemnation of unjust social structures, of repressive cultural fictions. Drawing upon a critical awareness of injustice, stage-three consciousness is more than an intellectual activity in its requirement of collective action in the struggle for social justice. Thus, conscientization, like post-formal thinking and teaching, refuses to only read or receive history—it makes history (Freire 1985, 63, 106; Britzman 1991, 25–26).

THE COGNITIVE VALUE OF DIFFERENCE: CONSTRUCTING THE POSTMODERN ETHIC

In the struggle to make history, to act on our deconstructive knowledge of the dominant cultural fictions, we make use of marginal and excluded voices. Such voices help us situate what exactly constitutes the central cultural values, in the process precluding power from freezing dominant ways of knowing into modes of dominance. With these understandings critical postmodern teaching utilizes marginal voices such as black writers, black musical forms, the perspectives of indigenous people, and women's ways of knowing to create a counterdiscourse, a running deconstruction of cultural power. As teachers inject such perspectives or as students bring them into the classroom, students come to see their own points of view as only one in a galaxy of socially constructed world views. Engaging with many excluded voices, students and teachers expand their epistemological vocabularies, in the process reaching new plateaus of meaning. For example, when teaching on a Sioux reservation I came to realize that my native American students saw dreams very differently than did those in mainstream Anglo culture. I listened carefully as students told stories of how their grandmothers had taught them to attend to and make use of dreaming. Their personal examples of creative use of dreams made a profound impact on me. Taking their stories seriously, I learned traditional Sioux techniques of how to induce dreams and then to make use of them in waking hours. I still employ this unusual (in modernist Western eyes) perspective in my teaching, writing, and music.

Consider how this one simple piece of cultural knowledge could be incorporated into a postmodern classroom. A curriculum could be built around the concept, as students and the teacher studies native American use of dreaming. If the school was located near a reservation, natives could be invited to visit the classroom and share their tribe's or their individual relationship to dreaming. The teacher could use the opportunity to ask students to keep their own dream journals. Several books have been written on dream inducing and dream use in waking hours. The teacher and students could practice induced dreaming in conjunction with creative writing. In order to induce dreaming on a story one wanted to write, teachers could direct students to pause several times a day and think of the story topic and what one could dream about it. Shutting out all distractions, students and the teacher would pause on the hours and visualize the topic. Before going to sleep, students would consider the topic once again. I have practiced such dream inducement with students who were successful in using dreams in their schoolwork.

There are many benefits to such an approach. The value of culturally different ways of seeing opens students to an appreciation of native forms of knowledge. The exercise is a great motivator, as students get caught up in the excitement of expanding consciousness. Indeed, when I have introduced my students to native dreaming, I found that for many students it was the first time they had been excited by the life of the mind. Also, the exercise is a great starting point for deeper studies of native Americans, of the mind, or of dreaming in history. Teachers can use the exercise as a first attempt to incorporate the concept of difference into their classes and maybe their own lives. The concept of difference is an invaluable concept in postmodern conceptions of instruction. Let us explore the cognitive and political dimensions of the concept of difference.

Modernist scholars have long contended the foundation of political and ethical thinking has rested on a close-knit community with a common set of precepts. Sharon Welch challenges such a perception, arguing from a postmodern perspective that hetereogeneous communities with differing principles may better contribute to the cultivation of critical thinking and moral reasoning. A homogeneous community often is unable to criticize the injustice and exclusionary practices that afflict a social system. Criticism and reform of cultural pathology often come from the recognition of difference—from interaction with communities who do not suffer from the same injustices or who have dealt with them in different ways. We always profit in some way from a confrontation with another system of defining that which is important. Consciousness itself is spurred by difference in that we gain our first awareness of who we are when we are aware that we exist independent of another or another's ways.

Welch maintains that the concept of solidarity is more inclusive and transformative than the concept of consensus. Even if we perceive consensus to involve a common recognition of cultural pathology and the belief that we must work together to find a cure, we first have to accept the value of solidarity. Welch claims that solidarity has two main aspects: (1) The ethic of solidarity grants social groups enough respect to listen to their ideas and to use them to consider existing social values, and (2) the ethic of solidarity realizes that the lives of individuals in differing groups are interconnected to the point that everyone is accountable to everyone else. No assumption of uniformity exists here—just the commitment to work together to bring about mutually beneficial social change (Welch 1991, 87–95). In the classroom, this valuing of difference and its political and cognitive benefits exhibits itself in a dialogical sharing of perspective. In this process students slowly come to see their own points of view as one particular sociohistorically constructed way of perceiving. As the classroom develops, students are exposed to more and more diverse voices in various texts and discussions, a process that engages them in other ways of seeing and knowing (O'Loughlin forthcoming, 43). Thus, their epistemological circle is widened, as difference expands their social imagination, their vision of what could be. Students are emancipated from the pseudodualism of the dominant culture, the liberal–conservative alternatives.

As travelers have discovered, the attempt to understand the cultural schematas of peoples from other countries often allows for a recognition of belief systems and social assumptions in oneself. When students widen their epistemological circles by exposure to non-Western perspectives, they gain understandings that become extremely valuable in the multi-cultural postmodern world. Such understandings may be on the surface very simple. In an American future, for example, which will be marked by far greater non-Anglo populations, the basic ability for different groups to live together in solidarity may be considered a survival skill. The critical postmodern ethic of appreciating and learning from diversity may be essential to the survival of the planet. In the postmodern curriculum of difference students will learn about cultural differences revolving around perspectives on work, leisure, competition, success, individualism, or time.

Take time, for example. Modernist societies have been trapped in a time warp of speed and efficiency that affects all aspects of our consciousness. Postmodern teacher education students study the effect of time perceptions on teaching and perceptions of intelligence. They discover that while premodernist cultures may have found that "haste makes waste," modern-ist cultures believe that speed reflects alertness, power, and success. Ever-hurried Mad Hatters late for important dates, modernists educators speak of slow and fast students. Pondering, reflecting, or musing might be valued in some cultures, but not in the culture of the modernist West. In a study involving male undergraduates, psychologists Robert Knapp and John Garbut found that the highest scores on standardized exams were those who placed the most value on speed. Students from traditional, indigenous, and agrarian cultures tend not to place a high value on speed—thus, for cultural reasons, *not* cognitive ones, such students do not tend to score highly on the dominant modes of educational evaluation.

In addition, researchers have discovered a correlation between one's socioeconomic class and one's perception of time. Without the challenge of difference, educators coming of age in a modernist culture are hard pressed to overcome cognitive and epistemological unidimensionality. Hidden sociocultural assumptions, such as temporality, remain hidden. Students steeped in modernist values of speed and efficiency are deemed intelligent, those from the margins of modernity are deemed "slow." Hence, the status quo is perpetuated as difference is denied. The econom-ically and culturally different are condemned to school failure. Buoyed by our critical postmodern ethic of difference, we are empowered to step out of the limited modernist paradigm and view the temporality–intelligence dyad from a variety of frames. Students from outside the mainstream are viewed in new ways, as teachers uncover forms of intelligence previously overlooked. Emancipated by difference and grounded by solidarity, critical postmodern teachers learn from their students' uniqueness (Rifkin 1987, 71–72).

The possibility of schools escaping from the cognitive and political blinders of modernism is dependent on teachers' ability to act on their understanding of difference. The teachers' sensitivity to the transformative possibilities that emerge from the perspectives of those on the outside looking in can change not only the school but the world as well. For example, our perspective on how gender role constructs our consciousness can be sensitized by serious attention to those with sexual preferences different from our own. Our understanding on how our racial identity constructs our consciousness can be deepened by careful attention to those with racial identities different from our own. Our appreciation of how socioeconomic class constructs our consciousness can be enhanced by critically listening to those from social classes different from our own. Our cognizance of how geographical place constructs our consciousness can be sophisticated by engagement with individuals shaped by places different from our own. School cannot stay the same, the circumscribed discourse of the academic disciplines can no longer resist change when subjected to the power of difference, the commingling of a Babel of languages.

Despite the protestations of reactionary forces promoting a homogeneous culture that sees difference as a threat, particular groups within Western society have come to value the multiple perceptions of reality that emerge from encounters with difference. One aspect of this postmodern valuing of difference involves a growing appreciation for local cultures with their diversity of forms of human patterning. In *Curriculum as Social Psychoanalysis: Essays on the Significance of Place*, William Pinar and I promote this notion of difference within a regional context focusing on education in the southern place. In considering the nature of the southern curriculum, we explore the concept of cultural renewal, a process where one's cultural history is confronted with the notion of difference. Avoiding any tendency toward nostalgic romanticization, perceptions of the past are interrogated by the present, by the social theories of other places. Thus, the curriculum becomes a form of critical psychoanalysis, as it analyzes the etymology of present pathologies revolving around race, class, and gender oppressions. Southern students come to realize the specific nature of their consciousness construction, gaining the cognitive insights that come from such a realization. Such insights involve the understanding that they don't just happen to hold particular perspectives toward race, class, gender, religious, and political issues—particular historical forces have shaped those viewpoints (Kincheloe and Pinar 1991).

In the arts and politics we find a similar type of localistic or "place" impulse. Performing arts have witnessed a trend toward totalism, an appreciation of ethnic and racial traditions as they incite new possibilities of aesthetic or dramatic expression. In politics the move toward localism transcends traditional liberal–conservative boundaries. Localities are increasingly separating themselves from state and national subserviance, as they utilize technology to make connections to those who share their social and political concerns. All of these localizing impulses undermine the "bigger is better" standardization tendencies of modernism. As place becomes more valued, the modernist dream of one great truth retreats and the subversive postmodern concept of difference becomes more influential (Gergen 1991, 250–51).

The growing pluralism of our student constituencies has forced Americans to reconsider, whether they want to or not, the nature of a multiracial, multiethnic society. At the same time that some people read the projected twenty-first-century demographics of diversity as testimony to the need to value difference, others, such as all-American racist David Duke, see it as a clarion call to fortify the armaments and protect the "traditional Western heritage" at all costs. Americans have not yet recognized the significance of the early battles between Bloom and the multiculturists, William Bennett and the feminists. These are not simply struggles over the curriculum at Stanford or the one presented by the New York regents. These skirmishes are the first outbreaks of a larger struggle to define who we are, to determine how we see the world and even how we learn to think. We are in a fight between a modernist traditionalism of consensus and a postmodern ethic of difference.

The postmodern politics of difference sees no fixed, transcultural view of self. In a pluralistic cosmos, the individual experiences multiple forms of intelligence, multiple epistemologies, diverse spiritualities, and a variety of ethical systems. Making use of a multiculturalist education, critical postmodernists search through premodernist societies in their quest for unique and practical ways to avoid the nihilism of modernism and reestablish human solidarity. The cognitive disease of modernism may best be cured by a postmodern broth of seven taro leaves—a recipe that borrows the democratic and egalitarian impulses of modernism, the communitarian and ecological respect of premodernism, and the self-awareness and the ethic of difference of postmodernism. The recipe leads to a critical constructivist meta-awareness of the fact that not only has our conscious-ness been historically constructed, but that once we realize this construc-tion the critical postmodernist can reconstruct his or her consciousness in a more emancipatory manner. The pedagogy that results from this ethic of reconstruction induces us to step outside our cultural incarceration, releas-ing ourselves on our own recognizance (Gergen 1991, 249; O'Loughlin forthcoming, 38).

FROM THE BOTTOM UP: SUBJUGATED KNOWLEDGE AND THINKING

As the cognitive illness of modernism infects more and more victims, we are rendered passive to an army of scientific experts who bulldoze our intuitions with their official answers. Our schizophrenic perception of the cult of the expert is well illustrated by the deliciously naive science fiction movies of the 1950s which revealed a logical faith in the scientific expert while intuitively sensing that something was wrong with his ('50s scien-tists were almost always men) way of thinking. The irony of this paradox pervaded the genre. In the *Beginning of the End*, scientists inadvertently produce a plague of giant grasshoppers by attempting to produce giant vegetables with atomic radiation. On a search and destroy mission against the grasshoppers, one soldier highlights the paradox as he attempts to comfort another soldier: "Mr. Wainwright's a scientist. He's trained to see things right." In *The Neanderthal Man*, a scientist conducting research on early humans goes on a Neanderthal murder spree after injecting himself with a compound that causes living things to revert to atavistic forms. Reflecting on the reversion of an injected cat to a murderous saber-toothed tiger, the scientist confides: "Everything has a logical explanation. I refuse to believe the supernatural. There must be some logical cause and effect to this unholy adventure."

In the postmodern world, personal authority has been undermined by this cult of expertise. Individuals depend on expert organizations, citizens depend on the state, workers depend on managers, and teachers depend on administrators and supervisors. When the centralization of decision-making power and the prerogative to validate school knowledge are placed in the hands of educational experts, the result is the reduction of teachers to mere executors of the experts' conceptualization of the teaching act. Students in this process become little more than repositories of predigested factoids, passive consumers of knowledge infected by the cognitive dis-ease. This is why our critical system of meaning is so important, it gives us a starting place, a cognitive and moral grounding to begin our analysis of the perils of modernism. When the critically grounded system of meaning meets the ungrounded postmodern critique of metanarrative, a dialogical relationship is formed. The interplay of the ungrounded produces a cognitive tension that undermines certainty but forces us to constantly reconsider moral and cognitive principles in light of new information. Thus, we are thrust into a never-ending internal and external moral and cognitive dialogue. This raising of our moral and cognitive consciousness is a revolutionary feature of critical postmodernism.

This is why liberation theology is so important to our attempt to develop an emancipatory system of meaning. Liberation theology, with its roots deep in the Latin American struggle against poverty and colonialism, morally situates our attempt to formulate an explicit set of assumptions from which to begin our formulation of educational questions. Liberation theology makes no apology for its identification with the perspective of those who are excluded and subjugated. Proclaiming their solidarity with the marginalized, liberation theologians work alongside them in their attempt to expose the existing social order as oppressive and unethical. All aspects of our critical system of meaning and the education that grows out of it rest on this notion of identification with the perspective of the oppressed. Accordingly, one of the main goals of critical postmodern education is to reveal the ways that dominant schooling serves to perpetuate the hopelessness of the subjugated (Welch 1985, 31). On the basis of this subjugated knowledge, of their "dangerous memory," we can formulate an approach to teaching that reveals at whose expense the structure of dominant culture is maintained, as it designs strategies for overcoming this oppression.

The deployment of an emancipatory, critical system of meaning as a grounding for our educational thinking will elicit charges of politicization, of tainted, unobjective teaching with predetermined results. Critical constructivism asserts that such forms of pious pseudo-objectivity must be confronted. If critical postmodern teachers cave in to such pious critics, the possibility of taking a moral stand in education, of seeing education as something more than a technical act, will be destroyed. As they argue that we must keep politics out of education and avoid emancipatory thinking à la Freire's stage-three conscientization, the pseudo-objectivists misrepresent the basic tenets of critical postmodern pedagogy. A recognition of the ideological nature of thinking implies that teachers by necessity must take a position and make it explicit to their students. They do not impose their interpretations as truth; their students and their colleagues have the right to reject everything asserted.

The objectivist critics don't seem to understand that teaching often has served the interests of power elites. Critical postmodern pedagogy, with its commitment to subjugated knowledge, seeks to confront such educational outcomes. The view from above of the traditional modernist paradigm gives way to views from below. Emerging from an understanding of and respect for the perspective of the oppressed, such an epistemological position (or at least a way of knowing) uses the voices of the subjugated to formulate a reconstruction of the dominant educational structure. It is a radical reconstruction in the sense that it attempts to empower those who are presently powerless and to validate oppressed ways of thinking that open new cognitive doors to everyone (Mies 1982, 123; Connell 1989, 125). As we expose the way dominant power invalidates the cognitive styles of marginalized groups, we begin to examine testing procedures and their political effects. Objectivist experts devise tests to evaluate student performance, forgetting throughout the process that evaluation is based on uncritically grounded definitions of intelligence and performance. When well-intentioned liberals attempt to develop curricula based on a recognition of the existence of marginalized experiences, they miss the lessons provided by an understanding of subjugated thinking. Liberal reform involves the inclusion of women or African-Americans in a history curriculum that has traditionally emphasized the contributions of famous (especially military) men. The cognitive orientation of the curriculum is not changed by such additions; it simply adds a few new facts to be committed to memory. Indeed, it is tokenism that perpetuates the power relations of the status quo—a kinder, gentler oppression (Connell 1989, 125–26).

The advantage of subjugated perspectives, the view from below, involves what has been termed the "double consciousness" of the oppressed. If they are to survive, subjugated groups develop an understanding of those who control them (e.g., slaves' insight into the manners, eccentricities, and fears of their masters); at the same time they are cognizant of the everyday mechanisms of oppression and the way such technologies shape their cognition, their consciousness. Because of their race, class, and gender positions, many educational experts are insulated from the benefits of the double consciousness of the subjugated and are estranged from a visceral appreciation of suffering. Contemporary social organization is viewed through a cognitive lens that portrays it as acceptable. Why would such educational leaders challenge cognitive styles, modes of interpretation that justify the prevailing system of education? What lived experience would create a cognitive dissonance within the minds of such leaders that would make them uncomfortable with the status quo? The oppressed—while often manipulated by mechanisms of power to accept injustice and to deny their own oppression—often use their pain as a motivation to find out what is not right and to discover alternate ways of constructing social and educational reality (Mies 1982, 121; Jaggar 1983, 370).

Theologian Sharon Welch describes this appreciation of subjugated knowledge as a "standpoint epistemology." This perspective on knowing realizes that the "master's position" tends to produce distorted visions of causation in sociopolitical concerns (Welch 1991, 90). Harvey Kaye insightfully writes that teachers must draw upon this perspective as they demystify the contemporary world. Specifically, this means revealing the social origins of the present especially the etymologies of the structures of power and the means of oppression which have come to be seen as inevitable. Kaye concludes with Walter Benjamin that social and political struggle is "nourished more by the image of enslaved ancestors than liberated grandchildren" (Kaye 1991, 156–57). Consider from the perspective of standpoint epistemology the teaching of history in the schools.

You are teaching American history to juniors in high school. Of course, you want them to understand rules of historical evidence, to know how to evaluate sources, to understand the complexity of causal relationships—you want them to understand the structure of the discipline of history. When we apply our understanding of standpoint epistemology, subjugated knowledge, to this teaching situation, we realize there is much to explore. History, especially the history learned in high school, has traditionally been taught from the top down; subjugated knowledge forces us to cognitively frame history from the ground up. Like Paulo Freire and Harvey Kaye, we attempt to connect with the culture of silence. Doing so, we discuss what ordinary people thought about the world around them. As the voices of central players or peripheral players (dissenters, deskilled or unskilled workers, soldiers, housewives, slaves, union organizers, welfare mothers) are heard, new dimensions of cognition begin to appear—ways of thinking with distinct political dimensions. Indeed, the power of voice is a key political issue. Maxine Greene maintains that when history teaching meets subjugated knowledge, new spaces for study are created—"metaphorical spaces," she calls them, "for speculative audacity." When like surrealistic painters, we view history from subjugated perspectives, the imagination is unleashed in unexpected ways. Cognition is pushed across familiar boundaries and in its new environs it sees new questions, unexamined avenues, and heroic men and women recognized neither in their own time or in history. The concepts of subjugated knowledge or difference form a starting point for a postmodern commitment to intelligence, to rewriting the traditional notions of cognition. History is not the only discipline that can be reconceptualized in this context—the entire curriculum is vulnerable to the power of difference (Greene 1988, 126–28).

PATRIARCHAL THINKING AND HUMAN SURVIVAL

As we move the concept of difference into the arena of gender, we apply the work of feminist theory to the politics of teacher thinking. Few sources provide more insight than feminist epistemology into development and limitations of modernist cognition. Few institutions reflect the patriarchal nature of modernist ways of seeing more than the school. Bastions of male supremacy and dominant cultural power, schools have been shaped by what patriarchy has viewed as acceptable behavior and appropriate ways of being. Sophisticated thinking, indeed humanness itself, has equated with maleness. As alluded to previously, even most liberal reform has reflected patriarchal assumptions as it defines critical thinking in terms of an androcentric rationality (Anderson 1987, 8–9). Because of this male-centered nature of schooling, white male students from middle-class homes are inbued with a confidence that allows them to see failure as more a reflection of the teacher's inadequacies than their own. Because female cognitive development proceeds along a different path, women's interpersonal and connected qualities are sometimes viewed as inferior to the androcentric notion of intellectual autonomy. Women find it risky to "go with their intuitions" in school in that such cognitive styles are so seldom recognized as valuable. Over the years women students begin to lose confidence, often coming to feel that their failure is a result of their own inadequacy (Maher and Rathbone 1986, 222).

What is it that we can learn from the feminist critique of thinking? Do we teach little girls to think more logically, that is, changing women to meet the modernist definitions of sophisticated cognition? Employing our critical postmodern system of meaning, the answer, of course, is no. Instead, we use the feminist critique to reconceptualize the dominant definitions of what constitutes higher order thinking. Utilizing a critically reconceptualized vision of thinking, we come to realize that sophisticated cognition comes in a variety of shapes and sizes. We understand that male-centered abstract math and science skills are important forms of higher thinking, but many other cognitive abilities are as valuable as well. In the patriarchal culture, however, mainstream white males do not value these "other cognitive abilities." Males see themselves apart from others, as independent entities. Such cognitive perspectives hold powerful political implications, as they shape social policy on everything from the social role of government to economic theory to the vision of community that guides us. For example, is the role of government to be a caregiver, a provider of social services to those in need? Or is it to be the guardian of "fair" competition? Recent political leaders have opted for the latter role, emphasizing androcentric autonomy and separateness.

The last couple of decades have witnessed a dramatic change in the discourse about women. Carol Gilligan's *In a Different Voice* (1981) and Mary Field Belenky, Blythe McVicker Clinchy, Nancy Rule Goldberger, and Jill Mattuck Tarule's *Women's Ways of Knowing* (1986) have exerted a dramatic impact on how we see women's cognition. Despite problems with decontextualization in regard to race and socioeconomic class, both works challenge traditional assumptions about gender and cognition. Because of the different nature of women's experience when growing up, the way they see the world, their values and moralities differ from mainstream white men. Drawing on both books, we come to understand that women's choices are often made in a context of mutuality and caring, of authentic conversation, of cooperation, and of play rather than rule governance. Instead of thinking in terms of rights in human interaction, women feel more comfortable thinking in terms of responsibility. It was these recognitions that Kohlberg failed to make, Gilligan argues, that led him to leave out one half of the population in his "universal" stages of moral reasoning.

Patriarchal cognition tends to involve less consideration of consequences than women's ways of knowing. As a result, male thinking will encounter more difficulties in situations that require an understanding of how individuals are affected by particular actions. Being more relational, emotional, and process-oriented than male thinkers, women often are thrown off stride when patriarchal schools require a logic that demands that things be viewed as right or wrong. Attention to consequences encourages a "maybe" orientation. Because of all the possible consequences that can be imagined, women tend to pause before deciding—a pause that males often take as a sign of weakness, an inability to make snap judgments. Thus, women tend to avoid the either–or thinking that can serve as an obstacle to the post-formal ability to imagine a variety of solutions to perplexing situations. Either–or thinking promotes less investigation of the "whys" in a situation; post-formal thinking values the asking of why questions. Why questions lead to uncertainty and humility in a cognitive culture of certainty. Given the patriarchal rules, women operate at a substantial disadvantage (Greene 1988, 84; Anderson 1987, 8).

Indeed, the coming of modernity, the Age of Reason, in the seventeenth and eighteenth centuries cannot be separated from the concept of gender epistemology. As Western society moved away from the interdependent perspective on reality of the Middle Ages to the logocentric, mechanistic view of modernity, there came to exist an accompanying misogyny that associated feminist thinking with madness, witchcraft, and satanism. Intuition and emotion were incompatible with androcentric logic and reason, and, as a result, scientific knowledge became the "only game in town." The masculinization of thinking was a cardinal tenet of Western social evolution. Individuals came to be represented in a dramatic new form—as abstracted entities, individuals standing outside the forces of history and culture. Society was caught in the cognition of patriarchy—a matrix of perception that limited our imagination to concepts that stayed within the androcentric boundaries, far away from the No Trespassing signs of the feminine domain.

Standing outside of the forces of history and culture involved observing at a distance. Valid knowledge was produced exclusively by personally detached, objective observers. Knowers were separated from the known. Masculinist autonomy, abstraction, and distance denies the spatial and temporal location of the knower in the world and thus results in the estrangement of human beings from the rhythms of life, the natural world (Lowe 1982, 164; Mahoney and Lyddon 1988, 199–201; Anderson 1987, 7; Bowers and Flinders 1990, 6–7; White 1978, 197). Feminist theory has asserted that the autonomy and isolation of the logical, masculine individual have necessitated a mechanistic perspective on the universe. Such a perspective guards against the ascendance of feminine forms of meaning and identity based on connecting, caring, empathy, inclusivity, and responsibility. Devoid of such characteristics, masculinist modernism created a behavioral science which set out to manipulate individuals and an educational system that utilized the behavioral sciences to mold students and their consciousness in a way that would foster efficiency and economic productivity, often at the expense of social justice and creativity.

Maxine Greene argues that while feminine notions of caring and connecting are valuable, they are not enough in themselves to change the schools. Greene argues that first we must replace the masculinist discourse that negates body and feeling with a new female expressiveness that draws upon personal experience (Greene 1988, 85). As feminist theory draws upon the nonverbal communication forms of the body and emotion, the possibility of post-formal thinking is enhanced. Truncated communication that excludes body and feeling produces truncated thinking limited by its immersion in logocentrism. This truncated masculinist thinking tends to be more presentist than future oriented. Many of the problems that threaten our very survival as human beings, such as depleted natural resources, overpopulation, and the threat of nuclear war, emerge as the result of this modernist presentism. Thus, the development of more post-formal modes of thinking is not simply an educational issue but one of the most important sociopolitical issues of human history (Anderson 1987, 9).

While the ability to transcend androcentric modernist thinking in order to save the species is a rather important issue, masculinist cognition misshapes what goes on in the mundane, lived world of the classroom as well. The modernist discourse denegrates the relevance of connecting and caring in the classroom and the importance of integrating the knowledge that students bring with them into the curriculum. The feminist reconceptualization of cognition and education does not involve only adding on information about women to the content of courses. The feminist critique has challenged the central concepts of academic disciplines, teacher education in particular. Feminist theorists contend that feeling should be united with reason in a way that strengthens our emotional identification with life and its preservation. All assumptions within a discipline must be reexamined in relation to this feminine emotional concern with life. Teaching can never be viewed in the same way after feminist theorists assert that experience does not take place in an isolated and autonomous self and that the individual is the basic sociopolitical and psychological unit. This feminist thought is the key in the shift from traditional constructivism to critical constructivism—critical constructivism maintaining that all constructions of reality are created in a particular cultural, institutional, and historical context (Reinharz 1979, 7; Fee 1982, 379–80; Bowers and Flinders 1990, 7; Wertsh 1991, 2).

THE TROUBLE WITH LOGICAL AUTONOMY: THE FEMINIST ETHIC OF POSTMODERN CONNECTEDNESS

Feminist analysis of cognition and epistemology reveal two major perspectives toward thinking and knowing. The first impulse, separate knowing, focuses on traditional Cartesian–Newtonian science with its blind observations and its exclusion of emotion and personal knowledge. The second impulse, connected knowing, values intimacy and understanding instead of distance and proof. Separate knowing pursues autonomy, the highest state in the developmental taxonomies of Piaget and Kohlberg. Even some notions of critical theoretical emancipation privilege autonomous self-direction based on an understanding of how the influences of one's past shape and mold. A feminist reconceptualization of emancipation grounded on connected knowing uses this understanding of one's past not only to free oneself from its repressive characteristics but to facilitate connection with other people around visions of community.

The autonomy of Kohlberg and other liberals rests on the assumption that once individuals reach a high cognitive development their thinking is directed by principles of justice and egalitarianism. Simple rationality, then, is what is needed in the effort to create a just community (Lesko 1988, 28; Greene 1988, 118). Henry Giroux argues that this modernist rationalistic perspective on justice is not defined by results but through an obsession with process (Giroux 1988a, 55). Unconnected to real histories and lived experiences, modernist justice is conceived for a society of strangers who all have a relationship with the law but not each other (Siegel 1986, 27). The problem, of course, with this rationalistic, autonomous justice is what it excludes. As Max Horkheimer wrote decades ago, such rationalism fails to address the nature of happiness and the good life. Women have traditionally pointed out the importance of attachment in the human life cycle, conceiving their role as teachers as purveyors of support and connectedness. Instead of presenting political procedures for justice, the supportive teacher attempts to touch students, to grapple with them as world makers struggling to find their voice in the choir (Greene 1988, 120).

Logic and rationality retain their importance, but the ultimate end of cognitive development goes beyond simply grasping abstract principles. Cognitive development entails understanding everyday life from as many vantage points as possible. Indeed, a key to post-formal thinking involves the ability to gain new angles of seeing, to contextualize in unique ways. Kohlberg in his detached modernism glorified Clint Eastwood, the self-contained high plains drifter who asked "nothing from nobody." The man with no name had no need to establish connections with a core of friends, to seek new perspectives on the conditions that he faced. Feminist cognition, on the other hand, operates within a network of relationships connected by an ethic of caring. In this way, feminism establishes the basis for our critical postmodern way of seeing. Leaving behind the myth of autonomy, moral and cognitive decisions are seen not as the constructs of individual minds, but as the product of communion among people (Gergen 1991, 168).

BEYOND FACE VALUE: STUDENTS AND TEACHERS IN DIALOGUE WITH TEXTS

As our postmodern students form their communities of caring and inquiry and begin to think about their own thinking, a dangerous current is created—a current of interpretation. Once in motion this current takes on a life of its own, picking up momentum as more and more individuals get caught up in a dialogue about dominant culture's representations of their own lives and dreams. Taking a cue from Nietzsche and his conception of a universe open to interpretation, postmodern students and teachers challenge the "heuristiphobic" technicist schools. Ambiguous about the development of students who engage in higher order thinking, advocates of technicist schooling are not so sure they want students who are less likely to accept the world at face value. Indeed, a fascination with the critical and the imaginative is at odds with the technicist impulses that still run many American schools (Feinberg 1989, 136).

Critical postmodern teachers are willing to take a risk, to engage in the dangerous challenge of the purveyors of the cognitive illness. The challenge must not take place without support, without a community of fellow inquirers. Based on a cognition that is dedicated to freeing minds from the tyranny of meanings inflicted by advertising, politics, and, unfortunately, the schools, the postmodern protest awakens the anesthesized spirit of democracy. Teachers and students engage in dialogue with texts, treating them as human-made entities to be deconstructed—not as priceless museum pieces above interpretation, to be guarded by Pinkerton thought police. Jesse Goodman argues that critical teachers struggling for empowerment take their risk when they decide not simply to fit into the institutional norms, but to make a humane impact on the world of schools. Teacher educators can promote the taking of such risks, he contends, by exposing prospective teachers to critical alternatives rather than just platitudes concerning the need to be creative (Goodman 1986, 31–32).

I would add that to make the risk connected and emancipatory, teachers and students must act on a vision of a shared becoming. Such action is a form of praxis, that is, activity which combines social theory and practice for emancipatory ends. The empowerment of teachers as individuals is not enough; to change the unjust social and institutional arrangement which threatens democracy, teachers must see the connections between their individual situations and those of their colleagues. The connected cognition that emerges opens a new conversation on the talent of others; it seeks situations where previously isolated groups and individuals come to work together. Shared labor concretizes the post-formal spirit, as teachers work with community members whose talents were previously unrecognized. As they prepare food together, refurbish houses or schools, or mend clothing, teachers and students begin to learn from those who have been marginalized because of race, class, or gender differences. Students of mine who have worked for Habitats for Humanity share the emancipatory and connected experiences gained in the process, making dramatic connections between their work in the project and their role as teachers. Such drama cannot take place in schools where traditional definitions of thinking limit learning to a monkish transcription of texts, to a rationalistic accumulation of predigested data to be "cashed in" on a set of standardized tests (Greene 1988, 133; Welch 1991, 98; Zeichner and Tabachnick 1991, 9).

Our attempt to transcend the blinders of modernist thinking, difficult enough as it is, is complicated by the social changes resulting from the media landscape that has developed over the past few decades. Many postmodern theorists point to a decline of meaning in such circumstances, pushed by the bombardment of images and sounds it produces (Lash 1990, 42–43). While many may find a nihilism within this decline of meaning, critical postmodernists such as Peter McLaren and Henry Giroux find it a source of great opportunity for the development of democratic critique and action. Let us now turn our exploration of the politics of thinking to its relationship to this contradictory postmodern landscape replete with its dynamics of despair and windows of opportunity.

Chapter 5

Mr. Huxley's Neighborhood: Can You Spell Postmodernism?

Having discussed the attempt to transcend modernist thinking, let us expand our brief description of the postmodern condition and the postmodern critique presented in Chapter 1. The postmodern condition is extended by electronic systems of communication. As the texture of industrialized societies changes, we are confronted with yet another historical watershed that promises to alter both the formation of our subjectivities and the nature of our interactions with other people. The postmodern revolution will make as much of a social impact as the industrial revolution of the nineteenth century. The coming educational and political conflicts will center around the management of the revolution. Technocrats see a future of harmony where materially satisfied people inhabit a world of creative accord. Structural changes in our political, economic, and educational institutions will not be necessary in this technocratic world, as high-tech apparati such as advanced computers will remedy stubborn human ills.

Teachers operating in much the same fashion as technicist educators of the present will turn out standardized students with "good attitudes" and rationalistic cognitive styles. This "Jetsonesque" vision rings hollow when we find that high-tech jobs are often more tedious and deskilling than more traditional ones. Technocratic optimism turns sour when we discover that electronic communications (telephones, TVs, video recorders, stereos, and computers) have increased our isolation from one another, locking many into private cells. Instead of making for a close-knit global community, high-tech communications have exaggerated the power of dominant elites

by granting them more media exposure and new techniques of surveil-
lance. Technophilia is a blind love that eclipses our view of technology's
dark side (Poster 1989, 124–25).

SOCIAL VERTIGO: POWER IN THE
POSTMODERN HYPERREALITY

Students of the late twentieth century face a different world, a
postmodern hyperreality marked by a social vertigo. In the same way that
John Dewey called for a new education to address the industrial world of
the early twentieth century, critical postmodern educators call for new
ways of thinking, new pedagogies to address the social lack of balance
that comes from postmodern hyperreality. This cultural landscape, marked
by the omnipresence of electronic information, has begun to lose touch
with traditional notions of time, community, self, and history (Gergen
1991, 74; Aronowitz and Giroux 1991, 115). The distinction between
reality and image blurs as Robert Young (a.k.a. Marcus Welby) repeats
over and over that he may not be a doctor but he plays one on television,
the entire time selling us pain relievers. And we buy them! A book about
Gen. George Patton pictures George C. Scott on its cover, as the image
chokes reality. People suffering from social vertigo attack soap opera
actress Susan Lucci on the streets of New York, angry over the way her
character behaved in an episode of "All My Children."

New structures of cultural space and time generated by bombarding
electronic images from local, national, and international locations shake
our personal sense of place. Electronic transmissions move us in and out
of different geographical and cultural locales instantaneously, juxtaposing
nonlinear images of the world with comfortable personalities who have
won our trust. Allowing these personalities to become our trusted guides,
we are rendered vulnerable to the image, relinquishing the desire for
self-direction in the thick informational jungle of hyperreality. As we
involve ourselves in hyperreality, we relinquish our ties with our once
close-knit community. Trading community membership for a sense of
pseudobelonging to the mediascape, residents of hyperreality are temporarily comforted by proclamations of community offered by "media
personalities" on the 6:00 "Eyewitness News." "Bringing news of your
neighbors in the Tri-State community home to you," media marketers
attempt to soften the edges of hyperreality, to medicate the social vertigo.
The world is not brought into our homes by television, as much as
television brings its viewers to a quasi-fictional place—hyperreality
(Luke, 1991, 14).

Our contact with hyperreality diminishes our ability to find meaning, to engender the passion for commitment. With so much information bombarding our senses, we lose our faith that we can make sense of anything. If nothing makes sense then what possibly merits commitment. This condition is what David Byrne and the Talking Heads addressed in their album, *Stop Making Sense*. If the postmodern condition is doomed to hyperreal meaninglessness, they assert, then stop trying so hard to deny it, stop making sense. Raised in the hyperreality, our students (though unable to name it) reflect the emotions (or lack of such) that hyperreality engenders. The postmodern pedagogical mission involves rescuing meaning even as we understand its destruction by the postmodern information landscape (McLaren 1991a, 233–36).

Some may feel that this attempt to rescue meaning runs against the grain of postmodernism. Isn't postmodernism itself an attack on meaning and the coming to terms with its loss? Throughout the preceding four chapters, I have attempted to build a case for a critical postmodernism or a postmodern critique grounded on critical theory's concern with egalitarianism and justice. In so doing I align myself with the politically oriented impulse of contemporary postmodern social theory. The other impulse, the "postpolitical" or what Teresa Ebert labels ludic postmodernism addresses the world as a stage for free-floating play (thus, the term "ludic") of images, eviscerated signifiers, and difference. Ludic postmodernists seek to separate signifier (word) and signified (meaning), in the process undermining traditional relations between language and the world. Such acts, when ungrounded by larger political concerns, tend to reduce reality to rhetoric, as they destroy the repressive totalities of official narratives. Obsessed with the dismantling of repressive totalities, ludic postmodernism undermines the will to act politically. Praxis becomes a totality to be undermined, thus subverting political engagement.

Critical postmodernism, on the other hand, views the relation between the word and the world not simply as the result of rhetoric or textuality but as the effect of power and social struggle. Language derives its meaning not from merely its linguistic system, as Saussure maintained, but from its relationship to power struggles over meaning. From the critical postmodern perspective the sign becomes a playing field of social struggle. Based on such recognitions, critical postmodernism utilizes textual analysis and deconstruction as methods to uncover the way power operates. On the basis of such exposures, critical postmodernist educators construct a transformative pedagogy that liberates individuals from race, class, gender, and place oppression (Bakhtin and Voloshinov 1986, 15–23; Ebert 1991, 886–88).

Thus, in our search for meaning in hyperreality our critical postmodern concerns push us to explore the relationship between informational technology and power. As industrialization and technology have evolved, power has become increasingly difficult to identify. Perpetually disguised, power has exerted its influences so subtly that most are unaware of the insidious oppression at work in their own lives. Of course, this is why the right wing can enjoy such dominance in contemporary life. In hyperreality power seems to require coproduction by those who generate electronic information and by those who consume it. Those who produce information must seduce the consumptive public into collaboration. The production and dispersion of seductive images requires so many financial resources that it can only be accomplished by extremely large firms and industries. In this context class and racial inequalities are perpetuated by new technologies and at the same time rendered more impervious to exposure by the removal of those with limited access to information from those who produce it. In hyperreality television viewers are continuously baffled by the nebulous "they" who control information in the process exercising some mysterious form of control over their lives (Luke 1991, 15–17).

This mysterious form of control, this exercise of power in hyperreality is chameleonlike in that it can assume a variety of forms. One of the most important forms, however, involves its power to seduce. Utilizing advertising representations of subjectivity, power interests in hyperreality absorb the antogonistic and irreconcilable resistances that grow in relation to dominant society. Rebelling, properly managed, is not only not a threat to the social order, but it also can be appropriated for the benefit of the status quo. All citizens can style themselves as something of a rebel similar to Jeff Daniels' "Charlie" character in Jonathan Demme's *Something Wild*. A little bit rebel, a little bit yuppie businessman, Charlie poses no threat to the status quo with his occasional failure to pay his check at restaurants. Affecting a James Dean persona or joining in the Nike Revolution as John Lennon sings the theme do not require a stakeout by the ghost of J. Edgar Hoover. As a dominant motif in selling products and services, the image of the rebel enlists us all as collaborators (Ashley 1991, 72; Luke 1991, 15).

Peter McLaren captures the point when he writes that postmodern power organizes life along affective or emotional structures as it mobilizes desire, mood, and pleasure (McLaren 1991a, 234). Social control in the mediascape involves the organization of attractive conditions for collaboration. Seduced by the pleasure of the image, individuals imagine themselves as self-managed entities who are too rebellious to be controlled. Failing to understand their own seduction, the conditions for collaboration, they jump headfirst into the society of consumption. Science fiction has long played with the themes of individuals controlled by an electronic device implanted in their brains. The electronic information providers of hyperreality bring science fiction (maybe cognitive science fiction) to life, controlling postmodern men and women not by coercion but by the "freedom" of consumer gratification or choice of lifestyles (Langman 1991, 185; Luke 1991, 15–16).

HYPERREALITY AND SOCIAL SATURATION: REFIGURING OUR SELVES

Hyperreality is a world of social saturation. In the information society individuals bombarded by ever-increasing images find their identities and sense of self changing. The drama of living has been portrayed so often on television that we, for the most part, know how it goes. As many postmodern analysts have put it, we become pastiches, imitative conglomerations of one another. In such a condition, we approach life with low affect, with a sense of postmodern ennui. Our emotional bonds are diffused, as television, computers, VCRs, and stereo headphones assault us with imagery. Traditionalists circle the cultural wagons and fight off imagined bogeymen such as secular humanists, extreme liberals, utopianists, and the like, not realizing the impact that the postmodern hyperreality exerts on their hallowed institutions. The nuclear family, for example, has declined in importance not because of the assault of "radical feminists" but because the home has been penetrated by electronic communication systems. Particular modes of information put individual family members in constant contact with a specific subculture. While they are physically in the home, they exist emotionally outside of it through various forms of communication. The construction of their consciousnesses and the formation of their emotional investments take place in a manner far different than is assumed by most educators (Gergen 1991, 15, 71; Poster 1989, 168).

As we confront this social saturation of hyperreality, we enter into a postmodern consciousness. Although we appear to one another as single, bounded identities, we are socially superabsorbent, hiding beneath the surface a maze of personality fragments. We are all part television game-show host, evangelist, interviewee in a breakfast cereal commercial, cop or criminal, and local news anchor. All personalities are latent and given the right stimuli are ready to come alive. Thus, the boundaries of individualism begin to fade like the chalk lines of a late inning batter's box. As they do, we become more aware of critical constructivism's notion of the social construction of the individual. Indeed, we even begin to recognize the limitations of middle-class notions of individualism. In the name of individualism we are taught a "me-first" perspective on self-gratification that renders us vulnerable to appeals such as "read my lips, no new taxes." This emphasis on self-gratification trivializes critical conceptions of citizenship, friendships, and sexual relationships, as each becomes something designed to get what we want. Of course, we use testing not only as a sound way of assessing the value of education but as a means of motivating our individualistic students. As we gain a meta-awareness of the construction of our postmodern consciousness, maybe it becomes possible to critically reconstruct our understanding of the nature of individualism.

In our reconstruction of individualism we cannot ignore the nature of our changing relationships to others. Small, unchanging, geographically based communities, with their small troupe of significant others, are quickly being supplanted by an expanding galaxy of relationships. The Andys, Opies, Barneys, Gomers, Goobers, and Aunt Beas and the cohesive Mayberry they signify is only thirty years old, yet it is light years away from America of the 1990s. No matter how hard we try, hyperreality has fossilized the Mayberry of the early 1960s—no one can go back "home" again. We have learned that "live" presence is not necessary to postmodern relationships. What does it say about us that Andy, Barney, Opie, and the rest may be the best example of community we can conjure? Moreover, they may have become our community. For many individuals, our students in particular, media relationships provide the most emotionally evocative experiences of their lives. Hyperreality thus inverts "prehyperreality"— the question is no longer whether television relationships substitute for the "normal," but whether the normal can substitute for the relationships of television (Gergen 1991, 57, 242). As these postmodern realities shatter traditional conceptions of individuality and relationship, it seems obvious that our critical reconstruction of individualism must address the new ways that consciousness is constructed. To ignore the social and cognitive impact of hyperreality is to bury our heads in a traditionalist sand. It is to embrace a form of educational fundamentalism that seeks safety in the education of a premodernist past as the world we once knew collapses around us.

LEARNING TO THINK ABOUT THE SIGN: A CURRICULUM OF HYPERREALITY

The culture of hyperreality has produced a new form of communication, a communion of image which, Peter McLaren writes, celebrates the look, the sign. This communion of image promotes a form of social amnesia that turns us away from a knowledge of the historical shaping of our consciousness, as it engulfs us in a white-water river of signs—a torrent of changing images that dull our senses. Unlike many analysts of contemporary information culture, critical postmodern analysis recognizes a political dimension in these seemingly random signs. For example, while advertisers claim that advertising is predominately informative, careful study indicates that it is grounded on image. Also, its images do not simply attempt to market products by connecting them to desirable traits, but they sell an accompanying ideology, a system of values that further individuals' identification with a culture of consumerism (McLaren 1991a, 234; McLaren 1991b, 145–46; Kellner 1991, 67).

Miller Lite Beer advertisements of the last couple of decades provide good examples of the use of signs and images to sell a product and an ideology. After a series of beer company failures to successfully market diet beers, the advertisers who won the account for the Miller Brewing Company developed a new "game plan" for Miller Lite. Recognizing that in a health-conscious culture a new market for a low-calorie beer could be tapped, the advertisers understood that the predominately male beer drinking market would not respond positively to an effeminate image of a diet beer. Beer drinking is often a male bonding ritual, and, as such, it could not be compromised by the introduction of a feminine beer. Basing their actions on this reading of masculine culture, the advertisers took the status production of sports and the new ethic of health that had developed and connected them to the culture of masculinity.

Seeking the most publicly recognized macho characters available, the strategists set out to prove that drinking a low-calorie beer could be masculine. Football players Dick Butkus and Bubba Smith, baseball legend Mickey Mantle, boxer Carlos Palomena, outdoorsman Grits Gresham, detective novelist Mickey Spillane, and many others were enlisted to sell the ties that bound together masculinity, sports, health, and low-calorie beer. While the marketers achieved great success in selling Miller Lite, they also sold a life-style. The appeal of a heterosexual (but homoerotic) culture of athletic men playing hypermasculine roles was the image being promoted. Women were outsiders at least, decoration at best, as demonstrated by their absence except for the employment of Mickey Spillane's "doll"—a vacuous "blond bombshell" with the looks but not the savvy of Roger Rabbit's "toon" wife, Jessica Rabbit. Young males, increasingly Republican and antifeminist, were the targets of the ads which were wildly successful judging from the sales of Miller Lite and the spate of low-calorie beer imitators Miller Lite launched.

Douglas Kellner critically deconstructs the image of masculinity and its accompanying life-style in Marlboro cigarette advertisements. He uses his deconstructions as examples of how we might learn to read hyperreality. Integrating the Marlboro ads in his teaching, Kellner writes of the student empowerment that results when students learn to critically analyze taken-for-granted features of their worlds. More often than not, Kellner contends, students quickly learn to decode tacit meanings of media, uncovering in the process the way their consciousness has been constructed by the larger culture. Unlike Marshall McLuhan, who maintained that media literacy was a natural ability developed by those who live in a media culture, Kellner argues that teachers or somebody must teach such forms of reading and thinking. Once such skills are learned, students have a much greater possibility of understanding the ways that oppression works. Indeed, deconstruction of media may work to engage students in such important political understandings more quickly than does the critical reading of the traditional book culture. While both forms of reading are necessary, the media reading is quicker because it engages students with the form closest to their lived worlds, the formation of their subjectivities (Kellner 1991, 78–80).

By engaging students at the level of emotion and the formation of their subjectivities, the messages of hyperreality gain a power never before achieved. Indeed, in the advertisements, political pronouncements, and entertainment of much electronic information, we find a postmodern version of a culture of manipulation. Hyperreality, then, often creates a climate of deceit. Just as the CIA has been known to produce disinformation designed to undermine the enemy and create conditions favorable to CIA interests, advertising and political discourse often distribute a similar form of data. Such media disinformation creates a facade of understanding while actually moving individuals in an opposite direction. Does such disinformation and the powerful images it produces not demand in response a form of teaching that sees itself as part of a larger critical postmodern pedagogy that attempts to explore the genesis of our ways of seeing the world? Does it not demand a form of teacher and student thinking that is capable of understanding the way consciousness is constructed and uses this understanding to emancipate social actors from domination?

The critical postmodern pedagogy I envision teaches students to interpret how images are constructed, how they shape our consciousness, and what they mean in different situations. Such an approach to education appropriates Jacques Derrida's ludic postmodernism and uses its deconstructive strategies to understand the power of the sign, the image in electronic media. Drawing our methodological cue from Derrida, we begin to deconstruct the form of thinking embedded in contemporary television. So doing, we find that linear forms of Cartesian–Newtonian logic have little to do with the construction of political media campaigns or television advertising. Neil Postman facilitates our critical deconstruction of the electronic image, when he points out that traditional attempts to distinguish between true or false advertising claims are misguided in their assumption that such claims are couched in the language of logical propositions. If such a language is discarded, advertising cannot be analyzed under the same ground rules applied to other forms of communications. Advertisers on television appeal to a domain of symbols that cannot be validated or refuted.

Take, for example, a Levis 501 jeans commercial. No claims are made about the quality, durability, or stylishness of the pants. The viewer is rushed through a barrage of shots of young people indifferent to the camera who are wearing 501 jeans. The image created can be read as young, sensual, alive people wear these jeans—but that's not the major point. We (the people here at Levis) are so engaged in the culture of "cool," marked by its low affect and its knowing indifference that we are not going to make an overt appeal for you to buy our jeans. James Dean would have never done it that way. Now, associate that image with these jeans. While multiple readings are possible, many of them will involve at some level an emotional identification of Levis 501 jeans with the culture of "cool." We get it because we are experts in the media culture of advertising. We are tired of the more overt, less "cool" attempts to gain our attention.

At the center of the critical postmodern curriculum is a study of media that analyzes not only the effects of television, radio, popular music, computers, and such, but also teaches postmodern forms of research such as semiotics, film analysis, and ethnography. Such analysis can begin as early as elementary school as students begin to study where adults get their information and their opinions about the world. Neil Postman argues that this media education should involve not only contemporary analysis of information forms but a historical understanding of the origins and uses of ideographic writing; the etymology and sociopolitical consequences of the alphabet; the development and impact of the printing press, newspapers, and magazines; the technological origins of the computer and its present effects; and so on. Postman's point is clear—media should be made problematic to our students in a way that causes them to assess the impact of information and information sources in their lives (Postman 1985, 8). Before such study becomes commonplace, however, teacher education programs must prepare teachers for the role of media analyst. Also, critical postmodern educators must convince the public that, contrary to the pronouncements of William Bennett, Allan Bloom, and Lamar Alexander, media education is not a "trivialization" of the curriculum.

Teacher education programs sensitive to the existence of hyperreality would require that prospective teachers study the nature of information. Historically, information has been packaged in many forms. Long before the electronic image, information was communicated through speech, writing, print, and the painted image. The nature of our thinking has been shaped in part by the dominant discursive form for transferring information. In order to understand the way events are shaped and history flows we must understand the influence of information formats. We can talk at great length about the way politics has changed over the past decades, but we will never approach understanding the reasons for the alterations until we analyze politics in relation to information form. Not attentive to abstract and ambiguous ideas, television focuses our gaze on images. George Bush standing tall, smiling broadly, and waving to the crowd *like a leader* is the issue—not the question of trickle-down economics. Teacher education and schooling in general must address this change in information format, as they prepare teachers and citizens in a democratic society to protect themselves from this epistemology of hyperreality. Indeed, such a social change demands a new form of literacy—a postmodern literacy— to "read" the effect of 5,000 hours of television before we start to school, 800 or more television commercials a week (Postman 1985, 4–8), and a cultural knowledge dominated by Fred Flintstone, Teenage Mutant Ninja Turtles, Tiny Toons, Captain M, and Super Mario Brothers.

As we study information, we inevitably have to confront the ways media and popular culture shape the consciousness of teachers and students. Peter McLaren suggests, in this context, that we ask:

How are the subjectivities, dreams, desires, and needs of students forged by the media, by leisure activities, by institutions such as the family, and by cultural forms such as rock 'n' roll and music videos? How for instance, is the practical ethics by which students engage everyday life inscribed within a contestatory politics of signification? How are images of male and female socially constructed? How do the politics of signification structure the problematization of experience? How are the subjectivities of students constituted by the effects of representations which penetrate the level of the body? (McLaren 1991b, 165)

Without a form of critical thinking that comes out of our attempts to answer McLaren's questions and the application of our media research strategies, we are as vulnerable to tyrannical manipulators as those who are without education.

As we analyze the way information is shaped by the various electronic media, we learn that the leaders of hyperreality subsume their natural ways of relating to polished techniques of efficient communication. Local dialects are suppressed, annoying gestures are eliminated, controversial topics are removed, dress is homogenized, and pleasant facial expressions are rehearsed. For example, David Duke before media training was a fiery, rough-edged, often frightening Klansman. After learning techniques of effective communication, Duke appeared on television as a soft-spoken, smiling, friendly, mainstream Christian with the attending respect and courtesy the image entails, who advocated political policies that protected our traditional values, our Protestant work ethic. The political differences of the before and after Duke were minimal. The video-friendly image took precedence over the racist reality. Those with ingrained fears and distorted views of African-Americans could say, "I'm not a racist, but what Duke says makes an awful lot of sense." As Aldous Huxley foresaw in *Brave New World*, the threat to freedom would emanate not from tyrannical threats of pain but from pleasure. In Huxley's *Brave New World*, citizens came to love the technologies that oppressed them and destroyed their cognitive abilities. To avoid Huxley's nightmare, we must learn the effects of the technologies that we have grown to love. We must develop a media literacy that empowers us to subvert the construction of Mr. Huxley's neighborhood by uncovering the codes on which it is based (Postman 1985, 4–8, 17; Gergen 1991, 203). As we subvert the codes, we use them to build an emancipatory vision of a postmodern reality.

POPULAR CULTURE AND THE POSTMODERN SOCIAL IMAGINATION

While the school is the primary site for the construction of what constitutes valuable thinking and valid knowledge, popular culture shapes what Stanley Aronowitz and Henry Giroux call the social imaginary. The social imaginary is the venue where youth locate their desires and find emotional identification. Specifically, young people locate the content of what it means to be socially mobile in situation comedies, in the movies with their depiction of pleasure, in music videos with their celebration of style, and in advertisements with their depictions of life-styles. Thus, hyperreality is by no means simply oppressive, but holds within its imagery visions of a better life, of pleasure.

In a culture that is still ambiguous about pleasure there is something threatening about a cultural form, in this case popular culture, that overtly promotes pleasure. Next to popular culture, the role of schooling as vestige of a Victorian asceticism is highlighted. In its denial of pleasure school promotes a regime of discipline and devotion to the transference of play into labor. In this context, school has consistently attempted to devalue popular cultural forms with its accompanying pleasure. At some tacit level recognizing the power of popular culture, schools have worked to detach students from popular culture, reshaping them along the lines of more ascetic dominant cultural notions such as the work ethic and respect for authority.

The curriculum and the public conversation about it are almost entirely devoted to the vocational needs of business and the state. In the postmodern economy these vocational needs are primarily ideological and attitudinal, not technical. Just as many television commercials sell partic- ular life-styles conducive to capitalism instead of selling a particular product, schools emphasize particular forms of behavior instead of a body of specific skills and knowledge. Much of the content of school is forgotten—the important lessons involve learning how to get good grades, how to survive in an organization, and how to win points with authorities. The school offers a grand compromise—trade in your popular cultural pleasure for the material benefits of consumer society. Critical postmodern education rejects the compromise, maintaining that pleasure and pedagogy can be united. In their unification, popular culture is reclaimed as an authentic expression of a generation, just as meaningful, just as valuable as folk cultures have been throughout history. Within their own popular culture, students begin to construct emancipatory visions, ways of think- ing, that move them into unexplored territories (Aronowitz and Giroux 1991, 163–70).

In the socially saturated culture of hyperreality, this emancipatory trek into unexplored territories is a vacation package without a map. Postmodern teachers must draw upon both their own and their students' understanding of popular culture, combining this knowledge with a critical system of meaning, and the self-reflexivity that comes out of exposure to hyperreality. While the critical system of meaning would be employed as a basis for questioning and rethinking popular cultural experiences, the self-reflexivity would be used to examine the role of popular culture in the construction of self. This self-reflexivity has been cleverly characterized by Umberto Eco as the postmodern attitude held by a man who loves a very sophisticated woman and realizes that he can't say to her, "I love you madly," because he knows that she knows (and vice versa) that Barbara

Cartland has already written those words (Gergen 1991, 135–37, 225). Students in class confront this same idea in the pronouncements of their teachers: They've heard it all before on a rerun of an old "Leave It to Beaver," or in the movie *Teachers* or *Fast Times at Ridgemont High* or *Stand and Deliver* or. . . . Such reflexivity cannot help but modify our sense of self. Living within the multiple realities of social saturation, our consciousness is continually interrupted by awareness of other depictions of similar circumstances. How are our actions shaped by our familiarity with these depictions? Are they shaped in a way with which we are comfortable? Are our actions compatible with the ethical demands of our critical system of meaning? What new visions of action might we formulate from our exposure to popular culture? Indeed, through such questions we turn reflexivity into critical reflexivity.

THE POSTMODERN HETEROGLOSSIA OF BEING—THE PROTEAN SELF

Such critical reflexivity heightens our understanding of the social construction of self, of consciousness in the postmodern cosmos. Each time we identify an essence of self, our postmodern self-reflexivity with its questioning sense of irony undermines our certainty. The multiple voices of hyperreality won't leave well enough alone. Because of these assaults on the essence of self, we have come to speak of our subjectivity rather than our identity. Unlike the Cartesian, humanistic version of self as grounded and bounded, the postmodern subject is partial and often defined in contradictory ways. The multiple determinations of hyperreality tear across emotional, ideological, place, and gender boundaries, pulling us this way and that in its storm of imagery (Gergen 1991, 7, 16–17; McLaren 1991a, 242). The apparati of social saturation populates the self, inducing a multiphrenic condition—here rests the genesis of the postmodern consciousness.

This postmodern consciousness challenges the very concept of personal essence. The Cartesian, humanist notion of personal essence sees the individual as a free, rational being whose view of self and the world is constituted through the exercise of reason. Chris Weedon argues that postmodernism's challenge to this viewpoint revolves around its recognition that language *constructs* our sense of ourselves, our subjectivity. When we contend that subjectivity is constructed, we are implying that it is not innate—it is socially produced. Our subjectivity then is produced by a variety of economic, social, and political discursive practices, and, as such, is always involved with power struggles to determine the meaning of particular discourses. Unlike the Cartesian, humanist notion of personal essence with its rational basis, postmodernism sees subjectivity as a terrain of disunity and conflict (Weedon 1987, 21). The recognition of this disunity of the subject by no means should imply that it ceases to exist; subjectivity simply is constructed by historical forms of power that work to produce particular values, forms of behavior, and world views. Those who would imply the death of the subject would concede the possibility of any form of emancipation that hopes to overcome the malformations of power discourses and social structures. It is a nihilism that denies hope and the human need to resist domination by developing alternative forms of thinking and alternative conceptions of subjectivity (Aronowitz and Giroux 1991, 79–80).

Consider, for example, the educational and cognitive impact of the adoption of the Cartesian view of self which assumes an autonomous and enduring essence. When we assume that individuals possess a mechanical essence of self existing close to the surface, then measurement should be easy. Such measurement of self would enable educational psychologists to explain all varieties of behavior while predicting an individual's future. Grounded on the belief that individuals are consistent through time, standardized tests measure the essence of an unchanging cognitive ability that, like a fingerprint, will be the same twenty years hence. Stephen Jay Gould argued over a decade ago that developers of a psychological testing failed to take into account the environmental modifications of an individual's ability (Gould 1981, 156). Test makers viewed individuals as living in isolation booths, where ability was static and unaffected by a person's interaction with the surrounding environment.

With these ideas in mind postmodernism pushes us toward a new vision of the self, a vision informed by Mikhail Bakhtin's use of the term "heteroglossia." Originally employed to designate the multiple nature of language within a culture, heteroglossia exposes the ways that vestiges of languages used in various historical eras and in various subcultures shape the extant language of a particular culture (Bakhtin 1981, 5–14). Applying the notion of the postmodern analysis of self, we come to see that hyperreality invites a heteroglossia of being. Drawing upon a multiplicity of voices, individuals live out a variety of possibilities, refusing to suppress particular voices. As men and women appropriate the various forms of expression, they are empowered to uncover new dimensions of existence that were previously hidden. Such discoveries open the possibility of perceiving through a new modality that was unaccessible in an old one. This multiplicity of perception or heteroglossia of being reflects Robert Jay Lifton's concept of the protean life-style. Just as Proteus, the sea god of Greek mythology could alter his shape from wild boar to dragon, postmodern men and women drawing on their heteroglossia of selves see being as a continuous flow without an imposed coherence. Drawing upon a variety of contradictory images, protean postmoderns employ a form of *difference* to reach new levels of cognitive perception. Drawing upon a critical system of meaning, this postmodern subject is constantly remade, desperately seeking to transcend confining forms of consciousness construction (Gergen 1991, 248–49).

THE SYNERGISTIC CONVERSATION BETWEEN CRITICAL THEORY AND POSTMODERNISM: EMANCIPATION IN HYPERREALITY

Societies like the one in the United States may be seen as democracies, but critical analysis reveals that they are democratic in only particular ways. As we have discussed throughout this book, the voting public is a manipulated public—an outcome of the social management of public opinion. In this climate of deceit, individuals are acculturated and schooled to feel comfortable in relations of either domination or subordination rather than equality and interdependence. Given the social and technological changes that have led to hyperreality with its bombarding imagery and fragmented selves, critical theoretical concerns with self-direction and democratic egalitarianism should be reassessed. As we consider the politics of thinking in the electronic maze of hyperreality, we recognize the need for the serious conversation between critical theory and the postmodern critique. Indeed, the theoretical structure of this analysis is grounded upon a critical theory reconceptualized by its familiarity with the postmodern critique (Young 1990, 18; Morrow 1991, 28).

Drawing upon Foucault's genealogy and Derrida's deconstructionism, a reconceptualized critical theory brings new insights to the way consciousness is constructed, subjectivity is formed, and power influences action in the schools and the world. Genealogy focuses on the concrete mechanisms of exclusion and domination. Concerned with the workings of power, genealogy focuses on the history that has been suppressed and the subjugated knowledges that have been disqualified or insufficiently elaborated. Foucault contends that it is through the emergence or reemergence of these low-ranking knowledges that alternate emancipatory visions of society, education, and cognition are possible. Critical teachers taking Foucault's genealogy seriously become transformative agents who alert the community to its dangerous memory, in the process helping individuals name their oppression (Foucault 1980, 82; Welch 1985, 42–43; Harrison 1985, 250–51).

Deconstruction can be defined in many ways—as a method of reading, as an interpretive strategy, and as a philosophical strategy. For our purposes it involves all three of these definitions, as it views the world as texts to be decoded, to be explored for unintended meanings. Jacques Derrida has employed deconstruction to question the integrity of texts, meaning that he refuses to accept the authority of traditional, established interpretations of the world. This becomes extremely valuable in hyperreality, as deconstruction focuses on elements that others find insignificant. The purpose is not to reveal what the text *really* means or what the author intended, but to expose an unintended current or an unnoticed contradiction within it (Culler 1981, 14–15; Culler 1982, 85–88). By understanding the genealogy of forces of postmodern power and by deconstructing the social contradictions of hyperreality, critical postmodernism offers a means of getting a handle on the confusion of the postmodern condition.

The synergism of the conversation between the postmodern critique and critical theory involves the interplay of the praxis of the critical and the radical uncertainty of the postmodern. As it invokes its emancipatory system of meaning, critical theory provides the postmodern critique with a normative foundation. Without such a foundation the postmodern critique is ever vulnerable to nihilism and inaction. Indeed, the normatively ungrounded postmodern critique is incapable of providing an ethically challenging and politically transformative program of action. Stanley Aronowitz and Henry Giroux argue, in this context, that if the postmodern critique is to make a valuable contribution to the notion of schooling as an emancipatory form of cultural politics, it must make connections to those egalitarian impulses of modernism that contribute to an emancipatory democracy. Doing this, the project of an emancipatory democracy and the schooling that supports it can be extended by new understandings of how power operates and by incorporating groups who had been excluded by their race, gender, or place (Morrow 1991, 56; Welch 1991, 84; Codd 1984, 9; Aronowitz and Giroux 1991, 81).

As our reconstructed critical theory, our critical postmodern critique confronts the challenge of the new forms of mystification and oppression endemic to hyperreality, semiotics becomes one of the most powerful analytical techniques it employs. The development of information-based societies places a high value on a form of study that analyzes codes and symbols in the communication process. A critical semiotics can be used to dislodge hidden mystifications, power, and oppression in political communiques and the general fare of electronic media. As it uncovers such hidden dimensions of hyperreality, semiotics helps equip individuals with a new critical consciousness—a way of seeing that empowers men and women to move beyond beliefs that have been shaped by domination and manipulation. As individuals take what they learned through critical semiotics about the hidden power of hyperreality, they employ their critical system of meaning to develop a democratic vision of what they can become. This vision can be used to fuel the resistance groups that are always forming at the margins of hyperreality (Luke 1991, 21–22). As my graduate students, for example, learn to employ critical semiotics, they often uncover emancipatory meanings in particular television programs. They integrate such meanings into their own teaching, engaging students intellectually and at the level of pleasure in the emancipatory struggle. Their students, in the process, learn to identify with marginalized groups who traditionally have been ignored or degraded in the school setting.

This critical identification with the marginalized produces a postmodern suspicion of modernism's penchant for boundary fixing, its tendency to subordinate and exclude. Thus, the semiotic decoding of the media, of text, of school, of world becomes an irreverent reading, an exploration of embedded ideology, dominant cultural values, and oppressive stereotypes. Whether the text is the "sacred" canon of Western civilization or popular culture, such readings are consistent in their iconoclasm. This is critical theory in action, negating the dominant culture's tendency to use schools as training grounds for the marketplace. In this educational context students learn how to adjust to rather than to contest the established culture of power. As it counters the mainstream, critical postmodern reading decenters the unchallenged interpretations, employing Foucault's genealogy and its cavalcade of the previously unheard and unread to lead us out of the stagnant cultural pond (Aronowitz and Giroux 1991, 81, 98; Gergen 1991, 126).

THE COGNITIVE STAGNATION OF THE MODERNIST WEST

As we have read, the Enlightenment grand narratives of modernism justify the last several centuries of Western history on the grounds of progress—improvement, conquest, success, and scientific achievement. Not only can we observe this progress but we can measure it. Deconstructing the concept of progress and tracing its genealogy, we are faced with the realization that what has been labeled as progress in the modernist era may have actually moved the culture backwards. Often when labeling a particular outcome as progress, modernist observers are compelled to remove from view everything that falls outside the specific outcome in question. Thus, when we argue that a school's standardized test-score improvement is a sign of progress, we focus only on the numbers. If the scores are to remain as our proof, we cannot explore simultaneous deterioration of students' sense of well-being or their inability to find significance in the everyday life of the classroom. Indeed, a postmodern critique of the scores finds that the obsession with test-score improvement has destroyed the pleasant ambience of the school—the improvement is not progress, but antiprogress. Postmodern genealogy uncovers repressive contradictions in terms such as progress by raising questions about how modernist narratives come to be constructed and how they necessitate particular epistemological, political, and cognitive perspectives (Gergen 1991, 232–36; Aronowitz and Giroux 1991, 80–81).

Deconstruction alerts us to the important understanding of the limitations of words. As it frames our thoughts, language constructs barriers. Outside of a meta-analytical perspective, without postmodern's genealogy and deconstruction, we confuse the map with the terrain. The subtlety of different points in the process are missed—the raspberry of July 10 is very different from the sweet one of August 4 that borders between ripeness and rottenness. The process of change always attempts to escape the ability of our words to capture it. Losing sight of the *process*, modernism sees a world that consists of discrete entities, each demanding a particular form of analysis. Schooling and the thinking it promotes reflect this isolating tendency as they search for fundamental essences, an understanding of "things in themselves." Thus, the possibility of a process-oriented cognition that views an entity as part of a larger set of temporal, spatial, and conceptual relationships is severely reduced by modernism. Indeed, modernist words are full of hidden assumptions, of tacit ways of thinking that wait for a deconstructing Godot to wring out the meaning that has through the ages soaked into them (Poster 1989, 126; Ferguson 1980, 149; Gergen 1991, 87, 106).

The tyranny of the unexamined word, the unexamined cognitive styles, has silenced competing voices both inside and outside of the Western tradition. The narrative of progress, the obsession with things in themselves have served to silence competing voices. In the process Western society has suffered, cognition has stagnated, schools have become more concerned with honoring the past than inventing the future. Egalitarianism is fought off as an unfair procedure, not a challenging engagement with voices, perspectives, and knowledges that had been drowning in the modernist whiteout. The grand narrative, unhinged by genealogy and deconstruction, gives way to a round of "postwar" negotiations of suppressed and local histories (Kincheloe and Pinar 1991). Like postmodern architects seeking an age of recovery, of historical renewal, emancipatory educators seek out tradition but with an irreverence born of critical self-reflection (Aronowitz and Giroux 1991, 115; Ferguson 1980, 359).

LEARNING ABOUT BECOMING: THE LESSONS OF POSTMODERN PHYSICS

Contemporary physics has produced a body of understandings that have not only revolutionized our view of the physical world but have exerted a dramatic impact on sociology, philosophy, and education. Ilya Prigogine won the 1977 Nobel Prize in chemistry for his theory of dissipative structures. Many argue that the theory may exert as much influence on science in general as Einstein's relativity did on physics. The theory of dissipative structures bridges the chasm between biology and physics, that is, the missing connection between living organisms and the ostensibly lifeless world that gave birth to them. Prigogine described the dissipative structure as a flowing wholeness, highly organized but ever in process. Basing his idea on the contention that physical science often ignored the concept of time, Prigogine argued that the Cartesian–Newtonian universe failed to see time outside the context of motion. Radically departing from the modernist scientific tradition, Prigogine maintained that there were many dimensions of time: history, decay, evolution, and the development of new forms. Modernist science simply had not left room for becoming, as it attempted to make reality sit still long enough to study it. The true nature of reality could not be studied simply as a snapshot—its nature moved beyond that static form. In searching for discrete boundaries, trying to find well-defined edges, we often miss the "blur of reality," that is, reality in a time sequence (Ferguson 1980, 149–50, 163–64).

The work of physicist David Bohm compliments Prigogine's work and helps us understand the implications of contemporary physics for postmodernism and postmodern education. Bohm theorized the existence of an explicate and an implicate order of reality. The explicate order involves simple patterns and invariants in time, that is, characteristics of the world that repeat themselves in similar ways and that have recognizable locations in space. Being associated with comparatively humble orders of similarities and differences, explicate orders are often what is identified by the categorization and generalization function of formal thought.

The implicate order is a much deeper structure of reality. It is the level at which ostensible separateness vanishes and all things seem to become a part of a larger unified process. Implicate orders are marked by the simultaneous presence of a sequence of many levels of enfoldment with similar dissimilarities existing among them. The totality of these levels of enfoldment cannot be made explicit as a whole. They can be exposed only in the emergence of a series of enfoldments. In contrast to the explicate order (which is an unfolded order), where similar differences are all present together and can be described in Cartesian–Newtonian terms, the implicate order has to be studied as a hidden process, sometimes impenetrable to empirical methods of inquiry (Bohm and Peat 1987, 174, 187).

As we conceptualize a postmodern form of cognition (or what we have referred to as post-formal thinking), a familiarity with the work of Prigogine and Bohm is helpful. As post-formal thinking attempts to understand the deep structures that shape hyperreality, we are seeking to view the social world in a time sequence, at the level of its implicate order. Profound insight in any field of study may involve comprehending structures not recognizable at the explicate order of reality. Transcending common sense, we cut patterns out of the cosmic fabric (Combs and Holland 1990, 46). Schools, of course, are grounded in the explicate order. The dominant culture's conversation not only about education but the political process, racism, sexism, and social class bias revolves around the explicate order. In the critical postmodern analytical process, for example, we come to understand the most damaging form of racism is not an overt "George Wallace in 1963 blocking the entrance to the University of Alabama" variety, but an institutional racism built into the very structures of our schools, corporations, churches, and entertainment industry. Critical postmodern theory has taught us that little is as it appears on the surface. When post-formal observers search for the deep structures that are there to be uncovered in any classroom, they discover a universe of hidden meanings constructed by a variety of sociopolitical forces, which many times has little to do with the intended (explicate) meanings of the official curriculum.

Attention to the implicate order helps us transcend the fragmentation common to modernist ways of seeing. Bohm calls for an examination of reality that seeks to uncover the enfolded connections among events. Human and social experience has been reduced, Bohm and the postmodernists argue, to discrete and arbitrary pieces that are separated from the combination of forces that provided human experience its distinction in the first place. Cartesian–Newtonian love, for example, involves a raised heartbeat, a specific percentage increase in hormonal secretion, and a behavioral expectation of positive reciprocation. Modern curriculum is removed from the social realities that grant significance to the knowledge to be "mastered." Indeed, modern schools often see society as one cog of a larger machine that is to be studied. Critical postmodern analysts see human beings and society as interconnected aspects of a broader framework, an implicate order, which reveals itself when the evolutionary possibility of humanity is entertained (Britzman 1991, 35; Oliver and Gershman 1989, 30).

Modernists have routinely failed to think in terms of connectiveness, in terms of becoming. Schools fall into this modernist trap, manifesting infection by the cognitive illness as they allow compartmentalization to define importance. As we compartmentalize the world and knowledge about it, we draw boundaries between what is spoken and what remains unspoken. Students may graduate from high school never having given a thought to how their various subjects relate or why knowledge is segmented as it is. While "no man [sic] is an island," contemporary schooling through its curricular structure stipulates that knowledge is. Removed from its sociohistorical roots and its political impact, the decontextualized knowledge of the modernist school serves to foster *explicate* processes—thinking of a concrete and formal variety that emphasizes categorization and retention processes (Britzman 1991, 35).

As we begin to understand the limitations of the reductionism of modernism, we can see the coming end of conventional science. To avoid reductionism in our teaching and our study of cognition, we must learn to derive meaning from direct experience. Learning from and extending the knowledge derived from direct experiences such as the practical knowledge of teachers, we move into the realm of connectedness where new awarenesses carry us beyond the boundaries of conventional ways of thinking. As conventional science retreats, the West may overcome its creative malaise and move toward higher dimensions of human experience. Marilyn Ferguson uses the multicultural image of the Cheyenne Wheel of Knowledge to conceptualize this higher dimension of human experience, the realm of human becoming. Thinking in terms of the themes we have developed in this book, the Cheyenne developed a system of meaning to help them make sense of the world and their relationship to it. Thus, in the spirit of the Cheyenne we learn to think in a way that allows us to make sense of our place on the planet, our role in the pageant of history, our connection to the quantum world of the subatomic and the immensity of the universe, and of our relationship to birth, death, work, and family. Without an appreciation of implicate systems and the way their unfolding affects us, we are lost in the cosmos, incapable of transcending the formal cognition of modernist reductionism. Without our postmodern wheel of knowledge we find "being" easier than "becoming" (Ferguson 1980, 172, 308).

POSTMODERN PLAY—OVERCOMING THE ILLUSION OF CERTAINTY

As we confront hyperreality with all of its exploding imagery, our form of cognition begins to adapt to the self-reflexivity of the postmodern condition. No longer are we comfortable with macho proclamations of our ability to comprehend reality. We begin to speak in terms of constructions of reality. With our awareness of the various filters that are employed by the media and other power groups, we begin to understand the process by which things get constructed. Such knowledge leads to a postmodern humility, a realization, in the words of Julia Kristeva, "that at the deepest levels of my wants and desires [I] am unsure, centerless, and divided" (Kristeva 1987, 7–8). This postmodern humility is not a passing uncertainty but a critical resistance to all representations and interpretations that claim transhistorical certainty. In rejecting formalism's universal reason as the supreme form of cognition, critical postmodernism seeks alternative forms of thinking and knowing that are historically and socially contingent, partial as opposed to total. Postmodern teacher educators can no longer appeal to some sacrosanct body of professional knowledge that rises above all other bodies of information in value. The partial, historically and socially specific knowledge of the practitioner must be respected for its insight, not for its certainty. No longer can teacher educators maintain an uncrossable chasm between professional and everyday knowledge (Ferguson 1980, 105; Giroux and Aronowitz 1991, 133; Feinberg 1989, 137).

One way of examining postmodern cognition is to think of it as an infinite game. It is a game that makes fun of certainty and the fundamentalist excesses that accompany it. Whether the excesses be religious, political, pedagogical, or cognitive, they all denote an epistemological arrogance that impedes self-reflection and interpersonal communication. Postmodernists are fallibists who are unafraid to laugh at their own fallibility. No one wins the postmodern game, but all players benefit from the way it exposes the pseudocertainties that plague modernism. Inclusionary and nonhierarchical, the game allows us to challenge the traditional rules that penalize the outsiders, the players from the margins (Gergen 1991, 197–98). For example, the frightening power of leaders like Ronald Reagan and George Bush rested in their ability to deflect criticism away from the manipulative charades devised by their image makers. By careful implementation of public relations strategies, Reagan and Bush did not allow the postmodern game to be played on their turf. The emancipatory value of the postmodern game in this context would have involved its ability to expose the self-serving hypocritical rhetoric, the simplistic distortions of information, and the flagrant appeal to emotion common to contemporary political speeches. Without this form of postmodern play, of post-formal thinking, we remain at the mercy of the illusions of hyperreality.

Chapter 6

Critical Constructivism

The work of Jean Piaget, combining cognitive psychology and epistemology, has revolutionized how we understand human thinking and learning. Piaget's work, often referred to as constructivism, describes the learning process in terms of the way new knowledge is produced (or constructed) through a process of cognitive change and self-regulation. Assuming that there is no knowledge without a knower, Piaget argued that the human knower belongs to a particular, ever-changing, historical world. The human being as a part of history is a reflexive subject, an entity who is conscious of the constant interaction between humans and their world. This reflexivity recognizes that all knowledge is a fusion of subject and object. Stated another way, constructivism maintains that the knower personally participates in all acts of knowing and understanding (Poplin 1988, 402; Lowe 1982, 163; Gordon, Miller, and Rollock 1990, 17; Reinharz 1979, 245). Viewed from the historical perspective of modernism and postmodernism, the epistemological shift to constructivism may be a necessary prerequisite for the larger sociohistorical shift from modernism to postmodernism.

A BRIEF INTRODUCTION TO CONSTRUCTIVISM

Constructivism has implied that nothing represents a "neutral" perspective, in the process shaking the epistemological foundations of modernist grand narratives. Indeed, no truly objective way of seeing exists. Nothing exists before consciousness shapes it into something we can perceive. What appears to us as objective reality, Piaget argued, is merely what our minds construct, what we are accustomed to see (Leshan and Margenau 1982, 189; Bohm and Peat 1987, 64). The knowledge that the world yields has to be interpreted by men and women who are part of that world (Besag 1986, 21). Whether we are attempting to understand football, education, or art, the constructivist principle tacitly remains. For example, most observers don't realize that the theory of perspective developed by fifteenth-century artists constituted a scientific convention. It was simply one way of portraying space and held no *absolute* validity. Thus, the structures and phenomena we observe in the physical world are nothing more than creations of our measuring and categorizing mind (Leshan and Margenau 1982, 189; Frye 1987, 59).

Not believing that interpretive constructs preexist in the mind, Piaget avoided innatism. At the same time he rejected behaviorism, maintaining that we do not come to understand reality through direct experience. To Piaget, our interpretive constructs develop as a result of increasingly complex interaction with the environment. This developmental aspect of Piaget's theory reflects its biological grounding, as he characterized intellectual adaptation as simply one feature of a larger process in which organisms adapt to their environments. As an organism develops, it becomes increasingly more successful in the attempt to survive, to adapt to its environment (O'Loughlin forthcoming, 6–7).

For simplicity, think of constructivism this way. An environmentalist, a real estate developer, an artist, a hunter, and a bird-watcher are walking through wetlands. Each of them sees and responds to the wetlands in different ways. To the environmentalist, it is a source of life; to the real estate developer, it is land to be cleared so beachfront condominiums can be constructed; the artist sees it as something to paint; to the hunter, the wetlands are a cover for game; the bird-watcher sees a natural setting to explore. Thus, the backgrounds and expectations of the observers shape their perceptions. In the same way, consider how a classroom is perceived by a class clown, a traditionally good student, a burnt-out teacher, a standardized test maker, a bureaucratic supervisor, a disgruntled parent, or a nostalgic alumnus. The way our psychosocial disposition shapes how the world is perceived holds extremely important implications for teaching. Each of our students brings a unique disposition into the classroom. Indeed, each teacher carries a unique disposition with her or him.

Here is the point where we justify our study of constructivism in the larger analysis of the politics of teacher thinking. In addition to a variety of problems with Piaget's version of constructivism, including a dehistorization, a logocentrism, an essentializing tendency, and a postivistic impulse that will be discussed later in this chapter, a major question arises in relation to this notion of disposition: Are our psychosocial dispositions beyond our conscious control?; do we simply surrender our perceptions to the determinations of the environment, our context? Because individuals are often unable to see the way their environment shapes their perceptions (that is, constructs their consciousness), the development of cognitive methods for exposing this process must become a central goal of the educational enterprise. This is where critical postmodern theory collides with constructivism—hence, the etymology of our term, "critical constructivism."

As previously discussed, critical theory is concerned with extending a human's consciousness of himself or herself as a social being. An individual who gains such a consciousness would understand how his or her political opinions, religious beliefs, gender role, racial self-concept, or educational perspectives had been influenced by the dominant culture. Critical theory thus promotes self-reflection. In my undergraduate teacher education course I help students cultivate a critical, theoretically grounded view of the construction of their own consciousness as a prospective teacher. Why is it that I have decided to teach? What forces in my life have shaped this decision? How have these forces contributed to the type of teacher I will become? These questions combined with an introduction to critical postmodern theory initiate an introspective process that eventuates in not only self-knowledge, but also cultural and educational critique. As we study major issues in education, the students are analyzing themselves; the interrelationship of these parallel studies produces some interesting perspectives, as students come to see various school purposes and reform movements play out on the terrain of their own school lives. Students undoubtedly come to know themselves better by bringing to consciousness the process by which their consciousness was constructed. Action to correct pathological constructions can be negotiated once the self-reflection reveals the psychological, ethical, moral, and political foundations of the pathology.

This notion of critical constructivism allows teachers a critical consciousness, that is, an ability to step back from the world as we are accustomed to perceiving it and to see the ways our perception is constructed through linguistic codes, cultural signs, and embedded power. Such an ability constitutes a giant step in learning to teach, indeed, in learning to think. Critical constructivism is a theoretically grounded form of world making. We ask penetrating questions. How did that which has come to be, come to be? Whose interests do particular institutional arrangements serve? As we remake and rename our world, we are constantly guided by our system of meaning, our emancipatory source of authority (Slaughter 1989, 264; Schon 1987, 136). With these foundations in mind, the remainder of this chapter will address the specifics of this sociocognitive theory of critical constructivism and its implications for teacher thinking and classroom instruction.

EPISTEMOLOGY AND THE CONSTRUCTION OF CONSCIOUSNESS

Modernist philosophy has been trapped in an epistemology that locates truth in external reality. Thinking in this context often has become little more than an effort to accurately reflect this reality. Indeed, Cartesian thought is seen as simply an inner process conducted in the minds of autonomous individuals. The thoughts, moods, and sensations of these individuals are separate from their histories and social contexts. If thinking is to be seen as a mirroring of external events, the need for a theory of critical constructivism or consciousness construction is irrelevant. The ability to conceptualize has little to do with culture, power, or discourse or the tacit understandings unconsciously shaped by them. From the Cartesian perspective, the curriculum becomes merely a body of knowledge to be transferred to the minds of students. More critical observers may contend that this is a naive view, but the naiveté is recognizable only if knowledge formation is understood as a complex and ambiguous social activity. Mind is more than a repository of signifieds, a mirror of nature. A critical constructivist epistemology assumes that the mind creates rather than reflects, and the nature of this creation cannot be separated from the surrounding social world (Benson 1989, 329–30; Bowers and Flinders 1990, 10–13; Harned 1987, 11).

Knowledge emerges neither from subjects nor from objects but from a dialectical relationship between the knower (subject) and the known (object). Drawing from Piaget, this dialectical relationship is represented by the assimilation–accommodation dyad. Employing these conceptualizations, critical constructivist teachers conceive knowledge as culturally produced and recognize the need to construct their own criteria for evaluating its quality. This constructivist sense-making process is a means by which teachers can explain and introduce students to the social and physical world and help them build for themselves an epistemological infrastructure for interpreting the phenomena they confront. Critical constructivists realize that because of the social construction of knowledge, their interpretations and infrastructures are a part of the cosmos but they are not in the cosmos. As a result, when the recognition of need arises we can always modify our viewpoints (Brooks 1984, 24; Kaufman 1978, 30; Benson 1989, 342–43).

Thus, the Cartesian–Newtonian conception of truth and certainty is rejected by the epistemology of critical constructivism. We can never apprehend the world in a "true" sense, apart from ourselves and our lives. As living parts of the world we are trying to figure out, we can only approach it from the existing cognitive infrastructures that shape our consciousness. Limited in this way, we can see only what our mind allows. With this restriction we are free to construct the world anyway we desire. This is not to say, however, that the outcomes of our constructions will not be confused and may be even destructive. We may, for example, adopt a world view such as the medieval Europeans. In this view of the world, sanitation was irrelevant and thousands of individuals died as the result of the Black Plague. Obviously, this was not an adequate construction of the nature of the world. This recognition confronts us with calls to develop a way of determining valid constructions of reality. All that critical construc-tivists can do in response to such a need is to lay out some guiding principles for judging more adequate and less adequate constructions: (1) The constructions are consistent with our critical postmodern system of meaning; (2) the constructions are helpful in our attempt to attain emancipatory goals; (3) the constructions are internally consistent; (4) the constructions contribute to the ability of humans to function and survive; (5) the constructions are appropriate for the purpose of the inquiry; and (6) the constructions avoid reductionism, as they recognize the contextual complexity of the situation in question (Fosnot 1988, 19; Bohm and Peat 1987, 56–57; Leshan and Margenau 1982, 13).

The modernist view of self cannot stand up to the epistemological assault of critical constructivism. Taking the concept of knower–known inseparability one more step, postmodern analysis examines the socially constructed dimensions of language and discursive practices. Foucault observed that discourse referred to a body of regulations and structures grounded in power relations that covertly shape our perspectives and insidiously mold our constructions. Bakhtin complimented Foucault's observations maintaining that power functions in a way that solidifies discourses in the process erasing the presence of unorthodox or marginal voices. After Foucault and Bakhtin the notion of the autonomous self free from the "contamination" of the social is dead; as language-utilizing organisms we cannot escape the effect of the influence of discursive practice and the power that accompanies it.

Armed with such an understanding, critical constructivist teachers direct student attention to the study of discursive formations in the class-room. They are empowered to point out specific examples of power shaping particular discursive formats and the ways that power subse-quently works to construct consciousness (McLaren 1991a, 236; Harned 1987, 11). For example, consider a critical constructivist history teacher who alerts students to the androcentric construction of American history textbooks and school district curriculum guides. The teacher uncovers an approach to teaching American history that revolves around the principles of expansionism, conquest, and progress. The westward movement of America is a central organizing theme that serves to focus the gaze of the student on the "impediments to civilization," for example, natives, "unus-able" land, other nations such as Mexico and England, and so on. In this context student consciousness is constructed to ignore the ethical and moral dimensions of empire building, to identify those different from us as the "other," as inferior enemies. A nationalistic consciousness is con-structed that not only exonerates the sins of the past but tends to ignore national transgressions of the present.

ESCAPING FROM THE TEXTUAL TYRANT: THE CURRICULUM OF DECONSTRUCTION

The notion of civilization embedded in our history textbooks becomes what Jacques Derrida calls a "transcendental signified"—a transhistorical fixed meaning impervious to alternate interpretations. All texts, all signi-fieds, are open to alternate interpretations. The construction of a text and the laws of its organization are not obvious to the prevailing wisdom, to common sense. As Derrida puts it in *Dissemination*: "A text is not a text unless it hides from the first comer, from the first glance, the law of its composition and the rules of its game" (Derrida 1981, 63). It is with the rejection of the transcendental signified that deconstruction meets the epistemology (or postepistemology—is there still truth?) of critical con-structivism. Placing the responsibility for meaning making squarely on human shoulders, both deconstruction and critical constructivism attempt to survive the walk through a minefield of fixed meaning.

As Derrida informs our attempt to prevent any dominant group from certifying its signified, we are better equipped to resist the unwitting construction of our consciousness. Thus, through the postmodern play of Derrida's deconstruction, we disrupt the tyranny of the official text, we break the power of the author or the supervisor or the curriculum developer to impose authoritarian meaning (Harvey 1989, 51). If we are unaware of

Derrida's play, we are vulnerable to the mainstream seduction of the view of language as a neutral message system. This Cartesian–Newtonian perspective regards language as a transparent medium through which students and teachers talk to one another from unproblematized selves (essences). We remain ignorant of the tacit social dimension of language and the power dimensions it reflects in ostensibly innocent conversations. "What did you learn today?," the teacher asks his or her students in an attempt to fill in dead time before the final bell rings. "To raise my hand before I speak," Mary answers. "To make the highest score on the science test," says Bob. This is not some *natural* conversational ebb and flow (Gilbert 1989, 259). Gender relations of power and classroom authority structures are hiding behind the shadows of the words.

The teaching of interpretation becomes a central focus of the critical constructivist curriculum. Idiosyncratic readings protect students from the "correct" interpretations, as they, in the process, gain practice in recognizing the ways their consciousness are shaped. Contrary to the pronouncements of some critics, all meaning is not lost by the rejection of "correct" readings. If anything is destroyed in such deconstructive analysis, it is not meaning but the stance of the unqualified superiority of one way of signifying over another (Zavarzadeh and Morton 1991, 177). Indeed, the interpretative classroom discussions in which we participate should never end "for good." This is why critical constructivist teachers will study the same texts in different ways in different classes or in different semesters. While we are interested in the various interpretations, like good detectives we are interested in their origins. The search for the forces that generated the interpretations of the moment move us into a great cultural conversation—the heart of the critical constructivist curriculum. In this context, our personal experience is illuminated by our engagement in the cultural conversation, and the cultural conversation is illuminated by our personal experience. We make knowledge through our actions and comments. The critical constructivist curriculum leaves us not with a sacred, never-changing set of truths, but a tentative encounter with the collective consciousness and a lingering uncertainty about the language used in the process.

THE ANTIDOTE TO REDUCTIONISM

Another term for the Cartesian mode of analytical reasoning is reductionism. This method has formed the basis for Piagetian formalism and the forms of analysis we strive to encourage in school. Cartesian reductionism asserts that all aspects of complex phenomena can best be appreciated by reducing them to their constituent parts and then piecing these elements together according to causal laws (Mahoney and Lyddon 1988, 192). This reductionism coincided with René Descartes's bifurcation of the mind and matter/body. Known as the Cartesian dualism, human experience was split into two different spheres: (1) the "in here"—an internal world of sensation—and (2) the "out there"—an objective world composed of natural phenomena. Drawing on this dualism, scientists asserted that the laws of physical and social systems could be uncovered objectively; the systems operated apart from the "in here" world of human perception, with no connection to the act of perceiving.

Forever separate, the internal world and the natural world could never be shown to be a form of one another. Critical constructivism rejects the modernist dualistic epistemology and posits an alternative to the Western traditions of realism and rationalism (Lavine 1984, 124; Lowe 1982, 163; Mahoney and Lyddon 1988, 192–93). Briefly, realism presumes a singular, stable, external reality that can be perceived by one's senses; rationalism argues that thought is superior to sense and is most important in shaping experience. Our notion of critical constructivism contends that reality, contrary to the arguments made by proponents of realism, is not external and unchanging. In contrast to rationalism, critical constructivism maintains that human thought cannot be meaningfully separated from human feeling and actions. Knowledge, critical constructivists assert, is constrained by the structure and function of the mind and can thus be known only indirectly. The objectivism, the separation of the knower and the known implicit in the Cartesian tradition denies the spatiotemporal location of the knower in the world and thus results in the estrangement of human beings from the natural world (Lowe 1982, 164; Mahoney and Lyddon 1988, 199–201; White 1978, 197).

Alvin Gouldner extends this anti-Cartesian critique, arguing that the social sciences promote a form of cognition suitable for an alienated age and an alienated people. The dominant expressions of the social sciences serve to adjust students to sociocultural alienation rather than helping them overcome it (Reinharz 1979, 240–41). Descartes argued that knowledge should be empirical, mathematical, and certain, and the orientation toward research that emerged worked to exploit the forces of nature in a way that destroyed the landscape of the Earth. As a result of this objectivist epistemology, we now inhabit a human-made, artificial environment. Emerging from this modernist tradition was a behavioral science untroubled by the manipulation of human beings and an educational system that utilized the behavioral sciences to mold students and their consciousness in a way that would foster efficiency and economic productivity, often at the expense of creativity, social justice, and democratic work.

Thinking and learning, from the perspective of the reductionists, are developed by following specific procedures, specific measurable psychological processes. The acts are operationally defined and then broken into discrete pieces; we first learn the symbols of chemistry, the place of the elements on the periodic chart, the process of balancing chemical equations, the procedure for conducting a chemical experiment. It would be disorderly and "scientifically inappropriate" to think in terms of where chemistry is used in our everyday lives before these basics were learned, the reductionists argue. Reductionists operating under the banner of the Cartesian scientific tradition utilize basals and worksheets and rigid, sequential methods. Such reductionistic methods facilitate the development of materials and the training of teachers—it is far easier to write a workbook based on a fragmented form of knowledge with a list here and an objective test there than it is to develop materials that help connect individual student experience with the concepts of a particular discipline. Indeed, it is far easier to *train* a teacher to follow specific, predefined, never-changing steps than it is to encourage a reflective stance concerning the points of interaction between student experience, emancipatory concerns, and disciplinary data.

Critical constructivists believe that in teaching and thinking the whole is greater than the sum of the individual parts. They reject reductionist task analysis procedures derived from scope and sequence charts. Rejecting definitions of intelligence grounded upon a quantitative measurement of how many facts and associations an individual has accumulated, critical constructivists maintain that there are as many paths to sophisticated thinking as there are sophisticated thinkers. The best way to teach one to think is to research particular students, observing the social context from which they emerge and the particular ways they undertake the search for meaning. In this process critical constructivist teachers set up conditions that encourage student self-awareness and reflection, hoping to facilitate further growth through an individual awareness of the nature of prior growth (Poplin 1988, 405–13; Fosnot 1988, 20).

Many reductionistic teaching strategies emerge from research studies conducted in strictly controlled laboratory settings that have little to do with everyday classrooms. Informed by their own practical knowledge and the practical knowledge of other teachers, critical constructivist teachers have questioned the generalizability of laboratory research findings to the natural setting of their own classrooms. These teachers may have suspected the inapplicability, but the modernist research establishment was not so insightful. The technicist mainstream assumed that laboratory research findings were the source of solutions that could be applied in every classroom setting (Doyle 1977, 175; Ponzio 1985, 40). Cartesian researchers failed to understand that every classroom possessed a culture of its own, a culture that defines the rules of discourse in classroom situations. Thus, all classrooms are different, critical constructivists contend, and as a result the use of standardized techniques and materials with their obsession with the parts instead of wholes is misguided. In these unique particularistic classrooms of critical constructivist teachers, form follows purpose as students are protected from premature instruction in precise forms; interest and passion are cardinal virtues, as student rational development is viewed as simply one aspect of thinking; and learning and thinking problems are not viewed simply as the products of aptitude but of complex interactions between personalities, interests, social and cultural contexts, and life experiences (Poplin 1988, 414). Thus, in its recognition of the complexity of learners and learning situations, critical constructivism serves as an antidote to the reductionism of Cartesian pedagogy.

BEYOND PIAGET: THE CRITICAL POSTMODERN RECONCEPTUALIZATION OF EQUILIBRATION

To Piaget, intellectual adaptation is an equilibration between assimilation and accommodation. Assimilation involves the shaping of an event to fit into one's cognitive structure. No event, even if a student has never encountered it before, constitutes a new beginning. In other words, as assimilation fits an experience to the demands of one's logical structures, it is grafted on to previously developed schemes. Accommodation, on the other hand, refers to the restructuring of one's cognitive maps to take care of an event. In order to accommodate, an individual must actively change his or her existing intellectual structure to understand the dissonance produced by the novel demand. Piaget described accommodation as a reflective, integrative behavior that forces the realization that our present cognitive structure is insufficient to deal with the changing pressures of the environment (Kaufman 1978, 30; Fosnot 1988, 17).

Piaget argues that at the beginning assimilation and accommodation tend to move in different directions: assimilation as the conservative protector of existing cognitive structure subordinating the environment to the existing organism; accommodation as the subversive agent of change leading the organism to adjust to the imperatives of the environment. In the long run, however, Piaget contends that the ostensibly divergent tasks are inseparable in the larger process of equilibration—the dynamic process of self-monitored behavior that balances assimilation and accommodation's polar behaviors (Kaufman 1978, 30–31; Fosnot 1988, 17–19). Over the last twenty years, however, critics have asserted that as Piaget described higher orders of thought, he privileged assimilation over accommodation. The effect of this assimilation-centeredness has been the progressive removal of the individual from her or his environment. The emphasis, thus, becomes not so much what an individual can do in the world of objects, what actions she or he can undertake, but how quickly the individual can learn to think outside of reality. The more an individual engages in disembedded thought, the higher level of cognition Piaget will ascribe to him or her. In a Cartesian–Newtonian framework, the higher order thinker is detached from personal experience. The Piagetian image of the active learner in charge of his or her own fate is subverted by the lack of exchange between the thinker and the world of objects. Because of this removal of women and men from experience, Piaget's theory abstracts individuals from the cosmos in the process reducing the possibility of emancipatory personal and social change (O'Loughlin forthcoming, 19, 22–23).

To Piaget, knowing involves the transformation of contradictory experience into stable structures. When subjected to postmodernism's challenge to the stability of meaning, Piaget's confidence in the viability of structures is undermined. Meaning is far too ephemeral for a postmodern student of cognition to claim the existence of a stable structure, a balance between assimilation and accommodation—in Piaget's words, equilibration. The concept of negation, central to critical theory *and* to accommodation, involves the continuous criticism and reconstruction of what one thinks they know. For example, critical theorist Max Horkheimer argued that through negation we develop a critical consciousness that allows us to transcend old codified world views and incorporate our new understandings into a new reflective attitude (Held 1980, 176). Let us delve deeper into these connections between critical theory and constructivism.

Critical equilibration denies the possibility of any stable balance between assimilation and accommodation. Aware of the tendency of Piagetian formalism to deemphasize accommodation, critical equilibration recognizes the radical potential of constructivist accommodation. As accommodation changes consciousness in order to understand new aspects of the environment, subjects gain awareness of their own limitations. Horkheimer maintained that through the awareness gained by way of critical negation—the philosophical analog to the cognitive act of accommodation—an individual develops and becomes open to radical change (Held 1980, 185). Thus, a key cognitive dimension of any critical postmodern curriculum will involve accommodation—indeed, a critical accommodation. Critical constructivist teachers understand the value of difference with its power to initiate the process of critical accommodation, a reshaping of consciousness consonant with the concerns of a critical system of meaning. Such teachers see the diversity of classroom experiences as an opportunity for cognitive growth.

A critical constructivist teacher, for example, exploring the meaning of intelligence and its relationship to his or her students would assimilate an understanding of the concept based on his or her own experience. The teacher would accommodate the concept as he or she began to examine students who were labeled unintelligent but upon a second look exhibited characteristics that in an unconventional way seemed sophisticated. The teacher would then integrate this recognition of exception (accommodation) into a broader definition of intelligence. The old definition of intelligence would have been negated; through exposure to diverse expressions of intelligence, new ways of seeing it would have been accommodated. They would be critically accommodated in the sense that the new ways of seeing would emancipate us from the privileged, racially and class-biased definitions of intelligence that were used to exclude cognitive styles that transcended the official codes. In this and many other cases accommodation becomes the emancipatory aspect of the thinking process in question. Critical constructivists recognize this and use it in the struggle for democratic social and educational change.

Critical accommodation in the classroom is the key to the creation of new student attitudes. Dialogical encounters between critical constructivist teachers and their students often involve the presentation of information that disrupts assimilated world views. It is at this point of disruption—a point at which cognitive dissonance reaches its zenith—that students realize that something in their consciousness is out of order and adjustment is required. This moment of accommodation is not to be subverted by the unethical teacher who takes advantage of it to indoctrinate, to provide a facile resolution to the dissonance. Such resolutions are ethically tantamount to behaviorist manipulation or the indoctrination of religious or political zealots. The critical constructivist teacher prolongs the accommodation moment for days or weeks at a time, using it to stimulate searching, research-based student activities (Hultgren 1987, 33).

Critical constructivist teaching proceeds in no prearranged, standardized manner, but it does seem to embody a few common characteristics. At some point teachers and students are encouraged to examine the cognitive structures that impede transformative action, whether on the self or the environment. For example, an individual may be stuck at a

Piagetian formalism that emphasizes a procedural form of abstract logical thought—a form of thinking that removes the relationship among thinking and consciousness construction and praxis (informed action) from consideration. Such forms of thinking tend to delegate teaching and learning to a cognitive realm separate from commitment, emotion, and ethical action.

At the same time transformative action may be impeded not only by cognitive structures but by sociopolitical structures as well. This sociopolitical impediment may be found in economic and linguistic structures, in geographic place, religious dimensions, and many other ideological public domains. Critical constructivist teachers strive to identify these impediments and their effects on how individuals come to see and act on the world (Codd 1984, 16). For example, no matter how "intelligent" a young women might be, her identification with a religious sect that viewed women as the metaphorical body and men as the head would impede transformative action on her part. Such obvious forms of sociopolitical oppression would be exposed by critical constructivism. In both the cognitive and the sociopolitical situations, impediments serve to impede the disruption of critical accommodation. Critical postmodern teacher education would prepare teachers with the skills to map the assimilation and accommodation experiences of their students in relation to the cognitive and sociopolitical interactions that affect these experiences. Learning action research techniques such as semiotics, ethnography, phenomenology, and historiography, prospective teachers would be empowered to uncover the evidence to construct their sociocognitive maps.

This sociocognitive mapping of critical constructivist teaching consistently involves the revelation of irony at one or more points in the accommodation process. Irony, Hayden White writes, alerts us to the inadequacy of the grand narrative in question to characterize, to account for the elements that don't fit into the order of the narrative. Often in the context of critical accommodation the grand narrative may be an individual's story about her or his self-production, the person's self-identity. Irony may be seen as a linguistic strategy that sanctions skepticism as an explanatory strategy, satire as a form of employment, and agnosticism as an ethical approach (White 1978, 6, 73–74). The postmodern critique, infatuated with irony, is hard to separate from critical accommodation. Nothing is as closed, self-sufficient, autonomous, or consistent as it seems. All entities are riddled with contradictions. What we think of as real, profound, or stable is merely a reflection of conventions—indeed, the world in general is an imagined series of places (Hutcheon 1988, 125; Shapiro 1992, 147). With this in mind, critical accommodation becomes a postmodern act as it draws upon such ironic recognitions to initiate the disruptive process. As Paulo Freire characterizes emancipation as risk, so too is critical accommodation. As teachers and students ironically interrogate past understandings, they embark on an agnostic venture into the unknown. Exploring and rereading sedimented meanings, these "geologists" critically accommodate ironic perception into new, albeit tentative, perceptions of reality and self (Greene 1988, 25; Grimmett, Erickson, MacKinnon, and Riecken 1990, 27).

An important aspect of this accommodation of ironic perception into new understandings of reality and self involves the disembedding of personal knowledge from the specific experience in which it developed. Only after this disembedding takes place can accommodations be transferred into new contexts. This critical transference involves a form of anticipatory accommodation that moves beyond a traditional Piagetian notion of formal generalization. The formal thinker, according to Piaget, possesses the ability to construct pristine generalizations from systematic observations. Such a cognitive process accepts a one-dimensional, Cartesian–Newtonian, cause–effect universe. In the formalistic empirical context, for example, all that is needed to ensure transferability is to understand with a high level of internal validity (the extent to which observations of a particular reality are true) something about a particular classroom and to know that the makeup of this classroom is representative of another classroom to which the generalization is being applied. Individuals operating in this tradition argue that the generalization derived from the first classroom is valid in all classrooms with the same population.

When we apply our understanding of critical constructivism and disembedding, we begin to see that in everyday situations people don't make generalizations in this formalistic, empirical manner. Our notion of critical accommodation tells us that we reshape cognitive structures to account for unique aspects of what is being perceived in new contexts. Through our knowledge of a variety of comparable contexts we begin to understand similarities and differences—we learn from our comparisons of different contexts. The Cartesian–Newtonian concern with generalization and prediction is not the goal of our disembedding and critical transference, our critical accommodation. Instead, we begin to think in terms of anticipatory accommodation, that is we anticipate what we *might* encounter in similar situations, what strategies *might* work in our attempt to bring about emancipatory outcomes (Barrett 1985, 2–3; Benson 1989, 330).

CRITICAL POSTMODERN TEACHERS:
CATALYSTS FOR CRITICAL ACCOMMODATION

Often, discussions of psychological and social theories possess relevance only for the theorists, not for practitioners. Let us briefly consider the classroom implications of the sociocognitive theory of critical constructivism. At the most fundamental level of instruction, critical constructivism implies that more attention should be granted to assimilation and accommodation by students than to the coverage of content. Indeed, the information created in the classroom by way of the process of critical accommodation is of far greater worth to students and critical postmodern teachers than the secondhand content of standardized curricular data. This simple idea subverts the technicist tradition of instruction and the instructional strategies demanded by the right-wing reforms of recent years. Instead of clarifying content, making "the facts" palatable, explaining solutions to problems, and testing for memorization of the facts and the ability to apply learned material to prearranged problems, instruction works to construct situations that produce cognitive dissonance, to develop Socratic adversarial roles to students' conceptions (not to them as people), to formulate qualitative strategies for mapping cognitive development, to cultivate student ability to expand and monitor their own cognitive development, and to devise creative questioning which fosters student ability to accommodate (Posner 1987, 187–88; Leshan and Margenau 1982, 22).

George Posner has theorized a form of instruction very similar to our concept of critical constructivism based on a careful monitoring of student epistemological dispositions and the conditions surrounding their move to accommodate new information. Posner contends that whether or not learners decide to accommodate depends on at least three factors: (1) the intensity of their metaphysical world view; (2) the nature and potency of their epistemological commitments, for example the role of science in the determination of truth; and (3) the presence of anomalies in relation to a presently held perspective. The degree to which a learner is aware of an anomaly and an alternative interpretation that addresses the anomaly is a measure of whether she or he will accommodate or assimilate (Posner 1987, 185). Drawing upon Posner's analysis of the tendency to accommodate, critical postmodern teachers can sophisticate their research on their students. In a manner similar to the Piagetian clinical interview, they can develop ethnographic and semiotic methods to uncover student location in the critical accommodation process. Such methods can help teachers pinpoint the types of factors that impede the accommodation process—factors which in postmodern hyperreality are not hard to find.

It is hardly a revelation to point out that the mind tends to hang on to what is familiar. The tacit ideological infrastructure is subtly woven into the social and educational fabric. Scientists and educators hold tightly to these threads, for their professional security clings to them. Thus, the teacher or scientist who rocks the boat may evoke strong resistance from her or his peers. Guarding its comfortable equilibration, the mind is adept at creating the illusion that no fundamental change is required, when such change may be necessary to survival. When this tendency for cognitive inertia is coupled with hyperreality's climate of deceit, we find ourselves beset by a postmodern complacency—a retreat from the terrain of paradigmatic change (Reynolds 1987, 171; Bohm and Peat 1987, 21–22).

Cartesian–Newtonian cognition possesses its own special ways to impede accommodation. By fragmenting the world into discrete pieces, such thinking overemphasizes the separation between a specific problem and its context. The problem is thus conceived in isolation, removed from related concepts. Counterfeit boundaries are drawn between problems; their connections to wider fields of study are ignored. Such compartmentalization of knowledge thwarts accommodation as new information is prevented from confronting existing beliefs. In addition, the Cartesian–Newtonian commitment to absolute frames of reference is so pervasive, so much a part of our culture and our language that an accommodation that leads to a critical constructivist understanding of socially formulated frames of reference becomes quite difficult. Teachers who are interested in curing the cognitive illness and taking part in the cognitive revolution need to understand these impediments to critical accommodation; they need to be able to diagnose the forces that interrupt their students in their movement toward accommodation (Posner 1987, 178; Bohm and Peat 1987, 23; Luke 1991, 19).

CONSCIOUSNESS AND HISTORY

A key theme of critical constructivism and of this book in general involves the concept that consciousness and cognition cannot be separated from sociohistorical context. All cognition and action take place in continuity with the forces of history. Contextualization is inseparable from cognition and action; the role of critical constructivism is to bring this recognition to the front burner of consciousness. With such awareness we begin to realize that consciousness is constructed both by individual agency, individual volition, and by the ideological influences of social forces—it is both structured and structuring. Thus, consciousness is not deterministically constructed by sociohistorical formations that comprehensively shape our ways of seeing;

nor is consciousness autonomously constructed by free and independent individuals unencumbered by the burden of history.

Our attempts at accommodation are hegemonized by an ideological domination that thwarts our pursuit of individual goals. At the same time, particular forms of thinking and action mirror a volition or a genuine motivation that transcends the confines of extant social forces. Radical theorists have traditionally been guilty of not recognizing this ambiguity of consciousness construction and social action. Not until the 1980s with the influx of poststructural and postmodern theories of language analysis and deconstruction did radical theorists understand the way power was reflected in language and knowledge and the implications for such reflection in consciousness construction. Individuals are initiated into language communities where women and men share bodies of knowledge, epistemologies, and the cognitive styles that accompany them. Thus, the manner in which our critical accommodations are made or not made is inseparable from these language communities. The sociohistorical dimension of consciousness construction often is manifested on the terrain of language (Codd 1984, 14–17; Giddens 1986, 69–70).

Because of these linguistic and other factors hidden from our conscious understanding, individuals are often unaware of just how their consciousness is constructed. The schemas that guide a culture are rarely part of an individual's conscious mind. Usually, they are comprehended as a portion of a person's world view that is taken for granted. It was these ideas that Antonio Gramsci had in mind when he argued that philosophy should be viewed as a form of self-criticism. Gramsci asserted that the starting point for any higher understanding of self involves the consciousness of oneself as a product of sociohistorical forces. A critical philosophy, he wrote, involves the ability of its adherents to criticize the ideological frames that they use to make sense of the world. I watch my colleagues and myself struggle as critical postmodern teachers as we attempt to engage our students in Gramsci's critical philosophical task of understanding themselves in sociohistorical context. The work is never easy as we complain and moan about our students' lack of preparation for engagement in such theoretical and introspective analysis. No matter how frustrating the job may be, we have to realize how few experiences these students possess that would equip them for such a task (Reynolds 1987, 169; Mardle 1984, 53–54, 62).

RECONSTRUCTING THE SELF

I don't think that it is an overstatement to argue that a critical constructivist epistemology is very important in the effort to engage in an ideological critique of self-production in the postmodern era. Such a critique interrogates the deep structures that help shape our consciousness as well as the historical context that gave birth to the deep structures. It explores the sociohistorical and political dimensions of schooling, the kind of meanings that are constructed in classrooms, and how these meanings are translated into student consciousness. Students of cognition, especially those that foster the concept of uncritical critical thinking we discussed earlier, often speak of student and teacher empowerment as if it were a simple process that could be accomplished by a couple of creative learning activities. One thing our ideological critique of self-production tells us is that the self is a complex, ambiguous, and contradictory entity pushed and pulled by a potpourri of forces. The idea that the self can be reconstructed and empowered without historical study, linguistic analysis, and deconstruction of place is to trivialize the goals of critical postmodern pedagogy, it is to minimize the power of the cognitive illness (Codd 1984, 17; Gilbert 1989, 263; O'Loughlin forthcoming, 4).

How do we move beyond simply uncovering the sources of consciousness construction in our larger attempt to reconstruct the self in a critical manner? Critical postmodern teachers must search in as many locations as possible for alternate discourses, ways of thinking and being that expand the envelopes of possibility. In order to engage in this aspect of the reconstruction of self, students and teachers must transcend the modernist conception of the static and unified self that goes through life with the 106 IQ—it is 106 today, it was yesterday, and will be tomorrow. While the process of disidentification is urgent, we cannot neglect the search for alternate discourses in literature, history, popular culture, the community, and in our imaginations. Peter McLaren maintains that we need to find a diversity of possibilities of what we might become by recovering and reinterpreting what we once were. While we might use this to change our conception of reality, we must see this change of conception (this change of *mind*) as only the first step in a set of *actions* designed to change reality (Gilbert 1989, 263; McLaren 1991a, 247–51).

Chapter 7

Contextualizing Cognitive Development

Drawing upon our critical system of meaning, our understanding of the political nature of cognition, our familiarity with the postmodern critique, and our conception of critical constructivism, let us address the question: What does it mean to think at a higher level? Grounded in student experience, aware of the demands of democratic citizenship with its civic courage, cognizant of the ways power shapes consciousness, dedicated to the creation of loving, nurturing, and safe classrooms, the critical postmodern vision of school purpose revolves around the cultivation of student thinking that is cognitively sophisticated and morally responsible. Throughout this book we have alluded to post-formal thinking. This chapter will expand those references, laying a foundation for a post-Piagetian, critically grounded sociocognitive theory for a postmodern cosmos. In no way does this delineation of post-formal thinking propose to be a definitive expression of higher order thinking—it is simply a beginning, a hesitant first step in thinking about thinking, which transcends Piagetian formalism. As we begin to think about higher forms of cognition, we begin to expand our conceptions of teacher thinking and, in turn, the role of the teacher itself. In this discussion of post-formal thinking we begin to open our imagination to a creative socioeducational vision of what teaching can become in the twenty-first century.

TRANSCENDING COGNITIVE ESSENTIALISM

One of the main features of post-formal thinking is that it expands the boundaries of what can be labeled sophisticated thinking. One of the amazing things that happens when we begin to expand these boundaries is that men and women who were excluded from the community of the intelligent seem to cluster around exclusions based on race (the nonwhite), class (the poor), and gender (the feminine). The modernist conception of intelligence is an exclusionary system based on the premise that some people are intelligent and others aren't. Intelligence and creativity are thought of fixed and innate, while at the same time mysterious qualities found only in the privileged few. The modernist grand narrative of intelligence has stressed biological fixities that can be altered only by surgical means. Such an essentialism is a psychology of nihilism that locks people into rigid categories that follow them throughout life. Again the 1950s science fiction movie image of the mad scientist reappears, as cognitive essentialism abstracts "mind" from the historical development of knowledge and its social formulation. Indeed, the mind still can be transferred as a discrete, self-contained biological entity from a human to, say, a fly (Maher and Rathbone 1986, 224; Bozik 1987, 2; Lawler 1975, 2–3).

The developmentalism of Piaget while claiming a dialectical interaction between mind and environment still falls captive to the grand narrative of intelligence. The theory walks into its own captivity as it views intelligence as a process that culminates in an individual's mastery of formal *logical* categories. The development of thinking seems to come from thinking itself, separate from the external environment. This reflects the innate fixity of earlier Cartesian–Newtonian views of intelligence as a spectre emerging from innate inner structures. The early Piaget, in particular, maintained that the desired pedagogical course was to move students' development away from the emotions so that rationality could dominate the progress of the mind. Stages were thus constructed around this logocentrism—stages that would become key supports in the common-sense, unquestioned knowledge about intelligence. Feminist theory would challenge this metanarrative, arguing that cognizance of social construction of individuals and the inseparability of rationality and emotion cause us to question essential categories of human development. The feminists asked us to examine the difference between masculine and feminine ways of knowing. The masculine, of course, represents the "proper" path for human cognitive development. Proposing that intelligence be reconceptualized in a manner that makes use of various ways of thinking, feminist theorists taught us that intelligence is not an innate quality of a particular individual but something related to the interrelationship among ideas, behaviors, contexts, and outcomes (Walkerdine 1984, 176; Lawler 1975, 3; Bozik 1987, 2–3).

Developmental psychological principles have become so much a part of teacher education programs, so taken for granted that it is hard to see where questions about them might arise. Not understanding the etymology of cognitive developmentalism, we are unable to see it as a system of scientific classification. Developmentalism hides behind its claim of "freeing the child" from traditional methods of instruction, protecting its identity as an order of regulation on which child-centered pedagogy has been established. Critical constructivism and post-formal thinking want to expose developmentalism as a specific sociohistorical construction grounded on a specific set of assumptions about the mind—indeed, developmentalism is not the only way to view intelligence. As we have come to see individualized instruction and child-centered pedagogy as a set of regulated and normalized progressive stages, we miss the rather obvious point that individuals operate at divergent cognitive stages simultaneously. For example, an eight-year-old may employ particular skills with a computer that certainly reflect a formallike thinking while his or her understanding of American politics reflects a more concretelike cognitive stage. Indeed, is what Piaget described as formal thinking a "universal" stage in cognitive development? When we examine the percentage of adults who "fail" when assessed by this formal standard, its universality is brought in to question. The irony in the twentieth-century's history of developmental psychology is that in its concern with individual freedom and the production of a rationality that could save human beings in their struggle for survival, it produced a system of cognitive and pedagogical apparatuses that delimited and rigidly defined the normalized individual. The biological capacities developmentalism has designated have ensured that *progressive* teachers view the child as an object of scientific pronouncement, in the process undermining the liberation promised (Riegal 1973, 363; Maher and Rathbone 1986, 224; Walkerdine 1984, 154–55, 190, 199).

This betrayal of liberatory intent is what happens when we fail to address the critical constructivist concern with the social construction of mind. As Cartesian–Newtonian science strips away the layers of the social from our analysis, cognitive development is essentialized. The social features (race, class, gender, place) that influence patterns of development and definitions of development are ignored, allowing what are actually social constructions to be seen as natural processes. Here rests the practical value of the postmodern critique with its decentering of the subject. Not allowing for a preexistent essence of self, postmodernism denies the existence of men and women outside of the sociohistorical process. The grand narrative of liberal individualism is thus subverted, for objects of any type (especially knower and known, self and world) that cannot be defined in isolation to one another. Cognitive development, then, is not a static, innate dimension of human beings; it is always interactive with the environment, always in the process of being reshaped and reformed. We are not simply victims of genetically determined, cognitive predispositions (Lawler 1975, 3; Walkerdine 1984, 154, 195).

Not only does the postmodern critique undermine cognitive essentialism, but it also subverts sociocognitive reductionism. The normalization of social control along the lines of scientifically validated norms of development and conduct implicit within developmentalism is not the outcome of some repressive power broker determined to keep individuals in their place. Thus, power manifests itself not through some explicit form of oppression but via the implicit reproduction of the self. Thus, advocates of critical thinking will operate within the boundaries of developmentalism with its predetermined definitions of normality, they will teach and learn within its gravitational field. The task of the advocates of critical thinking—those who understand both the social contextualization of thinking and the postmodern critique of its discursive practices—is to overthrow these reductionistic views of the way power works. When we view the effect of power on the way we define intelligence or the way consciousness is constructed as some simple cause–effect process, we forfeit our grasp on reality, we lose our connection to the rhythms of social life (de Lauretis 1986, 8; Walkerdine 1984, 196). Post-formal thinking attempts to conceive cognition in a manner that transcends the essentialist and reductionist tendencies within developmentalism that couples an appreciation of the complexity of self-production and the role of power with some ideas about what it means to cross the borders of modernist thinking.

FROM ESSENTIALISM AND REDUCTIONISM TO AMBIGUITY AND COMPLEXITY

Michael Apple argues that one of the major problems in educational history has involved the inability of those concerned with schooling to deal with ambiguity, to perceive it as a valuable characteristic. Without such an understanding educational leaders have continually sought naive and simplistic answers to the complex social and cognitive questions that confront education. Indeed, such a situation is grounded on the epistemological predisposition of modernism to seek certainty in its inquiries about human and educational affairs. Critical postmodern education attempts to overcome our socially engrained discomfort with the enigmatic, our desire to have something we can all subscribe to together, our need for a shared certainty. This cult of certainty informs the way we approach all educational problems, forcing us to focus our attention on the trivial—on that which can be easily measured by empirical instruments. Rarely do the most significant questions of human affairs lend themselves to empirical quantification and the pseudocertainty that often accompanies numbers (Koetting 1988, 6; Greene 1988, 14).

Certainty cannot withstand the pressure of poststructural analysis. Jacques Derrida ridicules the certainty with which modernist science constructs valid arguments. Such arguments begin with primitive and undefined terms and premises, he maintains, and to ignore this situation is to seek a fictional security. Meaning, like an eroding hillside, slowly dissolves until language and texts take on a configuration quite different from the original state. A reader in 2008 may derive a very different meaning of this paragraph from what I intend. Different social experiences, different circumstances may alter the codes that give this paragraph meaning in the 1990s. Meaning derived from research data or frames of reference that serve as the starting place for educational inquiry cannot help but reflect the ideology and social norms that surround them. Unexamined frames of reference lead to claims of scientific certainty that perpetuate privilege for the privileged and oppression for the oppressed (Cherryholmes 1988, 121).

These ideas have important implications for teaching when they are used to analyze contemporary teacher education and to help teachers formulate questions about their own thinking and the thinking of their students. Unlike the tendency of formality, thinking cannot be conceived as mere problem solving—problems, as the poststructuralists would tell us, do not unambiguously present themselves. If a problem is identified as a result of particular ideologies and social frames, then the Piagetian formalist predisposition to look at it as a puzzle to be solved misses some cardinal aspects of the process of thinking about a problem (Altrichter and Posch 1989, 25–26). Formal thinking does not allow teachers and students to explore the origins of the problems, the assumptions that move us to define some situations as problems and others as not problems, or the source of authority that guides us in our formulation of criteria for judging which problems merit our thinking and teaching time. This is where our critical constructivist notion of post-formal thinking helps us understand the complexity of our role as teachers. Employing such a thinking style we begin to uncover the hidden ways ideology shapes the questions that underlie our classrooms. Thus, we see far more clearly the shaky foundation on which the quest for certainty rests.

Our modernist faith in the constancy of meaning shapes our lives as teachers. The meanings that students and teachers attribute to terms such as reading, teaching, or learning influence the forms our evaluations of teachers, students, and schools take. For example, think about a teacher as researcher seeking to determine whether a critical constructivist method of teaching geography produces more learning than an inquiry method. The researcher begins the inquiry by identifying what learning is and what behaviors should be examined to determine whether it has or has not taken place. There is nothing objective about such a process; absolute, certain knowledge does not emerge from such a study. The knowledge that does emerge is inherently conditional—dependent on an acceptance of a variety of assumptions about the goals of geography education, the definition of a good student, the nature of learning, and so on. From a post-formal perspective, these teaching issues are not technical questions, they are questions of meaning. As our perspective on thinking fashions our evaluation strategies, the designations of who is a competent or incompetent teacher or student is contingent on the system of meaning we employ. Without this notion of epistemological conditionality, of context, we find that teachers and students are easily hegemonized, co-opted into covert systems of meaning that undermine their emancipatory trek, their efforts to come to terms with ambiguity.

When teachers possess a cognitive style that has accepted ambiguity and prefers complexity, they seem better suited to encourage such higher order forms of thinking on the part of their students. This high-complexity teacher tends to challenge student thinking, as he or she expects more factual and conceptual support for student argumentation, greater analytical divergence, and more self-analysis in light of the concepts under study. The high-complexity teacher is better able to establish more pervasive and authentic interaction between students and students, and students and teachers. Such interaction heightens self-awareness, as students (and the teacher) are attuned to the power of their own words and those of others, and the nature of the contexts and codes and the way they construct the meaning of communication (Peters and Amburgey 1982, 98).

These higher-complexity teachers tend to operate on a post-formal level, as they encourage the active interpretation and negotiation necessary to the critical process of cultural reconstruction. As they gain the power to reconstruct their own consciousness, they are able to help their students reinterpret their traditions and reinvent their futures together in solidarity with other self-directed human agents. Teachers who are comfortable with ambiguity and prefer complexity operate at a post-formal level that seems to be more tolerant, flexible, and adaptive and employ a wider repertoire of teaching models. They are better equipped to enter a postconventional world where certainty is sacrificed in order to overcome bureaucratic definitions of the deskilled role teachers often play in school. This post-formal view of teacher cognition helps us move beyond the negative consequences of the quest for certainty, as teacher educators and teachers themselves begin to imagine emancipatory educational futures. If the act of teaching followed the modernist pattern and was constant and predictable, teachers could act on empirical generalizations and teacher educators would know exactly what teachers needed to know to perform successfully. But teaching is not constant and predictable—it always takes place in the microcosm of uncertainty (Schon 1987, 6, 11–13, 171).

CONNECTED CONSCIOUSNESS: POST-FORMALITY AND THE TRANSCENDENCE OF EGOCENTRISM

The social climate created by hyperreality with its constant commercial inducements to consume, to gratify the self contributes to an egocentric culture. As we contemplate a post-Piagetian theory of a higher cognition, post-formality, we maintain that this postmodern egocentrism holds serious cognitive consequences. Egocentrism (as opposed to connectedness) reduces our awareness of anything outside our own immediate experience. In our self-centeredness we tend to reduce everything to an individual perspective which ultimately causes us to miss meanings of significance. Many would argue that this self-absorption leads the way to an introspective self-knowledge that will move us to higher levels of experience, new dimensions of cognition. While self-knowledge is extremely important, egocentrism tends to reduce our ability to critique the construction of our own consciousness—we cannot get outside ourselves to recognize the social forces that have shaped us. Unless we learn to confront our egocentrism, the possibility of formulating critical perspectives in regard to ourselves and the world around us is limited. While we must make sure that students have confidence in their own perceptions and interpretations, we must concurrently work to help them overcome the tendency to see the world only in terms of self. In a way we must help them cope with a lifetime struggle between the tendency for self-confidence and the tendency for humility. We do not seek resolution, just a healthy interaction between the impulses (Greene 1988, 7).

Overcoming egocentrism is an important first step in our post-formal quest for a connected consciousness. Feminist theory has emphasized the value of such a consciousness, as it has argued the importance of the feminine tendency for connectedness—that is, to experience the self as essentially in relationship with others (Belenky, Clinchy, Goldberger, and Tarule 1986, 102). Feminist theory distinguishes connectedness from separateness, which often eventuates in a moral stance grounded on impersonal methods for establishing justice. Separateness is often associated with an epistemology that is based on impersonal methods for establishing truth. Separateness has granted meaning to many of Western society's sacred political beliefs such as freedom from interference or deregulation, self-dependence rather than an interrelationship with the community, and freedom as the right to do as we please (Greene 1988, 7, 43; Belenky, Clinchy, Goldberger, and Tarule 1986, 102).

Julian Jaynes is helpful in framing our attempt to formulate what a post-formal connected consciousness might entail. In *The Origin of Consciousness in the Breakdown of the Bicameral Mind* (1976), Jaynes discusses the elusive nature of consciousness. Using Jaynes's description of consciousness, we will formulate the nature of a post-formal shift to a connected consciousness. Jaynes maintains that human beings will always encounter great difficulty understanding the nature of their consciousness. Understanding, he argues, involves the formulation of a familiarizing metaphor for that which is to be understood. There is nothing in human experience that resembles consciousness; there is nothing to which it can be compared. Thus, it cannot be described by metaphorical means. This makes the task of describing consciousness very difficult. Aware of the perils of the attempt, Jaynes posits that consciousness is not a thing, it is an operation. It operates by analogy. The conscious mind uses bodily acts as analogues for mental acts. We "see" solutions to problems; we "grasp" the point; we make mental "leaps"; we "digest" the meaning of a book; and we "kick" ideas around. Human beings, Jaynes continues, create a mind space that allows us to picture our world and our role in it. In other words our conscious mind allows us to imagine ourselves, for example, climbing a mountain so that we can decide if we really want to undertake such an action.

In this context, Jaynes contends that consciousness has six main features:

1. *spatialization*—granting spatial qualities to things like time that do not actually have such qualities

2. *excerption*—since we cannot "see" anything in its entirety we think of a part of it as representative of the whole

3. *the analogue "I"*—our imagined self in our imagined world that helps us make decisions

4. *the metaphor "me"*—here we actually see ourselves as a character in our imaginings, in the third person
5. *narratization*—the assigning of causes to our behavior and the granting of logical sequence to the situations we encounter, or storytelling
6. *conciliation*—the assimilation of dissimilar entities in a spatial context.

Jaynes's categories provide a provocative context in which we may consider the meaning of connected consciousness. When we juxtapose Jaynes's categories of consciousness with critical postmodernism some interesting things happen: Previously unconsidered relationships begin to emerge and we find ourselves confronted with new categories for study. A new pathway emerges for exploring what the post-formal concept of connected consciousness entails. The following characteristics of connected consciousness represent a critical postmodern reconceptualization of Jaynesian consciousness.

Critical Spatialization

Jaynes describes spatialization as the first and most primitive aspect of consciousness. When we think of different entities such as the White House, the National Archives, the Capitol, and the Washington Monument, we by nature spatially separate them. This spatial separation takes up a mental space. This often is referred to as mind space. It is this metaphorical mind space that humans are always adding to or enlarging when we become conscious of new relationships—when we grasp new concepts. We must bestow things in the physical world that do not possess spatial qualities with such qualities in order to become conscious of them. Time is a good example of this process. Jaynes maintains that if asked to think of the last 100 years, an individual may view the succession of years in a left to right sequence. Obviously, there is no spatial quality at all except through metaphor. Thus, the subjective conscious mind is an analogue of the physical world. In academia we spatialize when we listen to a new argument presented by a colleague at a scholarly conference. The process involves these steps; we listen to the argument; we consider it by placing it "beside" the various theories on the subject to which we decide the argument relates; we then try to determine how the argument "fits" into the various theories; we decide the best fit, if any, by constructing a metaphorical view of the nature of the fitting.

In critical spatialization we interrogate the spatialization metaphors of others and ourselves. Keeping in mind the social construction of consciousness, we realize that we are mentally separated from others—especially those who are culturally different—by an unfamiliarity with their spatialization metaphors. Once aware of some of these metaphors we gain unparalleled insight into the way the consciousness of our students is constructed—indeed, we gain a far more connected insight into the way they see the world. When we bring our own spatialization metaphors into the "front of our minds," we gain insight into the construction of our own consciousness. We are engaging in a form of critical disembedding, for as we uncover obscured spatialization metaphors the very structure of our thoughts is unveiled. Such structures provide a rare perspective on the genesis of our values and world views, a new way of thinking about the connection between the knower and the known.

Critical Excerption

Excerption is a process which enables us to handle the vast storehouse of reminiscence derived from our past knowledge of a particular thing or a particular event in our life. Excerpts are selected by our consciousness in order that we may make meaning of our life and times. We call upon our inventory of excerpts in order for us to comprehend changes, make decisions, and create narratizations that enable us to understand the world. Julian Jaynes is careful to point out that excerption is not the same as memory. Whereas our memories represent the individual items within our storehouse, excerption is the method by which these items are separated and categorized. Excerption represents within each of us our own method of inventory control which enables us to reminisce about or have knowledge of a particular person, place, or thing.

When adults are asked to think of the experience of school, for example, they do not think of the concept in its entirety—that would be impossible. They think of a portion of it, a scene here or there. They may visualize their elementary school building or their first-grade teacher sitting behind her desk; they may smell the oiled wood floors; or they may hear the sound of their third-grade class singing folk songs during music class. Jaynes tells us that we never conceive things in their true form—we are conscious of them only in terms of the excerpts we make of them.

Since each person must create his or her own method of inventory control, the process of excerption is influenced by a number of factors. For example, an individual's social context directly influences the level within the storehouse where a particular memory will be placed. Filters formed by the social context separate the incoming information or inventory into sections having labels: "significant" or "insignificant," "appealing" or "unappealing," "exciting" or "frightening," "liberating" or "threatening," and so on. Other factors that lead to the creation of sections within a person's storehouse include an individual's cognitive orientation, educational level, emotional state, and such. One moves to a level of critical excerption when he or she gains the ability to recognize the nature of, and reasons for the section selected for the storage of a particular piece of information. When the individual comes to this meta-analytical conception of excerpts, critical analysis of the excerpts of other people and the society is possible. Again recognizing the connection between knower and known, critical excerption frees the individual from bondage to past experience by allowing him or her to view personal knowledge of a person, place, or thing separately from the biases that construct the sections in the storehouse of reminiscence. By understanding such personal biases, the individual is better able to understand such biases in others. Critical excerption provides another way for us to gain connection to the consciousness construction of others. In addition, we better understand how power operates, as it shapes the process of inventory control in individuals unaware of their own consciousness.

The Analogue "I," Metaphor "Me" and the Analogue "You," Metaphor "Us"

Included in Jaynes's list of features of the conscious mind is the analogue "I" and the metaphor "me." In the analogue "I," we imagine ourselves in various situations, engaging in various activities resulting in different outcomes. This is the way people learn to make decisions. The metaphor "me" is a part of the analogue "I." When conscious individuals imagine themselves in the imagined world of the mind, they see not only from the "eyes" of the imagined self; they can also "step back" and see themselves, much like a third person. The ability to see oneself in the imagination is the function of the metaphor "me."

As we critically reconceptualize Jaynesian consciousness in our move to post-formal connected consciousness, we uncover the analogue "you" and the metaphor "us." In this connected consciousness we not only "see" ourselves in the imagined situations and outcomes of the analogue "I," we can also "see" others—we "see" what they "see." This is the analogue "you." When we see others in our "mind's eye" and imagine their actions based on a contextualized appreciation of their personal histories, we have discovered the metaphor "us." Not only can individuals with connected consciousness derive meanings from their mental projections for themselves, but they develop empathy for others as they come to understand the derived meanings of individuals other than themselves. This critical empathy transcends merely "seeing" another's point of view; it also involves an understanding of why they hold that point of view.

Critical Narratization

Jaynesian consciousness assumes the existence of an experiencing self, a self that can reflect on memories. According to Jaynes, the ability to integrate one's self (analogue "I") with the external environment is the nature of narratization. We see our "selves" as the central actors in the stories of our lives. When a teacher is asked to take a job in a particular school, the mental process that helps formulate his or her answer is a form of narratization. The teacher imagines working in the school, imagines interactions with the principal and the other teachers. The teacher thinks about teaching particular lessons and the types of reactions they may invoke from this principal. The prospect of being subjected to the forms of criticism that the teacher anticipates from the principal presents a gloomy prospect. Based on such narratizations, she or he turns down the job.

It is easy to understand and "see" this narratization in our consciousness. However, as one begins to synthesize a conceptual perception dissimilar to one's own viewpoint, a new form of narratization evolves. Individuals with a connected consciousness narratize in a way which helps us connect with individuals with backgrounds different from our own. Such a narratizing ability is based on an appreciation of the personal histories and dissimilar individual contexts of peoples from various social and cultural groups. We gain the ability to narratize their particular way of seeing themselves and the world given their own life histories and personal contexts. Such critical narratizations require dedicated listening and attending to the circumstances of others. Critical postmodern teachers can utilize such a process, as they gain knowledge of their students and attempt to formulate teaching strategies based on this knowledge.

Critical Conciliation

Jaynes argues that in conciliation we are making excerpts or narratizations compatible with one another (we are reconciling them). Conciliation brings dissimilar entities together into a cohesive spatial combination just as narratization brings experiences together as a story. Jaynes writes that if you think of a mountain meadow and a tower at the same time, you naturally conciliate them by having the tower rising from the meadow. We use this process to put things together into patterns that make the world recognizable. In this manner we can make our way despite the confusion of sense perception. Conciliation in Jaynesian consciousness allows individuals to reconcile the ambiguities and perceived ambiguities of the world. Jaynes's discussion of conciliation emphasizes concrete properties.

Critical conciliation aids the individual in the search for connection in lived experiences. As the critical conciliator searches for the context in which concepts emerge, he or she is better able to understand the thematic connections between different phases of one's life. Because of his or her recognition of social context and the nature of power, the critical conciliator may see through manufactured connections supplied by power interests. By way of their contextual understandings, critical conciliators may discover more humane, socially beneficient, and individually emancipatory conciliations. At the same time, critical conciliation also involves the recognition of the absence of connections when they don't exist. With this understanding the critical conciliator abandons the need for certainty and external authorization. Paradox is viewed as one characteristic of the lived world. The critical conciliator no longer senses the need to resort to outside authority for reconciliation of contradiction.

Critical Volition

We are well acquainted with the concept of volition (or will) and how it affects our daily lives. For centuries we have debated whether or not we have free will. We speak of willpower in overcoming bad habits and even the term for the last wishes of someone who has died is called their "will." Critical volition cultivates an awareness of the limitations on human self-direction. In a society beset by discourses of manipulation individuals who possess connected consciousness recognize the vulnerability of human will. Based on their understanding of the limitations of the human will and the ways it often is shaped to serve the interests of power, those who achieve critical volition possess the will to act (Jaynes 1976, 59–66; Kincheloe, et al. 1987).

Our critical constructivist epistemology when combined with this post-formal notion of connected consciousness holds significant political implications. Critical constructivism overthrows the constraints of modernist one-truth epistemology, in the process opening the mind to multiple ways of seeing. Such multiple perspectives benefit those traditionally excluded from power. Connected consciousness serves as critical constructivism's vehicle for uncovering these other ways of seeing. Guided by their familiarity with the categories of connected consciousness, post-formal thinkers explore the spatializations, excerptions, analogue "I's" and met-aphor "me's," narratizations, conciliations, and volition processes of them-selves and others, focusing on the social and psychological factors that have shaped them. Teachers can revolutionize their classrooms by way of the knowledge gained through an understanding of connected conscious-ness as they plug learning into the images running through children's heads.

META-AWARENESS AND POST-FORMAL INSTRUCTION

Contrary to what modernist education has ultimately become, the idea behind it involved the human attempt to move beyond the randomness of natural selection. As they developed the ability to think and choose, men and women came to believe that through education they could shape the nature of future evolution. No longer bound by instinct, humans use education to pose questions about the way things were, to discern mean-ings of that which confused them, and to change that which impeded them. In this process, they would pay attention to the consequences of their actions, generate alternatives, and become increasingly aware of possibil-ities in their lives. This simply is the educational vision of post-formal teachers familiar with the goals of critical postmodern pedagogy.

Post-formal thinkers push away the modernist blinders that separate us from these "primitive" goals of education. Keeping in mind the goal of shaping the evolution of the species, post-formal thinkers value the notion of moving to a higher order of thinking. Post-formal teachers attempt to convince their students of the need for a leap to a higher sociocognitive level. Such teachers refuse to naively accept or reject validity claims of any body of knowledge without considering its discursive nature, that is, where information came from, what can be officially transmitted and what can not, and who transmits it and who listens. This form of discursive meta-awareness is essential to post-formal thinking, as it grants us a larger picture of the nature of the information that shapes our lives. Unfortu-nately, some research indicates that few teachers are presently able to operate at such a level of meta-awareness. Teachers too often view knowledge in terms of specific thinkers considering evidence for or against the truth of particular ideas rather than in light of certain regimes of truth and discursive communities. Robert Young reports that about 85 percent of teachers hold to a monological view of knowledge, monological mean-ing that they possess little awareness of the social dependence of knowl-edge construction (Greene 1988, 42–43; Young 1990, 2–3, 95–96).

Post-formal teachers understand that it is the experience of inquiring, questioning, and reflecting that is important. No text, no principle, no work of art, or no person should be beyond question, analysis, or criticism. Bertrand Russell wrote almost a century ago that philosophy's value has little to do with its ability to produce answers to our uncertainties. Individuals without philosophy, Russell wrote, travel through life imprisoned by the prejudices derived from everyday existence, from common sense. The habitual beliefs of an individual's age become tyrants to a mind unable to reflect upon their genesis. At its best, Russell concluded, philosophy expands our thoughts and liberates them from the prison of custom. Again, post-formal thinkers release themselves from the prison of custom on their own recognizance, as they attempt to make their own way, free from the pseudoguides of conventionality (Peters and Amburgey 1982, 98; Greene 1988, 126; Codd 1984, 9).

If we are, as post-formal thinkers, to expand our thinking, then it is essential to understand what our thinking is and why it is that way. In formal thinking and teaching it does not matter what constitutes student or teacher perceptions. Student or teacher meta-awareness of discursive practices, consciousness construction, or knowledge legitimation has little to do with traditional developmentalism and its attempt to move thinkers through a regulated progression of discrete cognitive stages eventuating in formal thinking (Walkerdine 1984, 178). While traditional developmentalism may have understood that teaching is enhanced when the learner is surprised by the discrepancy between his or her expectations and reality, it failed to follow up on the implication embedded in the concept. Expectation implied an awareness of one's own perceptions—but formal thinkers were simply uninterested in the nature of these perceptions or how they might have been constructed. Thus, they forfeited claim to meta-awareness, to the self-knowledge that leads to emancipation and the possibility of freedom it offers. Unaware of the irony of the emerging climate of deceit, traditional developmentalists were trapped in the masking of appearance, thwarted by expressions of intent. They were imprisoned in the sociocognitive twilight zone, the fractured dimension between what is supposed to be and what is.

RECONSIDERING COGNITIVE STAGE THEORY

The motivating concern of post-formal thinking involves the desire to cure the cognitive illness by transcending the boundaries of Piaget's notion of formal thinking. The 1980s witnessed numerous attempts to transcend the boundaries of Piagetian and other stage theories. As formulated within the Cartesian–Newtonian paradigm, psychological stage theories often have proved to be quite limiting. Too often they have circumscribed thinking by fostering discursive practices that assume that the individual is shaped to meet the norm set by the stage. Thus, the stage becomes the reality, not the infinite possibility of unrestricted human action. Also, stage theory tends to psychologize cognition, removing it from the sociohistorical context that shaped it—that is, ignoring the critical constructivist concern with consciousness construction. Critical postmodernism attempts to transcend these limitations with the notion of post-formality.

Post-formality recognizes that cognitive development is anything but a simple, linear process that is individually and biologically determined. Because of this complexity, post-formality insists that the notion of universally generalized stage theories designed to describe human development be qualified in a way that accepts a variety of avenues leading to a diversity of models of cognitive maturity. Feminist theory has served as the catalyst for much of the reconceptualization and the mother of many of the diverse models of cognition presented in recent years. For example, feminist theorists recognized that in research based on Piaget's definition of cognition boys generally surpassed girls, reaching formal levels of thinking earlier and in greater numbers. The Piagetian emphasis on abstraction as the zenith of cognition was challenged by Carol Gilligan and other cognitive researchers. As we discussed earlier, the feminist challenge to Piaget proposed that connected cognition, a way of knowing based on the primacy of relationship and care, was in no way inferior to the androcentric tendency for abstraction (Walkerdine 1984, 222–24; Belenky, Clinchy, Goldberger, and Tarule 1986, 101–2).

In addition, Piaget's cognitive system ends with adolescence and rejects the possibility of any adult or "post-formal" development. The influence of Piaget has been so pronounced in the field of cognitive development that research into higher order thinking has been retarded for decades. It also has retarded insight into teacher thinking as a form of adult cognition. Post-formality is very concerned with the examination of teacher and other practitioner thinking as a form of adult cognition that transcends the limitations of boundaries designed for adolescents. In no way does this interest in adult thinking assume that adolescents themselves are incapable of post-formal cognition, for examples abound of adolescent thinking that goes beyond Piaget's formal boundaries. Research based on Piagetian stages would fail to uncover such border crossings, such examples of post-formal thinking, as it has focused on puzzle tasks or well-structured problems.

The use of such problems illustrates the lack of imagination of modernist cognitive science. All of the elements necessary for the solution of a puzzle are already known—indeed, an effective procedure for its solution exists. The form of thinking measured by such problem solving–oriented research is a procedural cognition that tests one's ability to follow the steps of process. This research is tied to evaluation instruments that assume the biases of Piagetian cognitive theory. For example, much of research relies on the Watson-Glaser Critical Thinking Appraisal (WGCTA) which contains only well-structured problems. As a result, it is only capable of reproducing original Piagetian conclusions, as it measures formal thinking exclusively. Since the research has not attempted to define anything "post-formal," it does not recognize it even when it sees it. Thus, formal procedural thinkers have no interest in where or how problems were derived or who devised them. They are condemned to solving puzzles developed by others regardless of whose interests are served. In many ways they may be characterized as cognitive technicians (Downing 1990, 3–8; Young 1990, 110).

The reflective cognition needed to understand epistemological assumptions and thus to appreciate the origins of knowledge appears to be a different cognitive process than those linguistic and logico-mathematical abilities identified as formal thinking. Many cognitive researchers working in venue of adult thinking have recognized this distinction and have sought to account for it in their descriptions of adult cognition. Much has been learned from their attempts (Kurfiss 1988, 10). We have been granted a glimpse of how "post-formal" cognitive styles might manifest themselves. While much progress has been realized, the adult stage theorists, like Piaget, failed to understand the socially constructed nature of consciousness and the impact context exerts on cognitive orientation. While there is disagreement among the theorists, most adult stages follow the descriptions offered by William Perry in 1970. A brief delineation of these stages is important as they represent the initial efforts to describe cognitive abilities that transcend Piagetian formality.

The first stage identified has been labeled dualism/received knowledge. Remaining within the concrete boundaries of Piaget's stages, adults at the dualism/received knowledge level view knowledge as a collection of separate facts. College students operating at this level (research indicates that there are many) regard learning as simply a matter of acquiring data provided by the professor to accompany the text. Information is black or white, correct or not—thus, the term, dualism. Dualistic students do not comprehend how the information presented in a class or a text is manipulated, interpreted, and delivered. To them the teacher is the authority, presented validated knowledge that is simply correct. Why interpret?, they ask; doesn't the textbook mean what is written? Epistemologically, level-one thinkers believe that objective reality can be known with certainty— reality and knowledge are mirrors or copies of one another (Kurfiss 1988, 9, 52–53; Belenky, Clinchy, Goldberger, and Tarule 1986, 35–43; Bobbitt 1987, 62–63; Downing 1990, 8).

The second stage of adult intellectual growth has been referred to as multiplicity/received knowledge. At this stage, cognitive theorists claim, adults come to the understanding that conflicting interpretations are an inevitable aspect of knowledge, that is, there are multiple perspectives. Located in a Piagetian netherland somewhere between concrete and formal thinking, stage-two thinkers begin to develop faith in their inner voices as a fount of knowledge—the subjective feature of the stage. Level two is an important turning point in intellectual development, as students come to recognize the complexity of knowledge. Even though they understand that ambiguity exists, they still don't know how to deal with it. Devoid of criteria for making judgments, these thinkers retreat to the position that knowledge is simply opinion. Research indicates that the majority of college students fall into this category.

The third stage of adult cognition has been labeled reflective skepticism/procedural knowledge. This level of development corresponds to Piaget's notion of formality, as adult thinkers come to realize that interpretations vary in quality. Armed with such a realization, they come to rely on disciplinary procedures for interpreting information. Stage-three thinkers approach knowledge with skepticism, believing that what counts as truth is contingent on the rules used to evaluate it. The rules, they maintain, must be closely followed and must be appropriate to the context. Such thinkers abandon belief in an objective reality, sensing that truth is inseparable from the context that produced it.

The fourth stage of adult intellectual development represents the attempt to move beyond Piaget's formality. Referred to as commitment in relativism/constructed knowledge, stage four posits that individuals must take a position and commit themselves to it even though they have no certified way of knowing for sure that it is correct. Knowledge in this stage is constructed as it integrates personal knowledge with knowledge learned from others. Learners at level four enter into meta-analysis as they move beyond the proceduralism of formality. At this point they analyze who asks questions, why questions are asked, and the procedures by which questions are answered. When interpreting a poem procedural knowers consider the proper technique to analyze it; level-four knowers consider what the poet is attempting to say to them in a personal way. Constructed knowers are never ready to close inquiry into knowledge claims but are committed to leaving them open to further review and reevaluation. Interpretation is an ongoing, never-ending process (Downing 1990, 8–10; Kurfiss 1988, 54–56; Bobbitt 1987, 64–65; Maher and Rathbone 1986, 224; Belenky, Clinchy, Goldberger, and Tarule 1986, 120–21).

Level four grants us a good place to start in our attempt to formulate a post-formal sociocognitive theory. Sociocognitive is used to emphasize the critical constructivist concern with the social construction of consciousness, the inseparability of the psychological and the sociological domains. While stage four is helpful, it also falls victim to the psychologizing tendency of cognitive science, that is, the tendency to overvalue the causative role of the mental. While some theorists have acknowledged the value of social context, none have sufficiently dealt with the nature of the interaction between the social and the psychological in cognitive development. Power is an unknown force in most cognitive theory.

Our notion of post-formality transcends much of the language associated with Piagetian and most other theories of higher order thinking. While traditional cognitive science has associated disinterestedness, objectivity, adult cognition, and problem solving with higher order thinking, post-formality challenges such concepts: Post-formal thinking is not disinterested, it is committed to the critical system of meaning and the notion of social justice it assumes; post-formal thinking is not objective, it is unabashedly subjective with its celebration of intimacy between the knower and the known; post-formal thinking is not simply an adult stage of cognition, it recognizes expressions of post-formality in adolescents; post-formal thinking does not seek simply to solve defined and structured problems. Post-formal thinking is interested in the ability to see problems where others see tranquility. Instead of focusing on the solution to the puzzle everyone recognizes as a puzzle, post-formal thinking wonders where the puzzle came from and who recognized it as being in need of a solution. Life rarely presents problems that are well structured like a puzzle. Most of the problems we find in the lived world are of the ill-structured variety. They possess no single, unqualified solution that can be attained merely by plugging in the correct cognitive process (Downing 1990, 7–8).

Post-formal thinking resituates cognitive theory as a radical discourse. As Piagetian stage theory became institutionalized and normalized, it no longer served the purpose of freeing individuals from arbitrary descriptions of intelligence. In the case of the Piagetian and other cognitive systems, social decontextualization removed the theories from a dialogical interplay with other cognitive perspectives. These cognitive systems failed to understand that the methods we employ to transmit and to interpret our experiences are socially constructed because they are inseparable from linguistic forms that are culturally generated. Individuals do not exist in a decontextualized isolation booth, coldly analyzing the cosmos through thick glass and formulating logical, Mr. Spocklike conclusions about it. On the contrary, what we often designate as reason is always a sociopolitical process of meaning making. Reason is socially constructed since any references, allusions, or metaphors we might employ and any linguistic symbols we utilize are social forms that carry with them the baggage of cultural codes, symbols, and signs. Reason and the production of meaning are not simply psychological processes; they are always socially mediated. Social mediation shapes mental action by providing individuals tools such as language and social conventions (Wertsch 1991, 12). Postmodern analysis has destroyed the modernist conception of the autonomously formed individual.

Post-formal thinking leaves the quest for certainty to modernist cognitive science. Comfort with uncertainty allows us the freedom to experiment and to be transformed by the process. We are free to be fallible and to learn from our fallibility. Marilyn Ferguson writes that "uncertainty is the necessary companion for all explorers" (Ferguson 1980, 107). Once post-formal thinkers relinquish the formal need for certainty, they become more comfortable with being guided by a sense of general direction—a sense of direction provided by our critical system of meaning. Buoyed by the direction of our critical system of meaning and freed by our comfort with uncertainty, post-formal thinkers learn to interrogate the social rules and their impact on various individuals. Thus, we are capable of social critique based on carefully considered moral and ethical principles. With these ideas in mind we are ready to detail our formulation of post-formal thinking.

Chapter 8

The Nature of
Post-Formal Thinking

Since one of the most important features of post-formal thinking involves the production of one's own knowledge, it becomes important to note in any discussion of the characteristics of post-formality that no boundaries exist to limit what may be considered post-formal thinking. Post-formal thinking and post-formal teaching become whatever an individual, a student, or a teacher can produce in the realm of new understandings and knowledge. Much of what cognitive science and in turn the schools have measured as intelligence consists of an external body of information. The frontier where the information of the disciplines intersects with the understandings and experience that individuals carry with them to school is the point where knowledge is created (constructed). The post-formal teacher facilitates this interaction, helping students to reinterpret their own lives and uncover new talents as a result of their encounter with school knowledge.

This view of cognition as a process of knowledge production presages profound pedagogical changes. If knowledge is viewed, however, as simply an external body of information independent of human beings, then the role of the teacher is to take this knowledge and insert it into the minds of students. Evaluation procedures which emphasize retention of isolated bits and pieces of data are intimately tied to this view of knowledge. Conceptual thinking is discouraged, as schooling trivializes learning. Students are evaluated on the lowest level of human thinking—the ability to memorize. Unless students are moved to incorporate school information into their own lives, schooling will remain merely an unengaging rite of passage into adulthood. The point is clear; the way we define thinking exerts a profound impact on the nature of our schools, the role that teachers play in the world, and the shape that society will ultimately take. As we delineate the following characteristics of post-formal thinking, each point contains profound implications for the future of teaching.

THINKING ABOUT THINKING—EXPLORING THE UNCERTAIN PLAY OF THE IMAGINATION

Like William Pinar's notion of *currere* (the Latin root of the word "curriculum" meaning the investigation of the nature of the individual experience of the public), post-formal thinking about thinking allows us to move to our own inner world of psychological experience. The effort involves our ability to bring to conscious view our culturally created and therefore limited concept of both self and reality, thus revealing portions of ourselves previously hidden (Pinar 1975, 384–85). To think about one's own thinking in a post-formal manner involves understanding the way our consciousness is constructed, appreciating the forces that facilitate or impede our accommodations. Post-formal thinking about thinking involves our ability to engage in ideological disembedding, the ability to remove ourselves from sociointerpersonal norms and expectations. This post-formal concern with questions of meaning and attention to the process of self-production rises above the formal level of thought and its concern with proper procedure. Our conception of post-formal thinking about thinking never allows us to be content with what we have cognitively constructed. Never certain of the appropriateness of our ways of seeing and always concerned with the expansion of self-awareness and consciousness, post-formal thinkers engage in a running metadialogue, a constant conversation with self (Codd 1984, 13; Kegan 1982, 42).

Ancient Greek mythology was fascinated by how in a room filled with conversation, there periodically spreads a lull of profound silence. The Greeks postulated that at such moments Hermes had entered the room. By silencing the everyday babble, Hermes allowed the Greeks to tap their imaginations, fears, hopes, and passions. Through this awareness they were freed from acting out socially constructed expectations that they really didn't understand. Hermes came to symbolize the penetration of boundaries—boundaries that separated one culture from another, work from play, fantasy from reality, and consciousness from unconsciousness. With his winged sandals and cap of invisibility, a postmodern Hermes can now bring the power of the unconscious into another room, the everyday world of consciousness. With this power of the unconscious, Hermes delivers insight and the potential for disembedding. The room in question is the bicameral room of the human brain and the lull of silence involves the quieting of the conversation among the plethora of socially constructed voices of the mind. As he connects us with the unconscious, Hermes becomes another in a long line of trickster gods whom ancients associated with the power of the imagination.

Post-formal thinking about thinking draws upon the boundary trespasses of Hermes and the playful parody of postmodernism to transgress the official constraints of our consciousness construction, to transcend modern convention by exposing its ironic contradictions (Combs and Holland 1990, 62, 88; Hutcheon 1988, 22–37). As Peter McLaren explains the postmodern double reading of the social world, he writes of a teaching disposition that encourages students to think about their thinking in a post-formal manner. Students learn to construct their identities in a way which parodies the rigid conventions of modernism, thus assuming the role of postmodern stand-up comics, social satirists (McLaren forthcoming, 7, 30). Hermes, the playful trickster, mysteriously pops up everywhere with his fantasies, surprise inspirations, "border crossings," and other gifts of the imagination; they are ours for the taking if we can hold onto the silence long enough to listen to him, if we have not let social expectations crush our propensity for play.

To play with convention, to allow our imagination some freedom, to give in to our fantasies is to honor Hermes. Such a form of play can reveal hidden dimensions of self, it can expand our sense of who we are and what we want to become. Tibetan Buddhism contends that what separates humans from animals is not intelligence but humor. To confront life in a postmodern playful manner involves learning to see it with the eye of humor. Such an eye does not blind us to the tragedy of human existence; it simply balances the tragedy of life with the wonder of it. Postmodern play is a courageous act, for it insists that we refuse to run away from the uncertainty and irrationality of our public and private worlds. But school is not a place for play. Modernist education has failed to recognize that new thoughts generally come from "mind play," as it has portrayed thinking as a weighty and sober, no-nonsense enterprise. Ruled by a quest for certainty, modernist thinking has attempted to submerge the human desire for play. In the process it misses the quiet visits of Hermes and the insight we might have derived from his playful ability to engage us in thinking about our own thinking. Post-formal thinkers are comfortable with the uncertain, tentative nature of knowledge emerging from postmodern play and its critical constructivist epistemology. They are tolerant of contradiction and value the attempt to integrate ostensibly dissimilar phenomena into new, revealing syntheses. Indeed, they are ready to accept Hermes' invitation to cross the boundaries of modernist social convention (Bohm and Peat 1987, 48; Combs and Holland 1990, 136–38; Van Hesteran 1986, 214; Kramer 1983, 92–94).

EXPLORING DEEP STRUCTURES—UNCOVERING THE TACIT FORCES THAT SHAPE

Physicist David Bohm helps us conceptualize this aspect of post-formal thinking with his notion of the explicate and implicate orders of reality. The explicate order involves simple patterns and invariants in time—that is, characteristics of the world that repeat themselves in similar ways and have recognizable locations in space. Being associated with comparatively humble orders of similarities and differences, explicate orders are often what is identified by the categorization and generalization function of formal thought. The implicate order is a much deeper structure of reality. It is the level at which ostensible separateness vanishes and all things seem to become a part of a larger unified process. Implicate orders are marked by the simultaneous presence of a sequence of many levels, each enfolding, with similar dissimilarities existing among them. The totality of these levels of enfolding cannot be made explicit as a whole. They can be exposed only in the emergence of a series of enfoldings. In contrast to the explicate order (which is an unfolded order) where similar differences are all present together and can be described in Cartesian–Newtonian terms, the implicate order has to be studied as a hidden process, sometimes impenetrable to empirical methods of inquiry (Bohm and Peat 1987, 174, 187).

Post-formal thinking's concern with deep structures is, of course, informed by an understanding of the implicate order. Many have speculated that at higher levels of human consciousness, we often peek at the implicate process. Profound insight in any field of study may involve the apprehension of structures not attainable at the explicate order of reality. At these points we transcend common sense—we cut patterns out of the cosmic fabric (Combs and Holland 1990, 46). "Artists don't reproduce the visible, Paul Klee wrote, instead they "make things visible" (Leshan and Margenau 1982, 172). Similarly, Albert Einstein often referred to his physics as based on a process of questioning unconscious assumptions so as to reveal the deep structures of the universe. The theory of relativity itself emerged from his probing of the tacit assumptions underlying classical physics, in particular absolute conceptions of time and space (Reynolds 1987, 170–71). As Einstein exposed deep physical structures of the "shape of space," he was at least approaching an implicate order of the physical universe.

Post-formal thinking works to get behind the curtain of ostensible normality. Post-formal teachers work to create situations to bring hidden assumptions to our attention, to make the tacit visible. Virginia Woolf argued that artists do much the same thing: They uncover hidden realities and communicate them to their readers. These hidden realities are inseparable from implicate orders that ultimately are to be found at the base of all experience. Formal thinking has not been attuned to such a reality, possibly because the expansionist, conquest-oriented goals of the Cartesian–Newtonian paradigm emphasized the explicate order of things. The social world is in many ways like an onion, as we peel off one layer, we find another beneath. An outside layer of socioeducational reality is the standardized test performance of a school. The second layer is the assumptions behind the language that is utilized in discussing the curriculum. The third layer is the unspoken epistemological assumptions of the curricular reforms. A fourth layer is the body of assumptions about learning students bring to school, ad infinitum (Briggs 1990, 17–18); Greene 1988, 121–22; Bohm and Peat 1987, 190).

Unfortunately the formalist analysis of school is grounded in the explicate order where deep structures remain enfolded and out of sight. The dominant culture's conversation not only about education but also the political process, racism, sexism, and social class bias is formalist and focuses on the explicate order. Critical postmodern theory has taught us that little is as it appears on the surface. When post-formal observers search for the deep structures which are there to be uncovered in any classroom, they discover a universe of hidden meanings constructed by a variety of sociopolitical forces that many times has little to do with the intended (explicate) meanings of the official curriculum. A post-formal analysis of curriculum is grounded on the recognition that there are implicate orders of forces that shape what happens in schools—some complimentary, others contradictory, some emancipatory, others repressive. When this post-formal analysis of deep structures is applied to education, the implications for change are infinite. Imagine the way we might post-formally reconceptualize evaluation, supervision, administration, and so on. The reductionism of the explicate approach to these areas would be overthrown.

ASKING UNIQUE QUESTIONS—PROBLEM DETECTION

The technical rationality of modernism has long ignored the ability to ask unique questions and to detect problems as important aspects of higher order intelligence. This modernist tradition has often reduced intelligence and in turn the work of teachers to problem solving. Such cognitive reductionism restricts teaching to the level of formal thinking and captures practitioners in a culture of bureaucratic technicalization where they simply seek solutions to problems defined by their superiors (Munby and Russell 1990, 72; Schon 1983, 39–40). When the work of teachers is reduced to mere problem solving, a practitioner's ability to identify the problems of the classroom and to ask unique questions about them is neglected. Indeed, pedagogies of problem solving and tests of intelligence that focus upon problem solving ignore the initial steps of questioning and problem detecting—prerequisites to creative acts of learning, to post-formal thinking (Courteney 1988, 40).

Problem detecting is undoubtedly a necessary precondition for technical problem solving, although problem detecting is not itself a technical problem—it cannot be approached in a formalist procedural (technical) way. As we detect a problem, we formulate questions about a situation. In the process, we impose a coherence on the situation which exposes asymmetries and helps cultivate an intuition for what might need to be changed about the situation. We frame the context in which we will make an observation. In this framing process we draw upon a body of past experiences and understandings and apply them to the situation in question. Problem detecting and the questioning that accompanies it becomes a form of world making in that the way we conduct these operations is contingent on the system of meaning we employ. With their focus on meta-awareness post-formal thinkers are cognizant of the relationship between the way they themselves and others frame problems and ask questions about the nature of the system of meaning they employ. They often possess an understanding of the genesis of frames even when the individual involved doesn't recognize the origin of a question or a problem.

Without this meta-awareness of a system of meaning, teachers and administrators may learn how to construct schools but not how to determine what types of schools to construct. They will not grasp the connection between political disposition and the types of education that are developed. Grounded on an understanding of such connections, post-formal teachers, administrators, and teacher educators realize that school problems are not generic or innate. They are constructed by social conditions, cognitive assumptions, and power relations and are uncovered by insightful educators who possess the ability to ask questions never before asked, questions that lead to innovations that promote student insight, sophisticated thinking, and social justice (Munby and Russell 1989, 77; Schon 1987, 4; Ponzio 1985, 41).

Post-formal thinkers realize that most of the problems or questions posed in school to students are of the well-structured variety. Such questions/problems involve all of the data needed to solve the problem, procedures and operations are delineated, and the criteria to be employed to determine the solution are all provided. Indeed, the process for solution is often laid out in a step-by-step format that is guaranteed to achieve a particular goal. When confronted with these structured problems, students are assured that there is one "right" answer to be located—no more, no less. Research conducted in recent years indicates that little thinking or learning takes place if the teacher chooses the problems that students are to solve. When we examine the studies of questioning and problem solving over the last eighty years, we find that most of the problems addressed in a classroom are teacher-posed problems usually connected to questions with one correct answer.

Indeed, too many teacher education classes fail to address questioning, especially the connection between one's system of meaning and the types of questions posed. Post-formal teachers not only ask unique questions but create classrooms where student learning is grounded on questions that students themselves ask (Laster 1987, 36; Courteney 1988, 46). In the modernist classroom, on the other hand, teachers are encouraged only to ask questions in regard to the accuracy of data and the sequence in which information should be delivered to the students. In this context teacher questions about the interpretation of information or questions about the moral and ethical nature of the curriculum are deemed dangerous (Benson 1989, 330). Here the point emerges that the post-formal ability to ask unique questions and to detect problems never before detected is politically dangerous as it tends to juggle comfortable power relations. Thinking is indeed a political act.

SEEING RELATIONSHIPS BETWEEN OSTENSIBLY DIFFERENT THINGS— METAPHORIC COGNITION

Post-formal thinking draws heavily on the concept of the metaphor. Metaphoric cognition is basic to all scientific and creative thinking and involves the fusion of previously disparate concepts in unanticipated ways. The mutual interrelationships of the components of a metaphor, not the components themselves, are the most important aspects of a metaphor. Indeed, many have argued that relationships, not objects, should be the basis of scientific thinking. When thinking of the concept of mind, the same thoughts are relevant. We might be better served to think of mind not in terms of parts but in terms of the connecting patterns, the dance of the interacting parts. The initial consciousness of the "poetic" recognition of this dance involves a nonverbal mental vibration, an increased energy state. From this creative tension emerges a perception of the meaning of the metaphor and the heightened consciousness which accompanies it. Post-formal teachers can model such metaphoric perception for their students. Such perception is not simply innate, it can be learned (Fosnot 1988, 5; Talbot 1986, 115; Bohm and Peat 1987, 33).

Pondering the question of what is basic in education, Madeleine Grumet argues that the concept of relation, of connecting pattern is fundamental. Ironically, she argues, it is relation that we ignore when asked to ennumerate the basics. Education involves introducing a student to modes of being and acting in the world that are new to his or her experience. Grumet concludes that it is the relation, the dance between the student's experience and knowledge that separates education from training or indoctrination (Grumet 1992). Post-formal thinkers recognize that relationships, not discrete objects, should be the basis for definitions in the sciences and humanities. From this perspective the physical and social worlds are seen as dynamic webs of interconnected components. None of the parts of the webs are fundamental, for they follow the dance of their relationship with the other parts. The nature of their interconnections shapes the form the larger web takes. The educational implications of such a realization are revolutionary. The uncovering and interpretation of the dance becomes a central concern of teachers and students. Curricular organization, evaluation techniques, teacher education, definitions of student and teacher success cannot remain the same if this post-formal characteristic is taken seriously (Talbot 1986, 115; Fosnot 1988, 5; Capra 1982, 93).

Philosopher Gregory Bateson was obsessed with the attempt to teach his students the importance of the pattern. Yet, when he looked around him, he watched his colleagues teaching little but rote facts—bricks without the mortar to hold them together. Teachers, Bateson lamented, plant "the kiss of death" on their students when they ignore the most significant dimension of life, the dance of the interconnecting parts. This dance, this Bohmian implicate order, is still a stranger in far too many schools. Learning to learn and learning to think at a higher order are inseparable from the ability to see the relationship between things. Anthropologist Edward Hall argues that contemporary schools actually teach us *not* to make connections. The teacher has to become a synthesizer, one who possesses the contextual understanding to pull events and character-istics together (Munby and Russell 1989, 77; Talbot 1986, 115; Ferguson 1980, 303). Such synthesis can be quite disturbing when the dance uncovered involves patterns of consciousness construction, reflections of asymmetrical power relations. In such situations post-formal teachers will find themselves being pressured to retreat into the social safety of factual delivery.

CONNECTING LOGIC AND EMOTION— STRETCHING THE BOUNDARIES OF CONSCIOUSNESS

Feminist theory has raised our consciousness concerning the role of emotion in learning and knowing. Feminist constructivists have main-tained that emotional intensity precedes cognitive transformation to a new way of seeing. Knowing, they argue, involves emotional as well as cognitive states of mind. As such, emotions are seen as powerful know-ing processes that ground cognition (Mahoney and Lyddon 1988, 217). Formal thinkers in the Cartesian–Newtonian lineage are procedural knowers who unemotionally pay allegiance to a system of inquiry—in-deed, they often see emotion as a pollutant in reason. Post-formal thinkers grounded in feminist theory unite logic and emotion, making use of what the emotions can understand that logic cannot. Emotionally committed to their thoughts, post-formal thinkers tap into a passion for knowing that motivates, that extends, that leads them to a union with that which is to be known. Feminist scholar Barbara DuBois describes passionate scholarship as "sciencemaking, [which is] rooted in, ani-mated by and expressive of our values" (Belenky, Clinchy, Goldberger, and Tarule 1986, 140–41).

Utilizing this union of reason and emotion feminist thinkers have revealed unanticipated insights gleaned from the mundane, the everyday lived world. They have exposed the existence of silences and erasures where formal thinkers had seen only "what was there." Such absences were revealed by the application of women's lived experience to the process of analysis, thus forging new connections between knower and known. Cartesian–Newtonian formalists had weeded out the self, denied their emotions and inner voices, in the process producing restricted and objectlike interpretations of social and educational situations. Using empirical definitions, these formalist objectlike interpretations were certain and scientific; feminist self-grounded interpretations were infe-rior, merely impressionistic, and journalistic. Feminist theorists came to realize that the objective thinking described by Piagetian formality was released from any social embeddedness or ethical responsibility. Objectivity in this sense became a signifier for ideological passivity and an acceptance of a privileged socioeconomic position. Thus, formalist objectivity came to demand a separation of logic and emotion, the devaluation of any perspective maintained with emotional conviction. Feeling is designated as an inferior form of human consciousness—those who rely on logical forms of thinking operating within this framework can justify their repression of those associated with emotion or feeling. Feminist theorists have pointed out that the thought–feeling hierarchy is one of the structures historically used by men to oppress women. In intimate heterosexual relationships, if a man is able to represent the woman's position as an emotional perspective, then he has won the argument—his is the voice worth hearing (Belenky, Clinchy, Goldberger, and Tarule 1986, 19, 134; Reinharz 1979, 242).

The way of knowing ascribed to "rational man" defines logical abstraction as the highest level of thought—symbolic logic, mathematics, signifiers far removed from their organic function. Piaget's delineation of formality fails to transcend these androcentric forces of decontextualization. Unlike Piaget's objective cognition, women's ways of knowing are grounded on an identification with organic life and its preservation. Rational man contends that emotions are dangerous as they exert a disorganizing effect on the progress of science. Informed by feminist perspectiveness and critical constructivist epistemology, post-formal teachers admit that, indeed, emotions do exert a disorganizing effect on traditional logocentric ways of knowing and rationalistic cognitive theory. But, they argue, such disorganization is a positive step in the attempt to critically accommodate our perceptions of ourselves and the world around us. Emotions thus become powerful thinking mechanisms that extend our ability to make sense of the universe (Reinharz 1979, 7; Fee 1982, 379–80; Mahoney and Lyddon 1988, 216–17).

Madeleine Grumet and Peter McLaren extend our understanding of the feminist attempt to transcend logocentrism by connecting the language of the body, of feeling with inquiry and thinking. Social science, they argue, whether guided by conservative or progressive impulses, has been enmeshed in a male-dominated snare of abstraction. Grumet and McLaren have sought new methods of inquiry that are capable of drawing the body and feeling into the public conversation about education. Making use of qualitative methodologies such as history, theater, autobiography, and semiotics, they confront androcentric abstraction with the uncertainty, specificity, and ambiguity of the private, the corporeal, and the feminine

(Grumet 1988, 3–15; McLaren 1991b, 144–73). From the perspectives of the guardians of the formalist Cartesian–Newtonian tradition such epistemological confrontations constitute overt subversion. After exposure to such theorizing, higher order thinking can no longer be viewed as a cold, rational process. As emotion, empathy, the body, are injected into the thinking process, as the distinction between knower and known is blurred, as truth is viewed as a *process* of construction in which knowers play an active role, feminine passion can be admitted into the all-male lodge of cognition. Post-formal teachers see themselves as passionate scholars who connect themselves emotionally to that which they seek to know and understand. How can we possibly divorce the creative moment from passionate intensity (Bohm and Peat 1987, 267)?

Passionate thinkers use the self as an instrument of understanding, searching for new modes of cognition and methods of inquiry to sophisticate analysis and action. Soren Kierkegaard anticipated this notion of post-formal passion, arguing in the first half of the nineteenth century that there is an intimate connection between commitment and knowing. Subjectivity, he maintained, is not simply arbitrary—instead, it reflects the most profound connection between an individual thinker and the world. As inquirers grow passionate about what they know, they develop a deeper relationship with themselves. Such a relationship produces a self-knowledge that initiates a synergistic cycle—a cycle that grants them more insight into the issue under consideration. Soon, Kierkegaard argued, a form of personal knowledge is developed that uses empathetic understanding to move beyond the perception of social life as more than a set of fixed laws. Social life is better characterized as a process of being, a dialectic where the knower's personal participation in events and emotional insight gained from such participation moves us to a new dimension of knowing.

Another precursor of the feminist, post-formal notion of passionate knowing concerns the way indigenous peoples have defined thinking. Note the similarities of Afrocentric and native American ways of knowing with the anti–Cartesian–Newtonian perspectives of Kierkegaard and modern feminist and postmodern theorists. To such peoples reality has never been dichotomized into spiritual and material segments. Self-knowledge lays the foundation for all knowledge in the African and native American epistemologies. Great importance has traditionally been placed on interpersonal relationships (solidarity), and diunital logic has moved these traditions to appreciate the continuum of spirit and matter, individual and world. Indeed, indigenous ways of knowing and the European Cartesian–Newtonian modernist tradition come into direct conflict over the epistemological issues of mind and body, individuals and nature, logic and emotion, self and other, spirit and matter, and knower and known—a conflict that has generated serious historical consequences. It is only in the last thirty or so years that some Eurocentric people have come to recognize the epistemological and cognitive sophistication of the indigenous paradigm that recognizes unity in all things and a connected spiritual energy embedded in both human and natural elements. Thus, that deemed primitive by modernist Westerners becomes, from the critical postmodern perspective, a valuable source of insight in our attempt to reconceptualize a form of thinking that transcends the blinders of formality (Belenky, Clinchy, Goldberger, and Tarule 1986, 140–41; Reinharz 1979, 242–43; Myers 1987, 73–75; Nyang and Vandi 1980, 245).

Women crusaders of the 1800s were not attentive to passionate thinking, to women's ways of knowing. Bifurcating their own experiences, they said little in their public statements about the feelings they had about their families, their household duties, and the knowledge they had gained as a result of these feelings. As they assigned the lived realities of their lives to the realm of silence, they undercut their ability to confront the politics of the family and the character of their own exploitation as women. They simply could not obtain liberation via the securing of abstract political rights alone. They could be emancipated only by integrating the domains of the private and the public, feeling and logic, and the cognitive and the political. Though the nineteenth-century crusaders could not recognize it, the realities of women's history made it impossible for women to escape from their everyday lives. They could not lay claim to particular abstract rights without connecting those rights to their everyday worlds. What, for example, did freedom mean to a young mother of five children? The ground of women's being, Maxine Greene writes, is removed when the political and the emotional are separated (Greene 1988, 70–71). The same is true in the cognitive domain—thinking in which logic and emotion are estranged becomes a despiritualized, hollow form of cognition that exerts little positive effect on human lives. The realms of the cognitive, the political, and the emotional are inseparable in the post-formal paradigm. Here thinking is viewed as an act of emotional commitment which leads to political transformation.

SEEING FACTS AS PARTS OF LARGER PROCESSES—CONNECTING THE HOLOGRAPHIC MIND TO HOLOGRAPHIC REALITY

Post-formal thinkers see facts as more than pieces of information. They see them in relationship to the larger processes of which they are a part.

Twentieth-century physics has asserted that there is no absolute standard of time and no solid objects, only energy fields—that is, interconnecting processes and relationships. Indeed, relationships are the foundation of human consciousness. Post-formal thinkers understand that consciousness is a part of a larger process, that the universe is a continuous fabric not an empty shell with discrete pieces, that particles in reality have no simple independent existence but contribute to the constitution of the larger process of life. This appreciation of the larger process was lost in the wake of the Cartesian–Newtonian revolution which fragmented the world into bits and pieces. Post-formal teachers understand the impact of this Cartesian–Newtonian revolution on schooling and attempt accordingly to bring the study of the larger process to their classrooms (Frye 1987, 65; Combs and Holland 1990, xxiii).

Return to Bohm's notion of the implicate order, the level of reality at which separateness vanishes and all things appear to become part of a larger process. Bohm asks us to think of holographic photography to extend the notion of the implicate process; indeed, we also can use this holographic analogy to help frame and extend our notion of the post-formal recognition of process. In photography a lens is used to focus light from an entity, so that each part of the entity is reproduced in a section of the photographic plate. In holographic photography, however, a laser light shines through a half-silvered mirror. When the beams unite at the photographic plate, they produce a pattern that to the viewer produces a sensation of seeing a three-dimensional object. Contained on every portion of the holographic negative is the whole image that was photographed. Bohm argues that this holographic effect (i.e., that all parts contain the whole) is a very simple version of what is occurring in each region of space all over the universe and in each part of the brain. The hologram thus becomes a possible model for how the brain stores memory. Since memory seems to be more distributed than localized, it may be possible that it is holographic in nature. Possibly, the brain is constructed around the ability to deal in interactions, as it processes bioelectric frequencies. Within these frequencies the whole code exists—memory thus is not a *thing*, it's a set of abstract relationships (Bohm and Peat 1987, 175; Briggs and Peat 1984, 110–11; Ferguson 1980, 179).

This holographic notion of relationship and process extends into the social dimension and the critical constructivist and post-formal attempt to understand the construction of consciousness. The postmodern attempt to understand language and its socioeducational effects can be extended by our understanding of holographic process. Meaning is enfolded in the structure of language and thus unfolds into human thought, feelings, and activities that have been "discussed" or given words. In the act of communication, this meaning unfolds into the entire community and then to each individual. Thus, in almost a Jungian sense the implicate order of society is enfolded into our consciousness. Drawing upon holography, post-formal thinkers cannot think of individuals in isolation from their social context or individuals in isolation from one another. What is viewed from one angle as society enfolds into what is seen from another angle as individual consciousness. When post-formal thinkers look at education, they see it not as something separate but as an expression of the society's implicate order, as a manifestation of the larger social processes (Bohm and Peat 1987, 185).

ETYMOLOGY—THE ORIGINS OF KNOWLEDGE

Many descriptions of higher order thinking induce us to ask questions that analyze what we know, how we come to know it, why we believe it or reject it, and how we evaluate the credibility of the evidence. Post-formal thinking shares this characteristic of other descriptions of higher order thinking but adds a critical hermeneutic and historical epistemological dimension to the idea. In order to transcend formality we must become critically initiated into our own tradition (and other traditions as well) in order to understand the etymology of the cultural forms embedded within us. Antonio Gramsci noted that philosophy cannot be understood apart from the history of philosophy, nor can culture be grasped outside the history of culture. Our conception of self and world, therefore, can only become critical when we appreciate the historicity of their formation. Indeed, we are never independent of the social and historical forces that surround us; we are all caught at a particular point in the web of reality. The post-formal project is to understand what that point in the web is, how it constructs our vantage point, and the ways it insidiously restricts our vision. Post-formal teachers become aware of their own ideological inheritance and its relationship to our own beliefs and value structures, our interests, and our questions about our professional lives (Daines 1987, 4; Codd 1984, 13; Greene 1988, 126; Cherryholmes 1988, 115).

As historical epistemologists, post-formal thinkers understand the etymology of knowledge, the ways that knowledge is produced and the specific forces that contribute to its production. The *Zeitgeist* influences knowledge production as it directs our attention to certain problems and potentialities—for example, the questions of equity emerging from the civil rights movement, of the nature of fundamentalism coming from the rise of the New Right, or of gender bias growing out of the women's movement. As the *Zeitgeist* changes or as multiple *Zeitgeists* compete in the same era, some bodies of information go out of fashion and are forgotten for the time being. Other bodies of knowledge are shelved because they seem to be tied to one particular research methodology and are not amenable to extension into different contexts. Thus, social and educational knowledge is vulnerable to the ebb and flow of time with the changing concerns and emotional swings of the different eras. This vulnerability to the temporal probably will continue, for social science shows no sign of developing consistent universal strategies for evaluating the validity of these various forms of knowledge. Indeed, such a strategy would be positivistic and would regress to a more formalistic mode of thinking (Fiske 1986, 68–71).

Post-formal thinkers concerned with epistemological etymology and their own subjective etymology (their consciousness construction) have identified with Michel Foucault's notion of genealogy. Foucault uses the term "genealogy" to describe the process of tracing the formation of our own subjectivities. By recognizing the ambiguities and contradictions in the construction of their own subjectivities, post-formal teachers can better understand the complexities of their students' consciousnesses. As they engage in self-critical genealogy, draw on our critical system of meaning, and employ qualitative action research techniques (which we will examine in detail in Chapter 9), post-formal teachers become "ungrounded" and "unrigorous" from the perspective of the technicists who wag their fingers at their lack of procedure and systemization. Indeed, the self-critical genealogy and the critical action research that grows out of it, constitutes an emancipatory right of post-formal passage as they leave behind their cognitive "adolescence." Exercising their new cognitive maturity they come to formulate more penetrating questions about their professional practice, see new levels of activity and meaning in their classrooms, decipher connections between sociocultural meanings and the everyday life of school, and reconceptualize what they already "know." As post-formal teachers grow to understand the etymology of the race, class, and gender locations of the students and others they study, they come to appreciate their own etymology and their location and the social relationships such locations produce (Reinharz 1982, 165).

PERCEIVING DIFFERENT FRAMES OF REFERENCE—THE COGNITIVE POWER OF EMPATHY

Critical postmodernism cannot accept a linear, cause–effect reality, for the complex reality it uncovers demands recognition of multiple causations and the possibility of differing vantage points in the structure of the universe. Depending on the context from which a phenomenon emanates or the system of meaning observers employ to help formulate their questions about it, different realities will be perceived (Lincoln and Guba 1985, 51; Briggs and Peat 1989, 153–54; Slaughter 1989, 262). Post-formal thinkers understand that reality, schools, and texts of all types hold more within them to be discovered than first impressions sometimes reveal. In this sense different frames of reference produce multiple interpretations and multiple realities. Contrary to the problem solving finality of formality, post-formality sees the mundane as multiplex and continuously unfolding its implicate orders (Greene 1988, 21).

Post-formality values a spatial distancing from reality which allows an observer diverse frames of reference. The distancing may range from the extremely distant like astronauts looking at the Earth from the Moon, to the extremely close like Georgia O'Keeffe viewing a flower. At the same time, post-formality values the emotional intimacy of feminist connectedness which allows empathetic passion to draw knower and known together. In the multiplex post-formal vision of reality, linearity often gives way to simultaneity, as texts become a kaleidoscope of images filled with signs and signifiers to be deconstructed. William Carlos Williams illustrated such post-formal qualities in the early twentieth century as he depicted multiple, simultaneous images and frames of reference in a verbal manner. Williams attempted to poetically interpret Marcel Duchamp's *Nude Descending a Staircase* with its simultaneism serving as a model for what post-formality might label "cognitive cubism." Post-formal teachers use such ideas to extend the holographic nature of their own and their students' memory, as they create situations where students come to view reality from as many frames of reference as is possible. The single angle of the traditional photograph is replaced by the multiple angles of the holographic photograph (Dobrin 1987, 79; Mandell 1987, 137; Talbot 1986, 51–54; Talbot 1991, 46–48).

Armed with their cognitive cubism, post-formal teachers come to understand that the models of teaching they have been taught, the definitions of inquiry with which they have been supplied, the angle from which they have been instructed to view intelligence, and the modes of learning that shape what they perceive to be sophisticated thinking, all represent a particular vantage point in the web of reality. Like reality itself schools and classrooms are complex matrices of interactions, codes, and signifiers in which both students and teachers are interlaced. Just as postmodernism asserts that there is no single, privileged way to see the world, there is no one way of seeing the classroom, intelligence, or teacher or pupil success. Once teachers escape the entrapment of the Cartesian–Newtonian way of seeing, they come to value and thus pursue new frames of reference in regard to their students, classrooms, and workplaces.

In this spirit, post-formal teachers begin to look at their lessons from the perspectives of their black students, their Hispanic students, their white students, their poor students, their middle- and upper-middle-class students, their traditionally successful students, their unsuccessful students. They examine their teaching from the vantage points of their colleagues or outside lay observers. Thus, they step out of their teacher bodies looking down on themselves and their students as outsiders. As they hover above themselves they examine their technicist teacher education with its emphasis on bulletin board construction, behavioral objective writing, discussion skill development, and classroom management. They begin to understand that such technicist training reflects a limited formality, as it assumes that professional actions can be taught as a set of procedures (Nixon 1981, 195–96).

Drawing upon their critical constructivist epistemology, post-formal thinkers like liberation theologists in Latin America make no apology for beginning a cognitive process by attempting to understand the perspective of the oppressed (Welch 1985, 31). The way to find an alternative to the mainstream perspective, they argue, is to understand an institution from the vantage point of those who have suffered most as the result of its existence. These subjugated knowledges allow post-formal thinkers to gain the cognitive power of empathy—a power that enables them to take a picture of reality from different angles. The intersection of these angles allows for a form of analysis that moves beyond the isolated, fragmented analysis of modernity. With these ideas in mind post-formal thinkers seek a multicultural dialogue between Eastern cultures and Western cultures, as well as a conversation between the relatively wealthy Northern cultures and the impoverished Southern cultures (Bohm and Peat 1987, 259). In this way, forms of knowing that have traditionally been excluded by the modernist West move us to new vantage points and unexplored planetary perspectives. Understanding derived from the perspective of the excluded or the culturally different allows for an appreciation of the nature of justice, the invisibility of the process of oppression, and a recognition of difference that highlights our own social construction as individuals—insights often lost on less sophisticated observers.

CONTEXTUALIZATION—ATTENDING TO THE SETTING

The development of a context in which an observation can assume its full meaning is a key element in the construction of a post-formal mode of thinking. The literal meaning of context is "that which is braided together." Awareness of this braiding induces post-formal thinkers to examine the ecology of everything, as they realize that facts derive meaning only in the context created by other facts. Only in recent years has the medical profession begun to examine the context of disease; some physicians argue that we should study the milieu and not simply the symptoms. In the same way, post-formal educators have begun to acknowledge that the contextualization of what we know is more important than content. In response to technicist educators who argue the importance of content, the need to "master" the basics as an initial step of learning, post-formal teachers maintain that once a fabric of relevance has been constructed, content learning naturally follows (Ferguson 1980, 303).

An example of the way meaning is dependent on context involves a listener who lacks adequate context to understand the "order" of a musical form. In many cases, such a listener will judge an avant-garde composition as meaningless. Europeans upon hearing African music attempted to assess it in the terms of another musical form. Unable to appreciate the context that gave meaning to the African music, the Europeans did not hear the intentions of the composers and performers with their subtle rhythms and haunting melodies. They heard primitive noise (Bohm and Peat 1987, 130).

When I was an adolescent, my elderly uncle walked in on me while listening to the Rolling Stones at high volume. "What is that?" he asked. As I explained "Get Off My Cloud" to the bewildered old man, he interrupted: "There's no melody to this noise. I hear only boom, boom, boom." Rock's different structure and Mick Jagger and Keith Richard's intentions as composers were lost on my uncle. Without a context to make sense of the sounds, he was unable to understand the implicate order of the music. Indeed, he was defensive; he perceived that his own implicate order was under attack. This situation is not unlike what happens when traditional teachers are confronted with students with new hairstyles or new fashions. Unable to understand the context ("where the students are coming from"), these teachers sometimes reject both the fashions and the integrity of the students themselves. The cognitive dissonance that results from a lack of contextual understanding metastasizes into a cognitive defensiveness and a cognitive distance.

Cartesian–Newtonian thinking fails to convey a valuable perspective on cognition and teaching, as it fails in its reductionism to account for context. In modern empirical research, so-called scientific controls contribute to a more perfect isolation of the context being investigated. Attention to circumstances surrounding the object of inquiry must be temporarily suspended. This suspension of attention is based on the assumption that these extraneous circumstances will remain static long enough to allow the study to be validated. Of course, these extraneous circumstances never remain static. They are constantly interacting and shaping. To exclude them is to distort reality (Longstreet 1982, 136). In settings such as schools, student and teacher behavior cannot be understood without careful attention to the setting, to the individuals' relationships to the traditions, norms, roles, and values which are inseparable from the lived world of the institutions. The inability of Cartesian–Newtonian researchers to say very much that is meaningful about school life is due in part to their lack of regard for these often invisible, but foundational, aspects of organizational life—the context (Eisner 1984, 450; Wilson 1977, 247–48). John Dewey reflected this idea long ago when he argued that many thinkers regard knowledge as self-contained, as complete in itself. Knowledge, Dewey contended, could never be viewed outside the context of its relationship to other information. We only have to call to mind, Dewey wrote, what passes in our schools as acquisition of knowledge to understand how it is decontextualized and lacks any meaningful connection to the experience of students. Anticipating our notion of post-formality, Dewey concluded that an individual is a sophisticated thinker in the degree to which he or she sees an event not as something isolated "but in its connection with the common experience of mankind" (Dewey 1916, 342–43).

We have grown so accustomed to the fragmentation, the decontextualization of modernist science and formal thinking that we no longer attend to it. Teachers are acculturated to accept the twenty-minute visit of the supervisor followed by an evaluation of the quality of their teaching. Like African music, every classroom has a context of its own. Post-formal teachers and supervisors understand the absurdity of the twenty-minute observation, knowing that such a snapshot does not allow for an appreciation of contextual features such as previously negotiated codes and conventions which grant meaning and significance to the mundane. Thus, Cartesian–Newtonian empirical researchers or evaluators often make judgments based on fragmented information not viewed in context.

UNDERSTANDING THE SUBTLE INTERACTION OF PARTICULARITY AND GENERALIZATION

Grounded in the Cartesian–Newtonian universe, formal thinking often emphasizes the production of generalizations. The post-formal teacher's concern with the particular, the unique experience of each learner, seems rather unscientific to the modernist educational scientist. To the post-formal teacher, the scientism, the obsession with generalization of the formal thinker are not especially helpful in the everyday world of the classroom. Formal generalization is out of sync with the rhythm of everyday life with its constant encounters with the novel and the unexpected—the particular.

As post-formal thinking moves beyond a simple concern with generalization, it also transcends the desire to know only the unique. Viewed from Piaget's perspective, post-formal thinkers want to assimilate—that is, they want to understand the commonalities of particular categories. The act of assimilation, of seeking these commonalities, is a search for generalization. But assimilation without accommodation never moves beyond lower cognitive levels. Accommodation involves the reshaping of cognitive structures to account for (accommodate) unique aspects of what is being perceived in new contexts. Through our knowledge of a variety of comparable contexts we begin to understand similarities and differences and we learn to anticipate from our comparisons of different contexts. As we accommodate as post-formal teachers, we come to understand the unique particular aspects of our classrooms—aspects that allow us to connect the unique experiences of our students to the world at large. Uniqueness and particularity are flies in Cartesian–Newtonian ointment. The realm of the particular complicates the attempt to produce generalized laws that can be applied to the effort to predict and thus control human behavior. What is good for one citizen is good for all—at least citizens in that particular classification, that generalization. In the same manner what is good for one student is good for all—the justification of standardization.

When thinking is captured by Cartesian–Newtonian generalization, the nature of the particular is missed when it is treated as a sample of a species or a type—it is not itself, it is a representative. Viewed in this way the particularistic, the individualistic has no proper name; it is alienated and anonymous. Children are interesting to the empirical researcher only as they represent something other than themselves. William Pinar's and my theory of place to ground post-formality's transcendence of mere generalization or mere particularity fights formality's reductionist tendency. Place, as social theory, brings the particular into focus, but in a way that grounds it contextually in a larger understanding of the social forces that shape it. Place is the entity that brings the particularistic into focus; a sense of place sharpens our understanding of the individual and the psychological and social forces that direct her or him (Kincheloe and Pinar 1991, 1–23).

Again, anticipating post-formality, John Dewey distinguished between knowledge and habit. When a learner forms a habit, he or she has gained the ability to use an experience so that effective action can be taken into the future. Dewey argued that this was valuable because everyone will certainly be faced with such problems again and again. But habit, like Cartesian–Newtonian generalization, is not enough; it makes no allowance for change of conditions, for novelty. An individual who has learned a habit is not prepared for change and is vulnerable to confusion when faced with a new particularity, a previously unencountered problem. The habituated skill of the mechanic will desert him, Dewey wrote, "when something unexpected occurs in the running of the machine." The person, on the other hand, who understands the machine is the person who understands the conditions that allow a certain habit to work, and is capable of initiating action that will adapt the habit to new conditions. The type of teaching and the type of schools which engender such thinking are very different from technicist schools which view knowledge as something passed from teacher to student that lends itself to empirical measurability (Dewey 1916, 335–41).

DECONSTRUCTION—SEEING THE WORLD AS A TEXT TO BE READ

The post-formal thinker reads between the lines of a text, whether the text be, as with a physical scientist, physical reality or, for a teacher, the classroom and students. Thus, a text is more than printed material, as it involves any aspect of reality that contains encoded meaning to be deconstructed (Whitson 1986, 419, 425; Scholes 1982, x, 14). Deconstruction can be defined in many ways—as a method of reading, as an interpretive strategy, and as a philosophical strategy. For post-formality it involves all three of these definitions, as it views the world as full of texts to be decoded, to be explored for unintended meanings. Jacques Derrida has employed deconstruction to question the integrity of texts, meaning that he refuses to accept the authority of traditional, established interpretations of the world. He has characteristically focused on elements that others find insignificant. His purpose is not to reveal what the text really means or what the author intended, but to expose an unintended current, an unnoticed contradiction within it (Culler 1981, 14–15; Culler 1982, 85–88).

When post-formal teachers view the world as a text, deconstruction can revolutionize education. No longer can the reader be passive, a pawn of producers of texts. Whether the text is produced by an author or by tradition, "areas of blindness" are embedded within it—areas that, when exposed, reveal insight into the nature of how our consciousness is constructed. All texts are silent on certain points, and the task of deconstruction is to reveal the meanings of such silences (Scholes 1982, 13). Operating in the spirit of deconstructionism, post-formal thinkers come to realize that what is absent is often as important, or maybe more important, than what is present in a text. Employing deconstructive strategies, post-formal teachers and students gain a creative role which transcends the attempt to answer correctly questions about what the author meant. After deconstruction, we can never be so certain and comfortable with the stability of the world's meanings.

Deconstruction represents the contemporary postmodern extension of a century of attempts in art, literature, psychology, and physics to penetrate surface appearances, to transcend the tyranny of common sense, to expose the unconsciousness of a culture. Within a deconstructive framework consider what has happened to the Cartesian–Newtonian concept of reality in the twentieth century. The work of Albert Einstein, Werner Heisenberg, Sigmund Freud, and Carl Jung planted mines in the sea of modernity. Laying dormant until armed by the postmodernists, the mines were detonated by the ships of absolute truth. In the explosions certainty was destroyed. In the wake of the destruction, the postmodern critique has taught us that, like fiction, science is a text. It produces "truth" no more absolute than the truth of Mozart or Dickens—it is an inventive act.

Cartesian–Newtonian scientists, despite their protests to the contrary, have foisted their own order on chaos, just as sculptors, authors, and composers impose theirs. The order imposed always refers to particular aspects of reality and is always grounded on the observer's frame of reference. Frames of reference are historical entities that differ from period to period in the same way that a Gilbert Stuart portrait differs from a Picasso. Undeconstructed reality once had a specific (and ultimate) meaning. New problems, whether in science or education, could not be considered outside the boundaries of this modernist reality. Thus, the manner in which formal thinkers have confronted the unencountered was prescribed in advance—those expressions that did not fit the prevailing view were ignored. Thus, thinkers within the modernist boundaries could only see or hear what they were told existed. The curriculum of modernist lives (not to mention modernist schools) was standardized and set in concrete (Briggs and Peat 1984, 277–78; Rifkin 1989, 264).

Post-formal thinkers understand that reading a social text involves the development of the capacity for self-criticism of the historically constituted nature of one's consciousness. In this context, deconstruction becomes a subversive postmodern activity that allows post-formal teachers and students to read the world in new ways. Post-formality becomes not only a cognitive but a political act, as this new reading frees individuals from the official interpretations of the dominant codes. Employing such deconstructive analysis, post-formal teachers begin to see schools as arenas of contestation where power interests compete over control of representations of the world. Understanding the process of representation allows post-formal teachers to uncover the ways the consciousness of their students is constructed. Such teachers read their students as living texts with their life histories, their stories, their mysterious silences, and their enthusiastic digressions. Post-formal teachers as deconstructionists view these stories and the way they are told as texts full of signs and codes. Such critical reading abilities expand the cognitive envelope, as they break the procedural barriers of modernity. Seeing the landscape from this new cognitive altitude, post-formal thinkers come to realize the modernist artificiality that separated the domain of the cognitive from the political.

NONLINEAR HOLISM—TRANSCENDING SIMPLISTIC NOTIONS OF CAUSE–EFFECT

Post-formality challenges the hegemony of Cartesian–Newtonian logocentric formality, as it reverses the hierarchy of cause–effect, the temporality of modernist cause–effect rationality. In formalist thinking, cause always has been considered the origin, logically and temporally, prior to effect. Post-formality upsets the certainty of this easy hierarchy by asserting that effect is what causes the cause to become a cause. Such a displacement requires a significant reevaluation of common sense in the mundane, in everyday language. In this context, we begin to understand that while the formal operational orientation functions on the basis of the Cartesian assumption of linear causality, the post-formal perspective assumes reciprocity and holism (Van Hesteran 1986, 214; Kramer 1983, 92–94). Holism implies that a phenomenon can't be understood by reducing it to smaller units, only by understanding it as an integrated whole. It is the opposite of reductionism. For example, in a film the value and significance of a particular image is lost when viewed in isolation. When perceived in relationship to the rest of the film's images it is understood as part of an organic whole. The film is the totality, not a succession of discrete images (Talbot 1986, 95; Bohm and Peat 1987, 189).

This returns us again to David Bohm's conception of the implicate order. The implicate order of a film or a piece of music or a painting is constantly unfolding from an original perception in the mind of the artist. More traditional conceptions of the creative process use a machine model, implying that the whole emerges out of an accumulation of detail—the whole is built out of a set of pieces. Thus, we see an important distinction between formal and post-formal thinking: creative unfolding representing a post-formal act and the sequential accumulation of detail representing a formal act. In any creative act there is an implicate order that emerges as an expression of the creator's whole life. The formal attempt to separate this holism into parts misses the essence of the creative process. Indeed, the attempt to teach based on this formalist, linear assumption will contribute little to the cultivation of creativity (Bohm and Peat 1987, 157).

Thus, creative thinking originates in the holistic depths of an implicate order. Such an order does not operate in a Newtonian universe of absolute, linear time. Events happen simultaneously rather than in a particular order of succession. When Einstein or Mozart or Da Vinci saw whole structures of physics, music, or art in a single flash of insight, they grasped the implicate order, the overall structure of a set of relationships all at once. Cognitive theorists have spoken of simultaneity for years, but they have rarely dealt with how to accomplish it. Post-formality can be more specific as it employs Bohm's implicate order. The flash of insight where all things are considered at once involves connecting to the current of the implicate order. It is not easy to teach products of Cartesian–Newtonian consciousness construction to think in terms of the implicate order and the holism it implies. Modernist thinkers have become accustomed to thinking that formal cognition with its scientific method is the zenith of human consciousness. In the formal milieu we learn to direct our attention to partial aspects of reality and to focus on a linearity consistent with our metaphors for time. In this formalist partiality we leave the whole stream of continuity, as we separate the humanities from the sciences, work from play, love from philosophy, reading from painting, the private from the public, and the political from the cognitive.

UNCOVERING THE ROLE OF POWER IN SHAPING THE WAY THE WORLD IS REPRESENTED

The way we make sense of the world around us is not as much a product of our own ability to assimilate information as it is the result of dominant ideologies or forces of power in the larger society. This dominant power insidiously blocks our ability to critically accommodate. As it blocks our recognition of exceptions, it undermines our attempt to modify our assimilated understandings of ourselves and the world. When educational leaders use particular words, metaphors, and models when they design programs and policies, they reflect the effects of the influence of power.

When teachers unquestioningly accept these models and metaphors and employ them to ground their instructional practices, they unwittingly allow power to shape their professional lives. Power, as Foucault has argued, has served to censor and repress like a great superego; but, he continues, it also serves to produce knowledge, creating effects at the level of desire. As a censor in our thinking as practitioners, power serves to reward particular ways of seeing and acting. For example, teachers who desire to be recognized as successful learn to follow particular norms and conventions that may have little to do with teaching and learning per se. When teachers internalize these norms and conventions, they allow power to dictate their views of appropriate "ways of being" (Cherryholmes 1988, 116–17).

Post-formal thinkers, operating at a meta-analytical level, are able to understand the way power shapes their own lives. Post-formal teachers realize that in school, power often silences the very people that education purports to empower. This is the great paradox of contemporary schooling and teacher education: Educators speak of empowerment as a central goal but often ignore the way power operates to subvert the empowerment of teachers and students. Failing to ask how curricular knowledge is produced, educational analysts infrequently address which social voices are represented in the curriculum and which voices are excluded. When such questions are not asked, the attempt to move to a higher order of cognition is undermined as both teachers and students fail to explore the ways that social forces have contributed to the production of their identities, their ability to function in the world. Does it matter that we come from rich or poor homes, white or nonwhite families? These questions are not recognized as cognitive questions or questions of power; indeed, they often are not recognized at all.

Psychometricians and testing psychologists seem undaunted by questions of power in their attempt to measure the intelligence of students. For example, two students in elementary school are being tested. "Bill" comes from an upper-middle-class family, his mother a lawyer, his father a physician. "Robert" has grown up in a lower-middle-class family, his mother working in the home and his father working on an assembly line at a local bread factory. Bill's family subscribes to twenty-five magazines, two daily newspapers, and two book clubs. Reading is a way of life—there is even a library in the home. When Bill eats dinner, current events are hotly debated. Language is very important in this home, as Bill is taught standard English. By the time he is in the fourth grade, he possesses an extensive vocabulary. School is important; it is seen as a necessary vehicle to the life Bill has learned to value. The family has traveled to Europe and

Bill has an acquaintance with a wide geographical and political vocabulary. He discusses scientific issues related to his father's medical practice and political issues related to his mother's legal practice. Neighbors and playmates possess similar experiences and provide Bill linguistic exposure to areas not emphasized in his home. In addition, Bill takes music and tennis lessons which introduce him to more vocabularies, forms of knowing, and values rewarded by the school.

Robert's family provides a very different set of experiences. Neither of his parents finished high school, dropping out after the tenth grade. There are no books in his home, no newspapers, and no magazines. Robert and his parents enjoy watching television sit-coms together, later often laughing at one another's references to the plot. Robert's father enjoys working on cars and knows engines intimately. He has passed this passion along to Robert who already knows all about the parts of an engine. He and his father go to the stock car races a couple of times a year. Robert fantasizes being a race car driver like Richard Petty. Each year the family visits Robert's aunt who lives in a small town about ninety miles away. Robert possesses an excellent vocabulary in auto mechanics and knows more about stock car racing than most interested adults. He and his parents talk about cars and Robert's future as a mechanic or a driver; they don't have much to say about school. Bill knows virtually nothing about Robert's world, just as Robert knows little about Bill's world. But as we know, it is Bill's world that is positively connected to the world of the school.

Bill and Robert are tested for their intelligence and achievement. Contextual factors such as linguistic background and interest level in school-related activities are irrelevant in the testing. Bill outscores Robert on all categories of the tests and is deemed to have more innate ability than Robert. Since modernist schools emphasize the skills and knowledge measured on the tests, the tests predict quite accurately how Bill and Robert perform in school. This predictive ability works to validate the tests' accuracy, and thus few attempt to challenge their validity. What they measure, it is assumed, must be intelligence and achievement. No attention is given to the contextual factors, the fact that Bill's whole life has prepared him to do well on tests while Robert's experiences virtually guaranteed his lack of success. This is power in action, power hidden from the scientific testing community, the school, and the public. Those endowed with the power of upper-middle-class status, the cultural capital, and the familiarity with the discursive practices of institutions such as school that accompany it, start the school race (in Robert's terms) five laps ahead of those that come from less powerful backgrounds. What do the tests measure? Innate intelligence or the social context of one's background? Is Robert's *ability* to learn measured? Do the tests give us a picture of what Robert knows or what he does not know? Such questions are rarely asked.

UNCOVERING VARIOUS LEVELS OF CONNECTION BETWEEN MIND AND ECOSYSTEM—REVEALING LARGER PATTERNS OF LIFE-FORCES

As a result of a dinner conversation with Albert Einstein, Carl Jung theorized his notion of synchronicity, the meaningful connection between causally unconnected events. Jung maintained that at the center of the mind, a level of consciousness existed that connected the inner world of the psyche with the outer world of physical reality. The inner world, the psyche, Jung argued, is a mirror of the outer world—thus, the origin of his notion of the collective consciousness or deep unconsciousness as a collective mirror of the universe. Such a theory implies a level of connection between mind and reality or ecosystem that opens a realm of cognition untouched by cognitive science. Peter McLaren taps this post-formal level of connection when he writes of the realm of "impossible possibility" where teaching begins to search for connections between causally unconnected phenomenon. As we move beyond the Cartesian–Newtonian borders in the explosion of our postmodern cognitive revolution, we begin to transcend our current disposition of being-in-the-world, our acceptance of boredom, alienation, and injustice. In a way we become the science fiction writers of education, imagining what is admittedly not yet possible; but because of the fact that we can conceive of it, like sci-fi writers who imagined trips to the Moon, it becomes possible (Combs and Holland 1990, 67; McLaren forthcoming, 9).

Post-formality is life-affirming as it transcends modernism's disdain, its devaluation of the spiritual. In its postmodern deconstructive manner, post-formalism contests the "meaning of life"—that is, the actual definition of life. In the process of the deconstruction it begins the task of reshaping on multiple, possibly contradictory, levels the definition of living. Transcending Cartesian–Newtonian fragmentation, post-formal thinkers understand that life may have less to do with the parts of a living thing than with patterns of information, the "no-thing" of the *relations* between parts, the "dance" of a living process—that is, life as synchronicity. Postmodernism is the consummate boundary crosser, ignoring the No Trespassing signs posted at modernism's property line of certainty. It is possible that postmodernism and its sociocognitive expression, post-for-mality, will lead us across the boundary dividing living and nonliving. Those characteristics that modernism defined as basic to life are present in many phenomena in the universe—from subatomic particles to weather to seahorses. Because all life on the planet is so multidimensionally entwined, it is extremely hard to separate life from nonlife. Indeed, some scientists already have begun to argue that the best definition of life is the entire Earth. Seen from this perspective, modernism's lack of concern with ecological balance is suicidal on many levels (Talbot 1986, 53, 130, 146, 180).

The world around us (maybe, the world, an extension of us) is more like an idea than a machine. Post-formality's concern with etymology, pattern, process, and contextualization expresses a similar thought on the social level. Human beings cannot be simply separated from the contexts that have produced them. Post-formality assumes the role of the outlaw from this perspective, as it recognizes none of the official boundaries that define our separateness. This is the feminist concept of connectedness writ large, a holistic connectedness that opens cognitive possibilities previously imaginable only by the dreamers. As a hologram, the brain may interpret a holographic universe on a frequency beyond Newtonian time and space (Ferguson 1980, 182). The only definition left for life in the postmodern world is not some secret substance or life-force, but an information pattern. This elevates the recognition of relationship from the cognitive to the spiritual realm, for it is the relationship that is us. The same is true for consciousness, as meaning sensitive intelligence is present wherever an entity can tune into the woven mesh of cosmic information, the implicate order of the universe. Thus, from this definition, the ecosystem is conscious—the "no-thing" of perceived pattern is the very basis of life and mind. Post-formal thinkers thus become ambassadors to the domain of *the pattern*. The cognitive revolution initiated by post-formality reshapes the school in a way where life and its multidimensional connectedness rests at the center of the curriculum. Thinking is conceived as a life-sustaining process undertaken in connection with other parts of the life-force.

If knowledge and consciousness are social constructions, then so is post-formal thinking. In no way is this meant to be an essential list of what constitutes higher order thinking. I offer it simply as a heuristic, as an aid to further thinking about our investigation of thinking. Post-formal think-ing always includes an elastic clause—a rider that denies any claim of the objective existence of a post-formal way of thinking. Indeed, as a social construction, post-formal thinking is a product of a particular historical place and time. It is one perspective from a particular point in the web of reality. It is a mere starting point in the post-formal thinker's search for what constitutes sophisticated thinking.

Chapter 9

Action Research, Educational Reform, and Teacher Thinking

Research is a cognitive act, as it teaches us to think at a higher level. In this context we can appropriate the action research movement in teaching to further our critical postmodern vision of school reform and to serve as a pedagogical strategy to help teachers break out of the prison of modernist thinking. Critical action researchers equipped with an understanding of research methodologies truly operate on their own recognizance, as they stake their claim to independence from the oppressive regime of educational leadership. Action research that is critical meets five requirements: (1) It rejects positivistic notions of rationality, objectivity, and truth. Critical action research assumes that methods and issues of research are always political in character. (2) Critical action researchers are aware of their own value commitments, the value commitments of others, and the values promoted by the dominant culture. In other words, one of the main concerns of critical action research involves the exposure of the relationship between personal values and practice. (3) Critical action researchers are aware of the social construction of professional consciousness. (4) Critical action researchers attempt to uncover those aspects of the dominant social order that undermine our effort to pursue emancipatory goals. And (5) critical action research is always conceived in relation to practice—it exists to improve practice (Kincheloe 1991, 19–20).

ACTION RESEARCH AND DEMOCRATIC THINKING

With these criteria in mind, critical action research is the consummate democratic act, as it allows teachers to help determine the conditions of their own work. Critical action research facilitates the attempt of teachers to organize themselves into communities of researchers dedicated to emancipatory experiences for themselves and their students. When teachers unite with students and community members in the attempt to ask serious questions about what is taught, how it is taught, and what should constitute the goals of a school, not only is critical self-reflection promoted but group decision making also becomes a reality (Carr and Kemmis 1986, 221–23; Giroux and Aronowitz 1985, 81).

For example, when students, community members, and teachers join together in a research project to discover locations in the community where students could come to learn in ways that combined vocational skills, with personal empowerment, and the cultivation of post-formal thinking, a democratic dialogue is created. In the course of such a dialogue not only would democratic imperatives be strengthened but social imaginations also would be extended by the analytical conversation it would elicit. Students, community members, and teachers would all have to think about their respective roles in the selection process, while at the same time engaging in a dialogue about the goals of schooling and the nature of thinking. Wise teachers in this process could elicit from adult workers in the community a self-examination concerning what aspects of their jobs require post-formal thinking and what aspects do not. Induced to think about their own thinking in relation to its applicability to the selection of sights, community members would be able to make significant contributions to the ways that post-formal thinking could be cultivated among students. The democratic ties and the cognitive advances that could be generated by this simple example of action research point to the power of the form.

Critical action research is not only a catalyst for post-formal thinking and democratic action, but it is also an antidote to perception of teachers as low-level, blue-collar workers. Research and theory building are not the domain of teachers in the modernist teaching workplace. Experts will take care of such concerns; teachers should stick to the execution of their prescribed tasks. Such modernist hierarchical elitism precludes teacher-directed research and democratization of the workplace, as it reinforces authoritarian status distinctions that demean the role of teachers and perpetuate public perceptions of incompetence (Altrichter and Posch 1989, 25). Critical action research is incompatible with the modernist notion of vanguardism—the idea that institutions change only when small cabals of leaders force their will on the peons, leading them to a higher ground. Such an antidemocratic notion fails to allow for teacher-led movements that reject the top-down view of reform that is tacitly embedded in the right-wing educational reforms of recent years (Agger 1991, 132). Educational reform of a critical democratic variety will work only when promoted and theoretically understood by teachers themselves (Floden and Klinzing 1990, 16).

Paulo Freire, as we would expect, is very helpful in our consideration of action research and democratic thinking. Taking our cue from Freire's conception of inquiry, action research becomes not only a stimulus to democratic thinking but a powerful teaching tool as well. Freire engages his students as partners in his research activities, immersing himself in their perceptions of themselves and the world around them and at the same time encouraging them to think about their own thinking. Everyone joins in the investigation, learning to criticize, to see more clearly, to think at a higher level, to recognize the way their consciousness is socially constructed. When teachers put Freire's methods to work in their own classrooms, they teach students the research techniques that they have learned. Students are taught such fieldwork skills as observing, interviewing, picture taking, videoing, tape-recording, note taking and life-history collecting. Such activities provide an opportune context for teachers to engage students in meta-analytical epistemological analysis—the heart and soul of the movement to post-formality. Freire's lessons in action research are subversive; his invitation to students and those being examined to take part in the conceptualization, criticism, and reconceptualization of research can be correctly construed as a direct challenge to the modernist cult of the expert. At the same time, his insights provide critical postmodern teachers employing action research with a sense of direction, a consciousness that transforms the notion of research from a data-gathering strategy into a post-formal, consciousness-raising, transformative pedagogical technique (Freire 1972, 135–37).

Such critical orientations to research may reverse the usual flow of communications in the teaching workplace—teachers may come to speak with a more authoritative voice to their supervisors. Indeed, modernist pedagogies that reduce teaching to a technical act of delivering the information certified by experts are subverted by critical postmodern teaching grounded on action research. When critical action researchers develop a system of meaning that helps them design research, select research methods, interpret their research, and act on the basis of their research, their way of seeing, their way of constructing their professional self-identity, is forever changed. Never able to claim neutrality, critical action research can never avoid challenging the undemocratic, scientifically managed modernist workplace of teaching. Teachers as critical researchers find it hard not to climb into the ring to join the fight to reclaim knowledge and the schools in a way that exposes the political and cognitive consequences of modernist forms of school management and teaching. Action research is a force of considerable influence in the struggle to salvage the dignity of teaching from the ravages of narrow accountability (Bogdan and Biklen 1982, 209–10; Oldroyd and Tiller 1987, 18; Kroath 1989, 61–68; Longstreet 1982, 149; Torney-Purta 1985, 74).

As action research fights techno-teaching and procedural thinking, it seeks unity with critical democratic groups outside the school. Using their research skills to identify subjugated knowledges in the local community, teachers as researchers become cultural workers who develop unique post-formal pockets of people who come to think about cognition as a political activity. Once women, for example, come to understand that their connected ways of thinking have been socially devalued and connect their own personal stories to this larger concept, they become allies in the critical postmodern project to reconceptualize the purpose of the schools. Understanding that their insecurities regarding their own intellectual abilities often find their origin in the politically validated androcentric discourse on cognition, women are empowered to redefine themselves and the prevailing perceptions of what constitutes sophisticated thinking. These are the individuals with whom critical action researchers seek solidarity. Such teachers find that their connections with such groups provide two-way benefits: (1) Not only do the teachers awaken dormant curiosities and insights of individuals in some way connected to subjugated knowledges, but (2) such individuals also induce teachers to ask questions of their own practices previously unconsidered. A public democratic dialogue initiates dramatic social and cognitive changes.

CRITICAL ACTION RESEARCH AND THE STRUGGLE FOR TEACHER EMPOWERMENT

Educational reform of any stripe will not work unless teachers are empowered. In our democratic reforms, teachers have to embody critical postmodernism and post-formal thinking if such ideas stand a chance of success. Action research is an empty idea, another educational triviality unless teachers make it a part of their lives, their belief systems. This is why top-down educational reforms fail—you can no more mandate critical reform without teacher consent than you can stop Tammy Faye Bakker from crying on television. The right-wing reforms of the Reagan–Bush era cannot work for the simple reason that they can never garner wide-scale teacher consent. Any body of reform predicated on a view of teachers as deskilled functionaries who carry out the orders of the superiors cannot succeed. Indeed, the view of cognition implicit in many of the right-wing prescriptions is consistent with the larger deskilling impulse common in proposals grounded on scientific management schemes.

Student and teacher higher order thinking (what we have termed critical critical thinking) is viewed as a frightening possibility by technicist reformers. The social and educational climate created by Reaganism in the 1980s, extends into the 1990s, viewing the attempt to expand conscious-ness or think at a higher level as a malevolent act—indeed, sometimes a satanic act. Teachers all over North America who have fostered thinking programs often have been the objects of derision by the same fundamental-ist groups that have supported Reagan–Bush political and educational goals. If thinking is of a variety that could possibly shed unfavorable light on accepted mores, it is not to be supported by the conservative reformers.

Excitement over the life of the mind, the attempt to extend our notion of thinking is the lifeblood of schools. Such enthusiasm can generate interest among students, prevent the burnout of teachers, and engage parents and community members in the world of education. Ideas such as action research that have the capacity to latch on to and amplify excitement about thinking are the very innovations that right-wing reformers have attempted to squash. Those who seek to narrow human possibility, under-mine the quest for social justice, and impede the progress of the cognitive revolution need to be held morally accountable. Such is the political task of empowered, reflective teachers buoyed by a critical system of meaning. As they connect pedagogical theory and teaching practice to larger social issues, they gain the ability to fight for reforms that are grounded on an appreciation of the importance of the teacher role. When teaching is viewed as an important position, teachers will be allowed to work in conditions where they have time to be researchers, to engage in critical reflection, to work in the communities that surround their schools (Giroux and McLaren 1989, xix, xxiii).

ACTION RESEARCH AS AN OPPOSITIONAL ACTIVITY

Decades ago John Dewey wrote about the kind of research that con-sciously challenged the technicist desire for certainty. Critical action research fits Dewey's conception, as it undercuts the androcentric comfort with taken-for-granted sociocultural patterns. In a dominant culture that has not valued self-reflection on the part of its teacher professionals, action research becomes an oppositional activity as it pushes professionals in a variety of fields to reconsider their assumptions (Greene 1988, 126). Peter

McLaren argues that postmodern forms of inquiry do not claim truth in a way that is unaware of the metaphors that guide their meaning. Such research forms do not conceive knowledge as something to be discovered. Information produced by postmodern inquiry, McLaren continues, is a self-conscious social text produced by a plethora of mutually informing contexts (McLaren 1992, 1, 6). Students in teacher education programs may have difficulty understanding such oppositional notions of truth, having been schooled for fifteen or more years within the modernist parameters of certainty. In addition, the oppositional ambience of critical action research may sit uneasily with teacher education students whose main concerns revolve around fitting into the schools in which they are planning to student-teach.

Most teacher education students hold a very traditional view of the research act. Susan Noffke and Marie Brennan report that when their teacher education students were assigned action research projects, designs tended to revert back to more traditional research formats (Noffke and Brennan 1988, 5; Noffke and Brennan 1991, 189–90). Research is rarely a component in undergraduate teacher education programs. When it is included at the master's level, research typically has involved the study of controlled experimental design with statistical analysis. Teachers report great dissatisfaction with such experiences, frequently referring to their inability to make use of such coursework in their everyday teaching (Ross 1984, 114). If research is a cognitive activity, then the research experience of teacher education students must be a practical exercise that extends the potential teacher's ability to see, to hear, and to act in the interests of his or her students. Teacher education students must come to understand in the process why at this historical juncture action research ends up as an oppositional activity, as it exposes the authoritarian tyranny of many teaching workplaces.

If critical action researchers as post-formal agents encourage epistemological analysis and professional self-reflection on the nature of the construction of their consciousness, then such teachers cannot escape the adoption of a political role. Indeed, technicists will argue that such teacher roles politicize the schools. Their argument that the schools should remain politically neutral reflects the popular naiveté that fails to identify dominant definitions of neutrality as problematic. The role of the teacher as a neutral transmitter of prearranged facts is not understood as a politicized role. If schools are to become places that promote teacher and student empowerment, then the notion of what constitutes politicization will have to be reconceptualized. Battle with texts as a form of research, Paulo Freire and Ira Shor exhort teachers. Resist the demand of the official curriculum for deference to texts, they argue in line with their larger critically grounded political vision. Can it be argued that capitulation to textual authority constitutes a political neutrality (Shor and Freire 1987, 8–9, 145, 184)?

In their refusal to accept the authority of texts, the dictates of the official curriculum, post-formal action researchers come to understand that they and their students are knowledge producers. This is one of the hardest lessons for teacher education students to learn, for most of their public school and university experience contradicts the concept. Research has been defined for them as finding information produced by experts. Many college students have become quite comfortable with the passive student role by the time they enter teacher education programs. They must only finish their assignments on time and pass exams that call on low-level cognitive abilities to memorize factual data. Such students have been taught to operate in the first three levels of William Perry's conceptualization of adult cognition discussed in Chapter 7. For those who have been influenced by such instruction, knowledge, at the least, is received—that is, it consists of isolated bits and pieces to be given back to instructors on tests; at the most, knowledge is something out there to be discovered via the application of proper procedures. Imagine students' cognitive and epistemological discomfort when confronted with the task of learning to become action researchers, producers of knowledge. Before such students are immersed in such research activity, they must be conversant with the cognitive, political, and epistemological issues that surround critical teacher research.

Once they are cognizant of such issues and experienced in action research, student teachers' and practicing teachers' professional lives are changed forever. As knowledge producers, such teachers begin to construct curricula around student experience, promoting student understanding of the social, economic, and cultural forces that have shaped their lives. Students are taught ethnographic, semiotic, phenomenological, and historiographical forms of inquiry, in the process learning to deconstruct the ideological forces that shape their lives. In such a context, they explore their place in the social hierarchy of their peer group, their romantic relationships, their vocational aspirations, their relationships with teachers, and their definitions of success. Teacher understanding of why critical action research is positioned as an oppositional activity deepens, as they step back from the world as they have been conditioned to see it. In the process, they uncover the constructing forces—linguistic codes, cultural signs, power-driven representations, and embedded ideologies. Here they are learning to research, to teach, and to think. Post-formal teachers as critical action researchers produce knowledge, that is, they remake their professional lives, they rename their worlds (Noffke and Brennan 1991, 189–90; Adler 1991, 79; Slaughter 1989, 264; Schon 1987, 36).

ACTION RESEARCH IS THE LOGICAL EDUCATIONAL EXTENSION OF CRITICAL THEORY

What else could critical postmodern educators do than teach prospective teachers to engage in critical action research? Since critical theory is grounded on a recognition of the existence of oppression, it stands to reason that the forces of this oppression have to be identified. Action research serves as a perfect vehicle for such a search. Without this critical recognition of domination and oppression, action researchers will simply consider the school site as value-neutral and their role as disinterested, dispassionate observers. Change in this context is irrelevant—and according to Cartesian–Newtonian perspectives on research, this is the way it should be. Researchers are to maintain an uncommitted view toward the actions they encounter. In a world of oppression, critical theorists argue, ethical behavior demands that such dispassion be confronted (Giroux and McLaren 1991, 70; Codd 1984, 10–11).

Whenever we dispense with values, political considerations, or historical context, our attempt to understand the situation we are researching is weakened. Our appreciation of an educational situation is contingent on the context within which we encountered and the theoretical frames we brought with us to the observation. Cartesian–Newtonian modernism has told us that our research must serve no specific cause, but critical postmodernism has caused us to realize that every historical period produces rules that dictate what nonpartisanship entails. In other words, different rules privilege different causes. Thus, what we "see" as researchers is shaped by particular world views, values, political perspectives, conceptions of race, class, and gender relations, definitions of intelligence, and so on. Research, thus, can never be nonpartisan for we must choose the rules that guide us as researchers; critical theory's exposé of the hidden ideological assumptions within educational research marked the end of our innocence (Aronowitz 1983, 60; Elliott 1989, 214).

To be critical is to assume that humans are active agents whose reflective self-analysis, whose knowledge of the world leads to action. Action research is the logical extension of critical theory in that it provides the apparatus for the human species to look at itself. Critical action research that is aware of postmodern perspectives on the production of subjectivity, the context of hyperreality, and post-Jaynesian connected consciousness can contribute to the sociocognitive emancipation of men and women. Such a sociocognitive emancipation is the first step in our cognitive revolution, our post-formal effort to see the world and ourselves from new angles. Based on a democratic dialogue, an awareness of historical moment, and a passionate commitment to the voice of the oppressed, the post-formal insurrection redefines research, in the process producing a knowledge between the cracks, information previously swept under the rug.

In schools the firsthand, up-close perspectives of teachers previously relegated to a lesser significance is valued by action research as kinetic knowledge—that is, knowledge with the potential to wreak havoc. This information gained through action research's emphasis on observation and reflection promotes democratic change grounded on the understanding of participants. In the modernist framework of scientific management such an emphasis constitutes a radical change of approach (Codd 1984, 27–28; Young 1990, 149, 158). Action that reflective individuals take to correct the social and individual pathologies uncovered by teachers can be negotiated after the action research process is completed. The critical core of critical action research involves its participatory and communally discursive structure and the cycle of action and reflection it initiates. Such a cycle does not produce a set of rules and precise regulations for the action it promotes. Critical action research provides a framework of principles around which action can be discussed rather than a set of procedures. Teachers who engage in critical action research are never certain of the exact path of action they will take as a result of their inquiry (Young 1990, 158; Popkewitz 1981, 15–16).

A central part of this action involves the redefinition of knowledge. There are many dimensions to this redefining process, but one of the most important involves democratizing access to knowledge in schools and society. If knowledge is a form of cultural capital, then lack of access to it spells major problems for those on the margins of the culture of knowledge. Foucault has convinced us that knowledge is power; and though it is a hard pill for advocates of teacher empowerment to swallow, part of the reason that the teaching corps is delegated to the margins is that too many of them are ill-educated in colleges and teacher education programs. Teachers with weak academic, theoretical, and pedagogical backgrounds must defer to the judgments of educational leaders, the certified experts. The culture of technicist teacher education has tacitly instructed teachers across the generations to undervalue the domain of theory while avoiding questions of the ideological, psychological, and pedagogical assumptions underlying their practice. The power that comes from such understandings is a prerequisite for the critical attempt to redefine knowledge. Teachers must understand the social and political factors that contribute to knowledge production—indeed, the gaining of such an awareness should be a central concern of critical action research (May and Zimpher 1986, 94–95; Porter 1988, 508; Maeroff 1988, 508; Tripp 1988, 19; Giroux 1992, 98–99, 238).

Critical knowledge production begins when action researchers illuminate the taken-for-granted. Dewey focused our attention on such a process when he argued that teachers should operate on the basis of a *reflective action* that disembeds moral, ethical, and political issues from mundane thinking and practice. As action researchers maintain such a perspective on their everyday experience, they are able to explore the tacit forces that have encoded their own lives and their students' lives. In a sense, critical action researchers relearn the way they have come to view the world around them; indeed, they awaken from the modernist dream with its unexamined landscape of knowledge and unimaginative consciousness construction. Once awake, critical teachers as researchers begin to see schools as human creations with meanings and possibilities lurking beneath the surface appearances. Their task becomes the interpretation of schools, not just the chronicling of surface characteristics devoid of context (Hultgren 1987, 28; May and Zimpher 1986, 94; Lesko 1988, 147).

What do particular forms of teacher evaluation tell us about the purposes and values of my school, teacher researchers ask. Looking below the surface of standardized-test-driven, behavioral assessment models of teacher evaluation, action researchers begin to uncover patterns of technicalization that erase teacher input into the determination of their own professional lives. Empowered with such knowledge, teachers gain the language to argue a case for their involvement in school policy. When principals and supervisors, for example, argue that teacher evaluation instruments necessitate particular forms of assessment, teachers will be able to point out that embedded within such instruments is an entire set of political, epistemological, cognitive, and pedagogical assumptions. Thus, teachers will enter into a sophisticated, theoretically grounded negotiation with administrators about the terms of their evaluations, the terms of their professional lives.

Obviously, critical theory–based action research attempts not simply to understand or describe the world of practice but to change it. Proponents of such inquiry hope teacher education students will learn to use action research in a way that will empower them to shape schools in accordance with well-analyzed moral, ethical, and political principles. Teachers who enter schools with such an ability are ready to make a cognitive leap; indeed, the stage has been set for movement to the realm of post-formal practitioner thinking. As critical action researchers endowed with a vision of what could be and a mechanism for uncovering what is, these teachers are able to see the sociopolitical contradictions of schools in a concrete and obvious manner. Such recognitions force teachers to think about their own thinking, as they begin to understand how these sociopolitical distortions have tacitly worked to shape their world views and their self-images. With a deeper appreciation of such processes, practitioners recognize the insidious ways power operates to create oppressive conditions for some groups and privilege for others. Thus, critical teacher research opens new ways of knowing that transcend formal analysis (May and Zimpher 1986, 94–95; Hultgren 1987, 27–30).

Such teachers as researchers cannot help but turn to biographical and autobiographical analysis in their inquiry. Aware of past descriptions of higher order thinking, such teachers would be alert to connections between biography and cognition. In other words, teachers in this situation become researchers of themselves, researchers of the formation of their own cognitive structures. Such inquiry produces a meta-awareness of an omnipresent feature of the role of critical postmodern teachers: They are always in the process of being changed and changing, of being analyzed and analyzing, of being constructed and constructing, of learning and teaching, of disembedding and connecting. The purpose of critical action research, thus, is not to produce data and better theories about education— it is to produce a metatheoretical cognition that is supported by reflection and grounded in sociohistorical context (Carr and Kemmis 1986, 39, 56, 123; May and Zimpher 1986, 94).

THE UNCRITICAL APPROPRIATION OF
TEACHER RESEARCH

Much of what comes under the heading of action research in the 1990s has not escaped the confines of Cartesian–Newtonian modernism, much is not conversant with the democratic dimensions of the research act. Many educational projects have viewed action researchers as implementors of theoretical strategies devised by researcher experts or administrators. The role of the teacher researchers is to test how well particular strategies work through analysis of particular techniques in their own classrooms. Such projects in the name of teacher empowerment promote a restricted view of the role of teachers. Teachers again take orders from superiors, executing, not conceptualizing, educational purpose and curriculum design

(Connelly and Ben-Peretz 1980, 98–100). Advocates of action research who support this teacher-as-implementor approach exhibit ideological naiveté. They are unable to recognize that the act of selecting problems for teachers to research is an ideological act, an act that trivializes the role of teacher. When hierarchical superiors select problems for teacher researchers to explore, they negate the critical dimension of action research.

Such perspectives toward action research illustrate the ideological naiveté of the educational establishment. Calls for action research within positivistic frameworks, for example, are self-contradictory, in that teacher research is grounded on an interactive and communicative (i.e., democratic) appreciation of the research process (Young 1990, 149). In other words, the uncritical appropriations of action research fail to understand the discursive construction of research traditions. Such "neutral" advocates incorrectly assume that the researcher speaks from a transhistorical and prediscursive locale outside of the assumptions of modernist social science. It is nonpolitical, such advocates contend, or at least it should be. When critical advocates such as Peter McLaren call for a postmodern exposé of the tacit political dimensions of modernist research methodologies, neutral proponents of action research claim politicization (McLaren 1992, 3–4). They don't recognize the social construction of consciousness or the ideological baggage of everyday language.

When the critical dimensions of teacher research are removed, action research can become a trivial enterprise. Uncritical educational action research seeks direct applications of information accumulated from inquiry to be applied to specific classroom situations—a cookbook style of formal thinking is encouraged, characterized by recipe-following teachers. Such thinking does not allow for a post-formal metaepistemological analysis, for complex reconceptualizations of knowledge. As a result, it fails to understand the ambiguities and the ideological structures of the classroom. In this context, teachers retreat to cause–effect analysis, failing to move to the post-formal recognition of the interactive complexity of a classroom. The point that educational problems are better understood when considered in a relational way that transcends simple linearity is lost. Thus, teacher research becomes a protector of the status quo, as teachers, like their administrators and supervisors, fail to reveal the ways that the educational bureaucracy and the assumptions that support it constrain one's ability to devise new and more emancipatory understandings of how schools work (Orteza Y Miranda 1988, 31; McKernan 1988, 154–57).

The cognitive illness thus strangles the reform impulse of action research. As its democratic edge is blunted, it becomes a popular grass-roots movement that can be supported by the power hierarchy—it does not threaten, nor is it threatened. Asking trivial questions devised by administrators, the movement presents no democratic challenge and offers no transformative vision of educational purpose, as it ignores the enfolded structures of schooling and prevailing views of knowledge. Teachers do not gain access to experiences that shake their cognitive foundations, inducing them to critically accommodate information gleaned from their research. They are deemed to be blue-collar couriers, that is, information deliverers; their status in the workplace is delegated accordingly (Ruddick 1989, 9; Ponzio 1985, 39–43). Uncritical action research fails to recognize the way the power hierarchy of the school holds the ability to cripple democratic inquiry by removing control of action research from the teachers engaged in it. Indeed, critical inquiry must always be self-directed and must always be free to subject its findings to some form of interpretation, to critical analysis. Like folk proverbs about the weather, critical analysis is dangerous in its unpredictability—it sometimes criticizes those who sense that they should be beyond reproach.

CRITICAL ACTION RESEARCHERS KNOW THERE IS NO VALUE-NEUTRAL WAY OF SEEING

How do action researchers come to understand the diversity, the hidden dimensions, the lived worlds of the silenced, the textured richness of education? One of the first things such researchers have to learn is the way ideology blinds them to particular dimensions of the lived world of schools. Ideology refers to the values, beliefs, ethical and moral judgments, their production and expression, and their influence on the way we assign meaning to the experiences of our everyday life. No aspect of schooling is ideologically innocent; no thoughts, theories, or pedagogies are completely autonomous. Ideas, perspectives, research orientations, and the actions that come out of them are always connected to power and value interests. It is extremely difficult to understand ideological forces, their educational effects, and their influence on all researchers. Cartesian–Newtonian researchers find it particularly difficult to understand the effects of ideology—not that they are really that interested. They have often attempted to quantitatively measure ambiguous educational processes. The ideological innocence that results supports the power relations of the status quo, the mythology of classlessness, the equality of opportunity, the political neutrality of school, and the creed of financial success as a direct consequence of an individual's initiative. When Cartesian–Newtonian forms of research focus on educational outcomes, the importance of innate cognitive processes is exaggerated and their role in learning is decontextualized. This decontextualization, this separation of cognitive processes from situations that shape them and grant them meaning paints a simpleminded picture of educational purpose, cognitive development, and the actual effect of schools on the lives of its students and teachers (Shapiro 1982, 157; McLaren 1989, ix, 176; Giroux 1983, 143–45).

Caught in the Cartesian–Newtonian research trap that tends to view research as outcome measurement, technicist researchers employ measurable but often trivial criteria to assess teacher effectiveness, assign students to curriculum tracks, and decide which schools receive excellence awards. As a result, we sometimes reward the most conventional teachers, assign creative students to nonacademic curricula, and decorate schools that possess a large percentage of upper-middle-class students. In these situations, research strategies are employed that examine only outcomes, not processes. The outcomes that were measured only partially reflect the life, the texture, the complexity, and the quality of the process: What is good teaching?; what makes a good student?; what does a good school do (Richards 1988, 496; Elliott 1989, 4)? Examining only outcomes we gain a very limited view of the educational process. Our capacity to conceptualize purpose, to understand the way our educational goals are socially constructed, is severely limited. We are not observing from an objective vantage point, for we equate talent with the outcomes we have chosen to measure. Indeed, our view of ability or intelligence becomes exclusive, as it regards only previously defined skills as worthwhile. For example, adult accomplishments were found to be unrelated to test scores, suggesting that there may be many kinds of talent related to later success that, unmeasured by modernistic research interests and thus unaddressed by schools, could be nurtured in educational situations (Munday and Davis 1974, i; Duke 1985, 674).

Action research conceived within a critical postmodern system of meaning turns inquiry into a higher order cognitive activity. Teacher researchers must confront not only what they see but *why* they see what they see. Post-formal researchers want to "see" the classroom as opposed to just "looking" at it for the purpose of fitting it into categories. When we learn why we see what we see, we are thinking about thinking, analyzing the forces that shape our consciousness, placing what we perceive in a meaningful context. We come to learn that all seeing is selective, filtered by the ways that power has constructed our subjectivity. We learn that we see from particular vantage points in the web of reality, coming to realize that there is no value-neutral way of perceiving. The post-formal observer uses this meta-awareness in combination with his or her critical system of meaning to tease out what is significant about an observation. This recognition of significance emerges from a larger post-formal appreciation of context, an understanding of the history, philosophy, and sociology of education. For example, an observation might be significant in that it illustrates the contemporary embodiment of the postindustrialization purpose of schooling as a method of social classification, the influence of positivism in shaping the way student evaluation is conducted, or the power of androcentrism to shape the definition of a "successful" school administrator.

Teachers as researchers, as passionate learners, as committed observers ask themselves after their inquiry: Are we empowered to improve the educational process as a result of our new ways of seeing?; can we transcend the clichés and shallow talk of so much educational discourse and move in the direction of authenticity?; does our action research equip us, in the spirit of anticipatory accommodation, to apply insight gained from one context to another? The purposes of critical action research are multidimensional and praxeological, as it attempts to engender understanding and promote transformative action on three levels simultaneously: the issue being researched, the research process itself, and the researcher (Koetting 1988, 7–10; Donmoyer 1987, 358–59; Reinharz 1979, 368). Critical action research as praxis (as action informed by theoretical understandings) encourages those it examines to break out of the culture of silence and reshape their consciousnesses. For example, empowered students and parents from a subjugated socioeconomic class or racial culture who were able to reconstruct a view of intelligence that was more sensitive to the talents that they already possessed could help reform both curricula and modes of evaluation that typically valued only dominant forms of intelligence. Indeed, critical action research becomes pedagogical, as it teaches both researcher and researched empowerment. Teachers as researchers through their understandings empower both themselves as professional agents in schools and their students and others, as they expose ideological restrictions on their own lives and the lived experience of others.

A SEMIOTICS OF INTROSPECTION—SEEING WHAT'S NOT THERE

Critical action research awakens teacher consciousness. John Dewey argued that we only become conscious when the obvious is extended by an understanding of what is absent in fact (Greene 1988, 125). This tacit dimension is present only in the potential of our imagination, only in the possibility of interpretation. Dewey peeked through the modernist veil, through the delirium of the cognitive illness and its propensity to perceive only the literalness of the visual. The illness is magnified by hyperreality and its media saturation. In this context individuals are unable, as Peter McLaren writes, "to penetrate beyond the media-bloated surface of things" (McLaren 1991a, 145). In their existence beyond the realm of the surface, concepts such as social context and consciousness construction are ignored as abstractions irrelevant to the world of living things. Our power as individuals, professionals, and members of social groups will be dramatically affected by our cognitive ability to see beyond the surface. Thus, the nature of our cognition is again exposed as a political act. When we refuse to take behaviors at face value, we demand analysis of consciousness construction, of intentionality, and of unreflective enactment of preexisting social patterns (Bowers and Flinders 1990, 10).

Action research conceived within a critical postmodern system of meaning becomes a post-formal effort to recognize profound meaning in the trivial. Drawing upon semiotics this post-formal research discovers new insights in unexpected places. Schools are diamond mines for semiological study, for they abound in codes and signs, in conventions that call for unique insight. The way teachers, students, and administrators dress; pupils' language when speaking to teachers as compared to conversations with classmates; graffiti in a middle school restroom; systems of rules of behavior; the use of bells in schools; memos sent to parents; and the nature of the local community's conversation about school athletics are only a few of the many school topics which semioticians could study. Teachers as researchers of the profound in the mundane begin to move beyond traditional questions of teaching into the uncharted territory of inquiries involving the question, who are we becoming as a result of this school experience (Whitson 1986, 418; Britzman 1991, 241)?

The brilliance of semiotics is that it makes the given an object of thought, of critical focus. Semiotics refuses the shallowness of lived experience, as it searches for ways of seeing that describe the invisible, the empty spaces of the picture. Viewed from this perspective of the post-formal inquirer, a gifted program involves far more than a set of enrichment activities for the smarter children. Levels of obscured assumptions begin to jump out of such programs when the light of grounded critique is shown upon them—assumptions unseen by even those making them. Thus, post-formal action research moves from the glorification of the novel to the analysis of the assumed. In this context language transcends its role as conduit for information. Post-formal analysts view the relationship between speaker and listener or writer and reader to be based on constant interpretation in the context of the semiotic matrices brought to the act of communication by all participants. Thus, we are faced with the realization that communication becomes not a matter of extracting meaning from communiques but of constituting meaning based on the cultural context, values, and social identities of those involved (Greene 1988, 122–24; Britzman 1991, 241; Bowers and Flinders 1990, 11).

When teachers turn such interpretative strategies upon their own practice, they engage in a semiotic of introspection. As teacher researchers analyze their actions with attention to ritual, metaphor, and questioning strategies, they begin to uncover hidden dimensions of their belief structures, their familiar cognitive strategies, their assumptions about students, and their attitudes toward the "proper" deportment of a teacher (Courteney 1988, 53–55). No longer can these teachers hide in the shelter of the Cartesian–Newtonian objectivism which shields the self from the deeply personal issues that saturate all educational acts. Post-formal teacher researchers cannot view themselves as transhistorical beings—they need to understand their place in the web from which they see reality. Contextualized in this way, the schemata, the values, the belief structures that defy recognition as they fade into the familiarity of our consciousness are highlighted as they are dyed by the ink of semiotics. Historical contextualization of self in this situation utilizes the insight of difference, as we finally begin to see ourselves when we are placed against a social backdrop of values and ways of perceiving that are unfamiliar.

ACTION RESEARCH AS THE LOGICAL EXTENSION OF CRITICAL CONSTRUCTIVISM

Critical constructivism assumes that consciousness is shaped by social forces with the dynamics of power playing an exaggerated role in the process. Critical education, critical constructivists argue, involves gaining an awareness of this procedure. When this awareness is combined with an appreciation of a critical system of meaning then the student is empowered to begin the reconstruction of his or her consciousness in a manner consistent with self-determined moral, ethical, and political projects. Action research viewed in this context is simply a logical extension of the concerns and assumptions of critical constructivism. Since critical constructivism is more concerned with what learning experiences mean to students (or for that matter to teachers), then critical action research provides a vehicle for uncovering and analyzing such meanings. As critical researchers discover students' perspectives and the ways they make sense of their educational experiences, they can begin to make pedagogical decisions based on such knowledge (Codd 1984, 23). Thus, curriculum can be renegotiated and subsequent teaching can be adjusted to meet the needs of various students.

ACTION RESEARCH AS A COGNITIVE ACT

When former doctoral students discuss their graduate programs, those who did more than a plug-in-the-data, procedural empirical study chosen by their dissertation director will often testify that the most valuable aspect of their program involved their dissertation. *The experience taught me to write, to use the library, to gather information, to make an argument, and to think*, they will say. When a student has a voice in the negotiation of the form a research project takes, the methodology of inquiry moves beyond a set of predetermined procedures and the research becomes a valuable cognitive experience. Few activities can move teacher education students and practicing teachers to new cognitive vistas as effectively as action research. The following is a tentative list of cognitive benefits to be accrued from participation in action research. Critical action research:

1. *Moves us to the critical realm of knowledge production, as it induces us to organize information, to interpret.* As active inquirers we no longer see ourselves as the passive receivers of expert produced knowledge. We become responsible agents who engage in our own interpretations of the world around us, of our classrooms. Thus, there is a power shift in this situation that democratizes the process of naming the world. Action researchers are "uppity," as they maintain that their interpretations are worthwhile. Such a perspective changes our view of how we approach knowledge—indeed, it changes the way we approach knowing in the first place.

2. *Focuses our attention on thinking about our own thinking, as we explore our own consciousness construction, our self-production.* Action research induces us to take seriously the ways that we are moved to see the world in the way that we do. As we become more familiar with the concerns of critical action research, we become more conversant with who we are. The genesis of the images we adopt of what it means to be an educational professional are interrogated for the ways that they reflect representations of conventionality and their manifestations of power. Such questioning grants us a higher perspective on who we are—a perspective that moves us in a post-formal direction.

3. *Creates an analytical orientation toward our work.* Simply put, we develop a reflective attitude toward our professional lives that motivates us to contextualize events that take place. We come to see events in ways that grant them meaning not readily apparent when they are viewed in isolation. In a post-formal context we begin to uncover the deep structures, the implicate order that connects events.

4. *Helps us learn to teach ourselves.* One of the key elements of a critical postmodern pedagogy is that it empowers students to teach themselves. Few activities better prepare one for such a task than an ability to conduct research. An individual who is able to conduct research not only has access to primary and secondary information sources, but is able to do for himself or herself what others rely on experts to accomplish for them.

5. *Improves our ability to engage in anticipatory accommodation.* Cartesian–Newtonian researchers assume that generalizations derived from one classroom are valid in all classrooms with that same population. In Chapter 6 we discussed anticipatory accommodation, the extension of critical accommodation which involves our ability to anticipate what we might encounter in similar situations and what strategies might work to bring about desired outcomes. In other words, when we engage in anticipatory accommodation, we learn from our knowledge of a variety of comparable contexts. Action research enhances our ability to make such accommodations by providing us with detailed pictures, interpretive understandings of the similarities and differences of the various contexts. Our ability to think as post-formal practitioners is significantly improved.

6. *Cultivates empathy with students and colleagues.* As a phenomenological act, critical action research helps us explore the consciousness of those we encounter. Our ability to understand the joys and pains, the dreams and motivations of our students and colleagues is significantly enhanced. Thus, critical action research becomes a vehicle for connected consciousness, a central form of knowing in a critical constructivist education.

7. *Negates reliance on procedural thinking.* Understanding the techniques and assumptions of critical action research releases us from the Cartesian–Newtonian rules for conducting inquiry. Thus, we gain a methodological freedom from rigid procedure, a freedom that allows us the right to change our strategies in the face of new circumstances. Not only do we gain a freedom to conduct inquiry in ways contingent on context, but we also are released from procedural definitions of cognition. When the need is perceived, teachers as researchers can embrace cognitive strategies more compatible with the situation encountered.

8. *Makes the attempt to improve thinking by making it just another aspect of everyday existence.* Action research becomes a way of life, a way of approaching the world. In line with higher orders of cognition, those who embrace action research view answers as tentative—findings are always in the process. Thus, our tendency to make up our minds and ignore the evidence is reduced; indeed, because there is always further evidence to be considered, we are less likely to resort to stereotyping and overgeneralization. Such cognitive orientations are essential to the democratic project, to the effort to make democracy work.

Chapter 10

Reframing the Debate about Teacher Education

Educational analysts have argued that around four separate paradigms of teacher education can be identified in colleges of education in the late twentieth century: (1) behavioristic, (2) personalistic, (3) traditional-craft, and (4) inquiry-oriented. Kenneth Zeichner contends that the most powerful orientation is the behavioristic perspective which is grounded upon a Cartesian–Newtonian scientism and a behavioral psychology. In this behavioristic professional education prospective, teachers learn knowledge, skills, and competencies that are thought to be the most relevant to the expert-produced definitions of good teaching. The criteria employed to measure success are explicitly announced and are understood to be the best measure of teaching excellence. Questions of the purpose or consequence of teaching are not important to advocates of behavioral teacher education, as they turn out unreflective functionaries who work in the interests of the state, who see their social role as "neutral" upholders of the status quo. Behavioral teachers are executors of the axioms of effective teaching, deliverers of content predetermined by empirical researchers who have identified links between certain strategies and increased test scores (Zeichner 1983, 3–4; Giroux and McLaren 1988, 160).

The personalistic paradigm draws up cognitive psychological theory and tends to privilege the teacher's ability to reorganize perceptions and beliefs over the mastery of particular behaviors and specific knowledge and skills. From this paradigm teacher education becomes a form of adult development, a quest for personal growth. As in the behavioral orientation, personalistic teacher education is socially and politically decontextualized.

Accepting the status quo as a given, teacher effectiveness in this context is measured within individual frames, not within the domain of the social. Teacher education becomes a process of adult development, a process of maturation rather than a process of instructing an individual how to teach. Traditional-craft teacher education views teachers as semiprofessional craftspeople who gain expertise through apprenticeship-type experiences. Behaviorism's dominance has cut into the support of this orientation and its emphasis on learning by trial and error. Unlike the behaviorists, advocates of the traditional-craft position assume that much teaching knowledge is tacit and is resistant to the scientific specification demanded by the behaviorists. Proponents of traditional-craft teacher education contend that learning a battery of technical skills of teaching not only is not valuable in promoting good teaching in particular situations, but that it also often causes teachers to lose sight of the purpose of teaching. Like personalistic and behavioral perspectives, traditional-craft advocates define teacher education within a sociopolitical context that is unchallenged, that fails to consider the battle for democracy and social justice. This naive acceptance of the status quo results in part from the absence of any attention to a social theory that focuses attention on the political dimensions of teaching (Zeichner 1983, 5; Giroux and McLaren 1988, 163).

Inquiry-oriented teacher education emphasizes the cultivation of research skills about teaching and the multidimensional contexts that concern it. Technical teaching skills are not seen as unimportant from this perspective, but are viewed as means to larger ends. Thus, advocates of inquiry-oriented teacher education value questions of purpose, and critical inquiry is viewed as a necessary feature of the attempt to achieve such goals. From this vantage point, teacher education becomes an attempt to produce professionals with teaching skills to teach and the research skills to analyze what they are doing in relation to students, schools, and the society. The more teachers are cognizant of the etymology of their actions and the social and institutional constraints on them, the greater is the possibility that they will control their own professional lives. This approach sees teacher education as moral resuscitation, a regaining of the political consciousness of teachers who are freed from the control of unwarranted beliefs that handcuff their quest for self-direction. Advocates of inquiry-oriented teacher education understand that teacher education is inherently political, as teachers always act in a manner that leads to either the maintenance or transformation of prevailing institutional arrangements of schooling and the social, economic, and political arrangements that accompany them. Rejecting the behavioristic, personalistic, and traditional-craft belief that teacher education should prepare young teachers to fit into schools as they presently exist, the inquiry perspective encourages students to problematize the "what is," to reflect on "what could be" (Zeichner 1983, 6–7).

THE POST-FORMAL EXPANSION OF INQUIRY-ORIENTED TEACHER EDUCATION

The proposals for the reconceptualization of teacher education offered here certainly fit within the tradition of the inquiry orientation. Our purpose is to expand upon this perspective through the application of critical postmodern social theory and a vision of post-formal teacher thinkers. Such expansion revolves around four features of a critical postmodern pedagogical consciousness.

1. Teacher educators are aware of the role of power in the various dimensions of teaching and professional education. Such an awareness produces a teacher education that is sensitive to both who exercises dominant power in the society and how power is organized and deployed in school curricula. Questions of the relationship between power and representation are central to the critical postmodern teacher education curriculum, as courses prepare students to critically deconstruct power relations in the culture of schooling and social context that supports it. Teacher educators don't have to look very far to uncover the exercise of power in education, as colleges of education themselves are primary victims of interest-driven legislative intervention in academic life. Responding to the needs of business and industrial leaders, legislators often impose policies that presuppose a view of an educational professional who acts in the interests of managerial elites. Appreciating such dynamics, critical postmodern teacher educators ground their curriculum on the notion that the social world has been constructed and thus can be reconstructed by human action and savvy political organization (Shaker and Kridel 1989, 4; Shor 1992, 34).

2. Teacher educators cultivate the ability to uncover the deep structures that shape education and society. Critical postmodern teacher education through the emphasis on action research encourages analytic habits of reading, writing, and thinking—habits that penetrate surface impressions and "common sense," as they approach the implicate orders of the social and political. Employing deconstruction, mundane school conventions are read for their deeper meaning. Teacher education students are provided ample opportunity to engage in such textual analysis in both methodological classroom settings and in the applied context of field experiences.

3. Teacher educators encourage desocialization via ideological disembedding. Critical postmodern teacher education coursework focuses on the ways in

which the values of postmodern hyperreality shape the consciousness of both students and teachers. The rigorous study of cultural context undertaken alerts prospective teachers to the ways dominant myths, behavior, and language dictate school practice and teacher expectation. With such consciousness, teachers are empowered to separate themselves from the racism, sexism, class bias, homophobia, macho patriotism, hyperindividualism, and militarism of the New World Order.

4. Teacher educators understand that self-directed education undertaken by self-organized community groups is the most powerful form of pedagogy. Teacher education in this context becomes a "prodemocracy" movement that attempts to promote forms of thinking and action that retrieves the impetus for educational change from business and industrial elites. Grounded on a conception of solidarity with the oppressed and the excluded, teacher education seeks to connect with democratic organizations dedicated to a cultural politics of emancipatory change. Here teacher education students can become part of social movements where they can employ their research and pedagogical skills to build new forms of democratic consciousness and counterhegemonic action. Such praxis can revolutionize the view of knowledge as an entity produced by experts in remote locales. Postmodern knowledge becomes a product of democratic cooperation, a manifestation of what happens when experience is interrogated in the light of historical consciousness intercepting personal experience (Shor 1992, 35; Giroux 1988, 212).

CONFRONTING THE GREAT DENIAL: THE POLITICAL DIMENSION OF TEACHER EDUCATION

A central tenet of the justification of a critical postmodern pedagogy involves the confrontation of the great denial of the political dimension of education. As Paulo Freire has long argued, politics does not influence merely one aspect of the educational process—it shapes all of it. Despite the denial, there are political dimensions to teacher-student relationships and to the way prospective teachers are taught to manifest their authority. It is difficult to enunciate one's emancipatory vision one day and to engage in authoritarian relationships with students the next. The choice of content for one's syllabus is a political decision, as it promotes the value of one body of knowledge over another. Yet, in the great denial such manifestations of politics are rarely acknowledged, syllabi being viewed as neutral documents presenting "essential" information. The daily choice of activities for the classroom holds political dimensions revolving around questions of who makes the choice—the class in negotiation with the teacher or just the teacher? What role does student voice play in a prospective teacher's professional education? Are the fears, concerns, and anxieties of future teachers important or are they immature prattlings best ignored? These are all questions of power (i.e., of politics) that must be answered in some way.

Many technicist teacher education programs, of course, offer little more than training in methods of transferring knowledge. Such a view of the role of teacher education already embraces several political assumptions about the act of knowing. Indeed, the way the knowledge is transmitted to us, the way the "deposit" is made contributes to the construction of our consciousness. Marshall McLuhan convinced us long ago that format may be as important as the content itself in shaping hearts and minds. Indeed, the way literacy is conceptualized can be politically empowering or disempowering. For example, many of the literacy programs initiated over the last couple of decades have adopted overtly utilitarian ends. Designed to adjust people to the logic of domestication—that is, adapting them to the needs of power elites in the status quo—literacy is viewed as a gift of philanthropy, given by the knowledgeable to those incapable of determining what they need to know. The illiterate learn about the indispensability of knowledge about obtaining credit, how to dress for specific forms of employment, the proper way to pursue promotion in the workplace, and how to deport oneself in an interview. Such literacy programs fail to see the importance of providing illiterates with information about collective wage bargaining, the prerogatives of organized labor, or the rights of tenants (Da Silva and McLaren 1992, 65; Torres 1992, 226; Lankshear 1992, 325–47).

Participants in the great denial frame "neutral" education as a neo-White Man's Burden, a missionary struggle between forms of civilized high culture and the poor or "off-white" unwashed masses. The culture of these masses is the disease to be cured, the Western canon is the magic bullet. In their confrontation with the denial, critical postmodern educators seek to reclaim the cultural capital of the oppressed. Hoping to employ it as a means of empowering the oppressed to reappropriate their history, linguistics, and culture, emancipatory teachers learn from this cultural capital. In the process teachers and learners join together, transforming this cultural capital into a new form of knowledge—a powerful and ever-dangerous subjugated knowledge (Da Silva and McLaren 1992, 5; Torres 1992, 226).

REDEFINING EXPERTISE IN TEACHING: THE POST-FORMAL PRACTITIONER

Mainstream educational researchers have been attempting for years to explain the knowledge structures used by expert teachers. The idea underlying the effort involved the belief that if teacher educators simply knew what expert teachers know then this knowledge could be passed along to prospective teachers. Recent analysis has exposed the inadequacy of such a perspective, as researchers have argued a case for a more contextualized or situated form of practitioner cognition. How an expert acquires and makes use of knowledge, how he or she constructs an environment with resources for knowing and reasoning may be as important as what knowledge is actually known. We will examine the way the post-formal practitioner acquires and makes use of knowledge and constructs an environment for knowing and reasoning (Lampert and Clark 1990, 22). First, let us examine the ways teachers are too often taught to think, to deal with the knowledge of the profession.

1. *Behavioristic rule following.* The knowledge of the profession is viewed as a verified set of facts and clearly delineated rules. The teacher thinks in terms of following the rules no matter what the situation or context. Though the dominant tradition of teacher education, behaviorism, follows this model of teacher thinking, very few teachers actually think this way in practice.

2. *Experience-based initiative.* The knowledge of the profession consists of intuitive understandings gleaned from teaching experience. The traditional-craft form of teacher education is comfortable with this form of practitioner thinking. Teachers learn to cope with a variety of situations, to maintain order in the classroom, to keep students occupied, and to survive in school bureaucracies.

3. *Emotionally involved intuitive.* The knowledge of the profession involves the development of emotional commitment to the goals of the profession and the lives of individual students. Teachers are taught to discard the rules that don't work and to focus on those rules that help them reach their goals. Teacher educators in this context adopt many of the objectives of the personalistic teacher education paradigm.

4. *Analytical procedural.* The knowledge of the profession involves a set of formal thinking skills characterized by analytical procedures. The teacher thinks as a pedagogical scientist, a consumer of empirical data on teaching and a developer of procedures that are derived from the information. Such teacher education encourages teachers to unite prior experience with the analytical procedures to produce "effective" action which leads to measurable outcomes. Teacher educators in the analytical procedural context draw upon the behavioristic and traditional-craft paradigms.

5. *Self-actualized expert.* Using modernist liberal frames of reference, self-actualized expert thinking is the goal of most teacher education programs. Here knowledge is based on mature understanding and becomes an intrinsic aspect of the teacher's subjectivity. Drawing on the analytical thinking of behavior-

ism, the emotional self-actualization of personalism, and the experience-grounded intuition of the traditional-craft paradigm, the expert is a creative thinker who understands general instructional procedures and can apply them to individual cases (Bozik 1987, 3–4).

With these perspectives on the teaching of teacher thinking in mind, we turn our attention to the thinking of the post-formal practitioner. Drawing upon our critical constructivist epistemology and our conception of post-formal thinking, the post-formal practitioner moves on to the terrain of a sociocognitive frontier that goes beyond the conceptions of teacher thinking we have discussed.

Post-formal teacher thinking is:

1. *Inquiry oriented.* Drawing upon the inquiry-oriented paradigm of teacher education, post-formal teacher thinking is cultivated and extended by research skills. Action research as a cognitive activity becomes a central concern of those devising teacher education programs. Teachers who are researchers are capable of helping to produce students who are researchers, inquirers who explore problems they have posed about their everyday life experience, the larger society, and the content of school.

2. *Socially contextualized and aware of power.* Unlike the other forms of teacher thinking—even the self-actualized expert—post-formal teacher thinking can never be separated from the sociohistorical context and the power dimensions that have helped shape it. Ever aware of the ways power shapes the discourse of education and thinking itself, the post-formal teacher thinker engages in a self-conscious metacognition. Attuned to the changing social context, such practitioners are monitors of hyperreality and its effects on themselves, their students, and the social fabric.

3. *Grounded on a commitment to world making.* Drawing on our critical constructivist epistemology, post-formal teacher thinkers understand that our perceptions and beliefs are based on worlds that they and the larger society have made. In this context knowledge is something to be produced by an interaction of teacher and student, not something to be imposed by outside experts (Shor 1992, 36; Schon 1987, 36).

4. *Dedicated to an art of improvisation.* Post-formal practitioners recognize that they operate in conditions of uncertainty, uniqueness, and conflict that demand an art of improvisation, a form of thinking in action. Such a form of reflective practice avoids the application of uniform rules and procedures to the fickle world of practice. As post-formal improvisational artists, teachers respond to unexpected situations by inventing new rules on the spot, extemporaneously. For example, a teacher recognizes that a group of students in the second grade have the test-taking ability to score well on standardized tests, but they have little understanding of how to use such

knowledge in their lives. Thus, the teacher as improviser changes his or her lesson plans and considers ways to connect students to the curriculum. Such improvisational skill can develop only in teacher education programs and field experiences where there is freedom to learn through experience and the risk factor is low.

5. *Dedicated to the cultivation of situated participation.* Post-formal teacher education programs provide practice for prospective teachers in the art of eliciting participation from colleagues and students. A key concern of the post-formal practitioner is the effort to encourage universal participation in culture of the classroom. Thus, teachers think in terms of promoting student discussion and writing rather than simple listening. One of the ways that this can be accomplished is to situate the class in the words, concerns, and experience of the students. Operating in an inquiry-based teacher education, prospective practitioners sophisticate their abilities to connect with student consciousness. In the process of learning their students' concerns teachers develop their ability to draw upon and expand those concerns in learning contexts. Such an ability draws upon a teacher's capacity to think empathetically, to make use of their understanding of the connected consciousness discussed in Chapter 7.

6. *Extended by a concern with critical self- and social-reflection.* As post-formal teachers learn to think of strategies to promote participation, their success allows them ways of knowing their students and ways of their students knowing them that produce authentic forms of dialogue. Thus, post-formal teachers conceptualize techniques to encourage such dialogical situations in ways that promote self-reflection. Such introspection demands a critical metaperspective on the nature of classroom conversations (how do we talk to one another?), the nature of classroom learning (what do we call knowledge?), curriculum decisions (what do we need to know?), and assessment (is what we're doing working?). When thinking advances and the dialogues grow in sophistication, students come to reflect about the sociopolitical nature of their school experience, asking whose interest it serves for them to see the world in the way they do.

7. *Shaped by a commitment to democratic self-directed education.* Post-formal teachers constantly consider and reconsider ways of expanding the democratic nature of their classrooms. Students understand that they possess the right to speak, to disagree, to point out the error of the teacher, and to call for a renegotiation of the curriculum. In these ways students gain an ownership of their own education, shaping it in light of their concerns and composing it in their words. Post-formal teachers are vigilant, frequently checking to make sure that they are not simply *providing* their students an education.

8. *Steeped in a sensitivity to pluralism.* Post-formal teachers are familiar with a variety of cultural expressions and the way education often brushes against

them. As action researchers, post-formal teachers develop the analytical ability to expose the insidious ways that dominant perspectives marginalize oppressed groups. Thinking in terms of race, class, and gender differences, post-formal practitioners survey their classes for patterns developing along these lines. This post-formal respect for such diversity allows such teachers the ability to conceptualize multiple perspectives on issues such as intelligence, student aptitude, evaluation, and creativity. Such perspectives allow for the acceptance of a diversity of expression which brings more students into the circle of school success.

9. *Committed to action.* As post-formal teachers challenge the passivity of modernist thinking with its anti-intellectualism and dependence on authority to provide meaning and initiate action, they subvert the disposition to inaction students often learn in traditional classrooms. Steeped in a notion of praxis, post-formal teachers come to see thinking as the first step to action. Post-formal teachers engage students with questions of the relationships between particular thoughts and actions, as students pose problems around current realities and their inadequacy.

10. *Concerned with the affective dimension of human beings.* Drawing from feminist conceptions of passionate learning and connectedness, post-formal teachers think in terms of developing both the emotional and logical sides of their students and themselves. In the dialogues that they and their students create, emotional reflection is encouraged. In their authenticity, the dialogues do not retreat from emotional expression, as humor, compassion, empathy, and indignation often are manifested.

THE FAILURE OF THE REFORM OF TEACHER EDUCATION

The types of teacher education reform that have been promoted over the last decade have done little to address the types of concerns posed by this analysis of teacher thinking. Marked by increased subject matter requirements, more fieldwork, five-year programs, and required arts or sciences undergraduate majors, reforms have generally ignored the structure of the programs. In most colleges of education content is still delivered in an efficient manner for the purpose of building a student's pre-service knowledge base. Social theory continues to be viewed as an exotic commodity, a strange European import with little relevance for the *practical* education of teachers. Without the analytical perspective provided by such theory, teachers remain unequipped to analyze the deep structures that shape their professional training and the schools in which they will teach. If teachers are to gain a post-formal meta-awareness of the forces that construct their consciousnesses, then social theory will have to become a part of their educational experience (Shaker and Kridel 1989, 5–6).

Without the cognitive and social benefits offered by feminist theory, for example, teacher educators and their students find it difficult to challenge many of the discursive assumptions of technicist teacher education. For example, the child to which technicist education refers is a male. The intellectual development that is provided *him* involves the cultivation of his abstract, rational, and problem-solving abilities. Thus, our definition of thinking is narrowed, all but white males are penalized by the rules of the discursive game, and teacher education is confined within a modernist force field of formal, procedural thinking. This modernist thinking accepts the universality of developmental theories and the viability of a single norm for assessing all members of the culture. Such an essentialized form of education leaves women, for example, to be defined as innately inferior, as they exhibit less competitive spirit, *rationality*, and "objective" standards of moral judgment. Indeed, it often views maternal thinking and sensitivity to the needs of others not as ethical virtues but as exploitable female characteristics (Maher and Rathbone 1986, 221–25).

Such views tend to reproduce the status quo, as they fail to question the belief that knowledge is a social construction and reflects tacit assumptions about the nature of the world. Without a critical skepticism a cognitive passivity is produced that frames social and educational phenomena as if they could have developed in no other way. The passivity often attributed to modernist public schools is very similar to the passivity produced by technicist teacher education classrooms with their replicative as opposed to applicative learning. While providing vocal support for reflective inquiry, technicist education professors model information transfer techniques. In the process they become one more brick in the wall of student passivity—even as they rail against it. Part of this passivity results from the use of Cartesian–Newtonian research techniques to produce simplistic prescriptions for teacher training, prescriptions that are passed along to students as part of the "knowledge base" of the profession. The passivity of the procedural thinking produced by such orientations is illustrated by the expectation that prospective teachers learn generic theories that they deploy once faced with particular classroom situations. The process is so passive, so unchallenging, so boring that teachers often lose their sense of wonder and excitement about learning to teach. Their enthusiasm rarely emerges from what they learn in their program; knowledge is not viewed as intrinsically of worth, but just as a means to the end of certification (Floden and Klinzing 1990, 16; Shaker and Kridel 1989, 6–7; Ross and Hannay 1986, 13).

In such professional education it is not difficult to understand how teaching is separated from its moral and ethical roots. Context-stripped by the view that teaching is a technical act, political issues are far removed from the consciousness of prospective teachers, as they memorize the generic theories and the fragments of the knowledge base. Delegated to a state of being, teachers in the technicist paradigm are conceived as a unit of production on an assembly line—a static self located outside of a wider social context. Reforms that decontextualize students in this manner are doomed to failure, as they fail to recognize that teachers are continually molded by the dynamics of history and social structure. Identity, the poststructuralists frequently remind us, is never complete and always subject to modification (Ross 1988, 10; Liston and Zeichner 1988, 4; Britzman 1991, 32).

Critical postmodern reforms must go beyond the morally "neutral" reforms of the technicists. At the same time they must not allow their calls for reflective inquiry to degenerate into slogans and buzzwords—a path traveled by many educational reform movements. Indeed, the call for reflective teaching has already taken a few steps down the path, as camp followers repeat the mantras of reflectivity without addressing just what it is that they should be reflecting about or what criteria for evaluation they should employ in the process. Without a system of meaning to help prioritize and assess the quality of reflection, the activity can become a vacuous enterprise. Already slipping into the realm of superficiality, reflective reforms often fail to extend beyond isolated individuals. Without a moral grounding and a political critique, reflection in practice comes to accept the injustice of the larger society and the hierarchical and alienating structures of contemporary schools. Lapsing into a form of pop therapy, teacher reflection becomes a means of adjusting teachers to the irrationality of the given. In this situation schools continue to be "dream killers" for students and teachers. Instead of locating and sophisticating the intellectually and ethically talented, schools of education continue to reward dispirited but conventional teachers, emotionally prepared to fit themselves into the bureaucratic expectations (Zeichner and Tabachnick 1991, 2; Bullough and Gitlin 1991, 39; Ferguson 1980, 310).

CROSSING THE LAST BOUNDARY: TEACHER EDUCATION AND THE CREATION OF KNOWLEDGE

Critical postmodern teachers understand that knowledge is not just created in the researcher's office or in the professor's study but in the consciousness produced in thinking, discussion, writing, argument, or conversation. It is created when teachers and students confront a contradiction, when students encounter a dangerous memory, when teacher-presented information collides with student experience, or when student-presented information collides with teacher experience. When we speculate on the etymology and deployment of knowledge, new knowledge is created. Generally speaking, Western culture is unaware of the origins of knowledge and the social process by which knowledge is legitimated. Without such understandings, teachers are unable to separate nonconventional thinking from expressions of intellectual deficiency, highly moral behaviors from deviant behaviors. Teacher education that is grounded on the attempt to produce knowledge must focus attention on linguistic analysis, the study of power and its relationship to the individual, and the examination of the rational process. As the teacher education curriculum focuses on these concerns, prospective teachers learn that language, individual production, rationality, and knowledge itself are never ideologically innocent.

Numerous factors work to disguise the ideological dimension of knowledge, language, subjectivity, or intelligence. For example, when schools teach about the industrial revolution and the subsequent evolution of industrialization in Western history, the focus is almost exclusively on the benefits of the process: the increased production, the contribution to our standard of living, the relationship between industrialization and geopolitical power relations. Rarely are questions of industrialization's social side effects raised: the despiritualization of labor, the ethic of deskilling, the irrationality of bureaucratization, the environmental destruction, and so on. In the process of denaturalizing the discourse of industrialization, critical postmodern teachers separate thinking from its identification with powerful ideological interests. As a result, a process of rewriting is unleashed—a process that produces new forms of knowledge, not only about industrialization, but also about other spheres where the apparatuses of power have constructed consciousnesses (Britzman 1991, 43, 216–17; Bowers and Flinders 1990, 14, 19–20).

Teaching in multicultural settings provides a situation where the creation of knowledge takes on an even more profound significance. When a critical postmodern teacher who doesn't share the culture, language, race, or socioeconomic backgrounds of students enters the classroom, he or she becomes not an information provider but an explorer who works with students to create mutually understood texts. Based on their explorations, teachers and students create new learning materials full of mutually generated meanings and shared interpretations. At a time when educational dilemmas resulting from the rapid increase of diverse students in schools portend the future of North American education, such a pedagogical perspective becomes extremely important. If educators are unable to meet the challenges issued by this expanding diversity, disastrous consequences will result. Feminist pedagogy provides us insight into the role of education in diverse settings. Teacher education must cultivate an understanding of various ways of knowing, whether it be women's ways of perceiving or subjugated knowledges of oppressed peoples. In other words, colleges of education must explore the connections between modes of social integration that individuals experience and the systems of thinking they embrace (Gomez 1991, 104–5, 110; Lesko 1988, 28).

Such explorations cannot take place until teachers begin to learn about the diverse lives of their students and the specifics of their thinking processes. Methods courses in critical postmodern teacher education programs teach beginning teachers to overcome the paucity of dialogue in classrooms and the impersonal relationships such as absence produces. One of the first lessons such students learn is to surrender their pose as an expert when they stand as a teacher in front of class. When we are ready to admit to our role as imposter, that we are not omniscient providers of truth to our disciples, we begin to actually listen to our students. We become open to the stories of students, listening and analyzing how the stories inform educational and social theory and how educational and social theory inform the stories. The cultivation of such abilities forms the core of the critical postmodern methods course curriculum. Prospective teachers learn to engage students in genealogical projects, autobiographical writings, journal keeping, and collaborative methods of assessing and interpreting these activities. Student lives become primary sources for writing and reading exercises. In the process teachers learn forms of linguistic analysis, which they use to engage students in meta-analytical examinations of their consciousness construction. Such examinations elicit the type of critical thinking that we have labeled post-formality (Greene 1986, 80; Maher and Rathbone 1986, 228).

Paulo Freire, as usual, facilitates our attempt to conceptualize a democratic form of teacher education. Our democratic post-formal teacher education prepares prospective practitioners to build curriculum around the construction of knowledge using the themes and conditions of people's lives as primary building blocks. Perspective teachers learn to study their students' experiences in classrooms and in their communities in order to identify the words, conditions, concepts, and ways of seeing basic to their lived worlds. Freire has taught us that it is from this information that teachers identify "generative words and themes" which signify the most important subject matter for an emancipatory curriculum. Contrary to the belief of some critics of our critical postmodern position, this subject matter is not simply passed uncritically along to students. The information is presented back to students for interrogation as part of a critical dialogue. As Freire puts it, the subject matter is "problem-posed," that is, students and teachers reflect on the lives they lead asking questions of meaning and value. From a post-formal perspective they come to think about their own thinking, about the political dimensions of their daily lives. Such reflection provides students and teachers with a cognitive distance that leads to transformative action (Shor 1992, 32).

While there are many teacher educators and teachers who base their professional work on an ethic of caring, such an orientation is necessary but not sufficient in the attempt to formulate a critical postmodern teacher education (Gomez 1991, 42). Caring education that fails to create knowledge from the critical connections between home and school, the unvalued skills that many children develop, and the experiences that young people live is unable to produce post-formal thinkers, to cultivate courageous citizens with the insight to redefine progress. Henry Giroux and Peter McLaren extend our thinking on this issue, as they envision a teacher education that provides teachers the skill to assist students in the analysis of their interpretations of events and cultural meanings. The critical illumination that grows out of such analysis allows participants to intervene into their own consciousness construction. The key aspect of the role of teacher education in this context involves prospective teachers learning how to engage student experience in a way that both affirms and questions it, all the time keeping alive the possibility of self- and social transformation (Giroux and McLaren 1991, 79). Such an idea can revolutionize the long-maligned methods course, as it transforms it into a subtle, academic, and practical pedagogical process of learning "how."

Right-wing critics such as Allan Bloom, Chester Finn, and Dinesh D'Souza will decry such proposals, claiming that they undermine instruction of a core curriculum grounded on the great ideas of Western tradition. There is no reason that a critical postmodern education wouldn't engage many of the ideas such critics hold dear—albeit not in the same reverential way Bloom, Finn, and D'Souza would. Indeed, our critical postmodern curriculum would go beyond the boundaries of the West and engage ideas from Asia and Third-World cultures as well. The central point of critical postmodern education, however, involves the epistemological shifts it demands. While traditional technicist education assumes a correct-answer-oriented curriculum with an unquestioned realist epistemological base, critical postmodern education envisions a conceptually oriented curriculum with a self-conscious critical constructivist epistemological base. These critical curricular and epistemological perspectives change the purpose of teacher education programs and schools in general from vocational orientations with an emphasis on the provision of an essential body of knowledge and a set of narrow skills to one of intellectual development and an attempt to rewrite and transform the world (Benson 1989, 343–44).

Student teachers do not learn to create and problem-pose knowledge by passive reception of lectures; such abilities are gained through experience and practice. Critical postmodern teacher education students learn sophisticated research techniques and deploy them in inquiries about student experience; the ways dominant interests manifest themselves in schools, society, and individual lives; and the ways that individuals resist the domination of these interests. Knowledge is no longer made to appear as if it is immutable, a secret known only by the elect, the privileged. Umberto Eco writes in *Name of the Rose* about the evils of immutable, secret knowledge that is viewed as an entity to be possessed rather than diffused among the people. Speaking of Aristotle's work, the blind monk who guards the great books in the monastery argues that if he were to allow the books to become objects open to anyone's interpretation "we would have crossed the last boundary." The last boundary is democracy, the right of individuals to create their own knowledge rather than having to rely on the official interpretations of the experts. We have yet to cross that boundary; critical postmodern education pushes us toward it (Ross and Hannay 1986, 12–13; Greene 1986, 79).

The view of teaching as a technical enterprise where privileged knowledge is passed along to students is contrary to our vision of post-formal teacher thinkers teaching in critical postmodern schools. With our concern with teaching and learning as the creation of knowledge, democratic interpretation becomes a cardinal virtue not the unthinkable evil of the blind monk. Such a perspective toward knowledge is germaine not only for conservative guardians of tradition but also for progressives who recognize the social malformations wrought by economic and social power interests. Critical postmodern teachers must refrain from the imposition of their viewpoints on students. As they present their perspectives in discussions, critical postmodern teachers must encourage students to interrogate and disagree with their interpretations. The democratic process is fragile and must constantly be nurtured and bolstered by careful adjustments (Greene 1986, 80; Shor 1992, 31).

As we reconsider teacher education in light of our post-formal concern with teaching and learning as processes of knowledge creation, several concepts begin to emerge. The following is a tentative list of principles on which a post-formal teacher education is grounded.

1. Prospective teachers learn to create situations where students learn about the world through their own efforts. Critical postmodern teachers know that understandings of the world cannot be delivered to students. Teacher education, thus, becomes a theoretical and practical activity where students learn to create situations that impel students to learn on their own. These teachers often measure their own success in terms of how well their students have learned to teach themselves, how well they engage in knowledge production.

2. Prospective teachers understand critical constructivism, that is, that the world is socially constructed and shaped by human action or inaction. As teachers learn the ways the world has been shaped, they come to realize that the world can be re-created and transformed. Such a perspective dramatically changes the way we approach the teaching act. Since the world is subject to change, students are viewed as active participants in world making as opposed to passive recipients of secondhand knowledge. Again, their own stories and life histories become important, as they formulate their own interpretations and create their own knowledge.

3. Prospective teachers must learn to see themselves in relation to the world before they can cultivate such an ability among their students. Critical postmodern teacher education moves beyond simple concern with teaching as a technical act, as students study the genesis of knowledge production in postmodern society and the ways such production shapes their view of themselves and their relation to the world. Combining social theory, information studies, and autobiography, our form of teacher education becomes a model for the reconceptualization of university teaching.

4. Prospective teachers participate in the rewriting of the world, in the making of a new history, in the revitalization of a democracy dissipated by the postmodern condition. Critical postmodern teacher education is concerned with the study of democracy. Analyzing democratic thought historically, philosophically, in relation to hyperreality, and as a benchmark for the conceptualization of the purposes of schools, prospective teachers engage in a collective social enterprise, a teacher education curriculum centered around democratic studies.

5. Prospective teachers learn to confront the myths that hold them and others in oppression. Myth succeeds as an instrument of domination as it undermines the complexity of human actions, resolves all contradictions, and strips lives and events of their historical quality. In this mythologizing process, individuals fall prey to social amnesia as they lose the memory that the world is humanly constructed; without such memory the attempt to overcome oppression is severely limited. Thus, critical postmodern teacher education is historically grounded as it emphasizes the genealogy of schooling with its focus on

social control and cultural imposition (see Kincheloe and Pinar 1991 for an expansion of this thesis).

6. Prospective teachers learn to read the word and the world in new ways, becoming in the process post-formal thinkers and critically reflective practitioners. Critical postmodern teachers learn to use action research techniques grounded upon ethnographic, historiographical, and semiotic methodologies. The cognitive benefits of such strategies are profound when they are learned in conjunction with social and educational history, epistemology, and information studies. When the understandings gleaned from such scholarship are contextualized with the pedagogical concern with "learning how," an unmatched context for producing post-formal thinkers and critically reflective practitioners is created (Lankshear 1992, 357).

What a major revision of teacher education these ideas would initiate—not simply in colleges of education but in the university in general. Most university coursework, not unlike classroom experiences in public schools, regards knowledge as something simply to be transmitted to students who have no participation in the determination of its relevance. Knowledge is divorced from how we come to know, the study of pedagogy dismissed as a trivial enterprise. Without pedagogical inquiry, knowledge is merely received, not constructed, and those dispensing it are positioned as confident authorities presenting the final word. Such teaching is grounded on a set of epistemological assumptions, including the belief that reality is a static entity, not an evolving set of relationships; knowledge is given, not created; the world is impervious, the change not transformable; and reality is something to which we adjust, not something we make. Such a fatalistic epistemological orientation allows for teachers to transubstantiate living knowledge of the world into a necrophilic set of artificial facts and generalizations redeemable only in the prosthetic evaluations of school (Britzman 1991, 41–45; Lankshear 1992, 359).

THE VALUE OF PEDAGOGY: THE COMPLEXITY OF "KNOWING HOW"

Traditionally, schools of education have been viewed as the American Motors of the university, inept and capable only of producing inferior products. While such a reputation has often been honestly gained, the devaluation of the study of pedagogy that accompanies it is unfortunate. The academy's separation of theory and practice and its condescension toward the "unsavory" world of the practical has constructed a view of teacher work more technical than intellectual. Eschewing pedagogical analysis of their own classroom work, university professors sense that teaching is somehow not as important as the higher status work of research and theory building. The academic community in general and the teacher education community in particular have theoretically failed to appreciate that "knowing how" is a coequal but different form of knowing than "knowing that" (Moore 1989, 4; Britzman 1991, 39–40).

Post-formal practitioners must operate on two levels of cognition where theoreticians are required to work on only one. In addition to the under-standings demanded by the debate over what forms of knowledge, social theory, political orientation, moral vision, and historical interpretation should be a part of schooling, post-formal practitioners must grapple with how to engage students with these knowledge forms and the multitude of contextualizing concerns such engagement demands. The separation of knowledge from practice has suppressed the study of these issues over the last seventy-five years, reducing pedagogy to a technical question of information delivery. In a critical postmodern context pedagogy is rescued from modernist technicalization, as it addresses the processes by which knowledge is certified in the larger society and democratically produced in the classroom. Critical postmodern teacher education asks how power relations contribute to the production of knowledge and the construction of consciousness. At the same time, it studies the conditions knowing demands, the negotiations and the social relations necessary for learning. Drawing upon a critical constructivist epistemology, post-formal teachers reject models that frame teaching as the provision of facts while embracing a view that considers the process as a dialogical reformulation (i.e., a critical accommodation) of the world (Codd 1984 10; Britzman 1991, 237–39).

When pedagogy is viewed in such a context every dimension of education changes, from everyday classroom practice to teacher education to the professional preparation of educational leaders. Education research changes as we become far more concerned with questions of context and interpretation rather than simply questions of frequency and mathematical relationship. Even our view of the teaching workplace begins to change from the modernist laboratory to an ambiguous and ill-structured social terrain. In such conditions our view of teacher thinking cannot remain the same.

Chapter 11

Preparing the Post-Formal Practitioner

Teaching is an uncertain and complex enterprise. If the act of teaching were known and constant, teachers could simply follow the dictates of empirical generalizations and teacher educators would know exactly what teachers needed to perform successfully. Unlike fast-food employees at McDonald's who are taught to follow precisely a ten-step process in making a Big Mac, teachers now realize that their practice is situation-specific. When practice is grounded on generalized formulas and quantitative measures typically conceptualized around student mastery of isolated but measurable bits of information, teachers are removed from the particularities of the everyday life of the classroom. Such practice assumes that teaching is constant and predictable, always occurring in a cocoon of certainty. Cartesian–Newtonian technicist teacher education prepares novices for classrooms that are "objects in general," not as if they were ambiguous and distinctly human situations unlike any other in the cosmos. Sophie Haroutunian-Gordon characterizes classrooms as ill-structured situations that must be viewed in their particularity to be appreciated. No longer can the argument be made that educational science can eliminate the uncertainty of professional practice and replace it with an empirical knowledge base about the teaching act. It won't work (Schon 1987, 6, 11–13; Floden and Klinzing 1990, 16; Greene 1986, 80; Haroutunian-Gordon 1988, 226).

LINKING THE ANTICIPATION OF THE
GENERAL WITH THE LIFE OF THE SPECIFIC

The Cartesian–Newtonian modernist rationality has sought the most general concepts and the most comprehensive axioms. Engaging quantitative characteristics, analyzing one variable at a time, education scientists formulated a rationalistic variety of teaching that attempted to direct the teacher gaze to children in general and knowledge in general. In the process, these tacit rational assumptions distanced teachers from their bodies, inducing them to treat themselves and their students as information transmitters and information receivers—as androids. On the other hand, poets, painters, novelists, and historians have established a tradition of focusing on the particular, on specific individuals, on particular situations, and on unique successions of events. This particularistic tradition has concentrated on the qualitative nature of the concrete. With its ostensibly necessary concern with the particular, education has been profoundly affected by the feminist reconceptualization of the specific (Greene 1986, 70; Courteney 1988, 8).

Madeleine Grumet expands our understanding of this feminist notion, as she maintains that androcentric empirical science in its emphasis on abstract generalizations has moved us away from the domain of specific human beings with their passions, their feelings, and their bodies. We must become more concerned with what matters, with the living. Perceptions and experiences of individual students are important, as feminist theorists caution educators and educational scientists to personalize their professional worlds. From the perspective of technicist educators and the guardians of the Cartesian tradition such pronouncements ring of treason. After exposure to such feminist theorizing, teaching and research about it can no longer be viewed as a cold, rational process. When we address the living, we find our concern with human connection growing. In this context, the connected consciousness we have discussed initiates a quest for community, an attempt to better understand and empathize with those who surround us. Teacher education can catalyze this concern with the living, as prospective teachers learn to focus on the *life* world of schooling. Instead of emphasizing the decontextualizing and context-stripping methods of the behaviorists and the positivists, teacher educators direct attention not only to the conversations and body languages of the school but to the context of these expressions as well. By directing prospective teachers to the connected consciousness of the teaching act, teacher education overcomes the tendency of Cartesian–Newtonian educational science to reduce living individuals to a "type," a derivative category (Grumet 1988, 3–15: Haroutunian–Gordon 1988, 235–37).

William Pinar and I extend this concern with the living in our discussion of place. Our effort revolves around the attempt to link the general and the particular in a synergistic manner that sophisticates our ability to perceive and to think about ourselves and our relationship to the world. To understand the significance of the individual, we must concurrently appreciate it on its own merit (a synchronic view of a phenomenon) and in the context provided by its contextualization in light of larger social structures (a diachronic view of a phenomenon). Place concerns the cultural location of where we start, where our consciousness is formed. Knowing where we started allows us insight into where we reside. Place is the venue where our feelings took shape, the locale where our consciousness turns for metaphorical reference in our attempt to understand the world of change, to accommodate the unexpected. Our sense of place when connected with anticipatory accommodation moves us in a post-formal direction. When we engage in anticipatory accommodation we make use of knowledge gained from a variety of contexts in order to accommodate the uniqueness of each situation. By taking into account our knowledge from these different situations we gain the ability to better anticipate what might happen and what we might do based on our recognitions (Kincheloe and Pinar 1991, 4–23).

Post-formal practitioners see their teaching in a way that goes beyond either the particularity of private experience or the generalization of socioeconomic pattern. Yet post-formality encompasses them both. Human beings are entwined in countless ways in the synchronic-dia-chronic synergism. Aware of this synergism, post-formal teachers direct their attention to the ways that socioeconomic and ideological forces construct consciousness while at the same time observing how individual children, real-life students, respond to this construction. This is why action research is so important to post-formal practitioners, semiotics in particular, as such inquiry helps practitioners uncover the tacit forces that construct consciousness at the level of everyday life.

THE CRITICAL GROUNDING OF THE
PRACTICAL KNOWLEDGE OF TEACHERS

Picking up on our post-formal interest in the cognitive synergism produced by the interaction of the general and the particular, teacher education needs to be considered in reference to such concerns. Maurice Merleau-Ponty anticipated our concern with the particular with his call for a return to the "there is," to the site and soil of our actual bodies. Teacher intuition is grounded on this consciousness of the particularistic "there is." Another way of approaching the subtle realm of teacher intuition involves an understanding of the *practical knowledge* of teaching. Residing in practitioner familiarity with specific schools and students, teacher practical knowledge occupies the realm of the particular. What is typically referred to as teacher intuition involves the ability to reshape cognitive structures to *accommodate* the novel situations routinely faced in the classroom. When we move to a higher order of teacher thinking, practitioners gain the ability to take the "there is" and highlight it with the insights provided by a general knowledge of social structure. The move to a more sophisticated cognition involves the ability to push accommodation to the critical realm, as we challenge particularistic accommodation with the theoretically grounded accommodations that consider the oppressive social consequences of particular teacher actions (Greene 1986, 70; Courteney 1988, 20–21).

If teacher education is to make any real difference in the attempt to improve teaching and heighten emancipatory consciousness, it must understand and ground itself on the practical intuition and knowledge of teachers. Post-formal teacher education must question existing practical knowledge of pre-service and in-service teachers, but at the same time respect it and draw upon the valuable insights it possesses. Thus, critical teaching methods come not simply from understandings of critical postmodern social theory and emancipatory pedagogical theory, but from the interaction of such theories in terms of the practical knowledge of teachers. The intuition that results from such interaction is not the product of the direct instruction of teacher educators, but the product of the knowledge that is created by the dialogical unification of practical knowledge with the theoretical domain. Classroom dialogues often are structured around the search for significance and meaning in the classroom experiences teachers share. Pre-service teachers are not excluded from such dialogue for they have over a dozen years of classroom experience as students, not to mention the possibility of field observations assigned by education professors themselves (Ross and Hanney 1986, 12, 14; Courteney 1988, 40).

The dialogue can become a powerful sociocognitive experience for pre-service and in-service teachers when they gain the realization that the problems of teaching are not structured puzzles resolved by standardized procedures. The problems of teaching are rarely consistent and possess no recognized method of solution. Such problems demand a form of practitioner thinking in action where on-the-spot alterations of plans are necessitated. Teachers who are thinking in action make use of larger theoretical concerns, pedagogical strategies, and bodies of knowledge, employing a system of meaning to produce judgments concerning what constitutes a good class or a desired outcome. The difference between this form of practitioner thinking and more traditional Cartesian–Newtonian scientific varieties is profound, as these technicist thinking styles apply rigid constructs to mercurial situations where they are inappropriate.

Often procedural practitioners will attempt to force a teaching situation into a framework that is amenable to the scientific techniques available. Thus, they will reduce the complexity of a classroom in order to make it easier to analyze or to measure the "important" variables. Such manipulations are often not purposeful or even conscious; practitioners are simply rearranging the situation in a manner that makes it understandable in a Cartesian–Newtonian context. Preestablished objectives still can be met as a result of these manipulations; the problem is that the specific needs of students in the living classroom may have little to do with these goals. Indeed, technical practitioners may have to ignore the aberrations, the problem students, the rebellious children who do not benefit from the techniques envisioned by the theory. The idea of reframing the objectives or discarding the prearranged measures of performance does not fit into the paradigm. Post-formal notions of reflection in action value practitioners who are empowered to change directions in midstream, teachers who make use of the evidence around them to construct new strategies and even new goals if they deem it proper (Moore 1989, 5; Clark 1987, 17; Greene 1986, 81; Schon 1983, 44–45, 165–66, 345–46).

CRITICAL POSTMODERN REFORMS REVOLVE AROUND THE DEVELOPMENT OF TEACHER THINKERS

It seems reasonable to assume that the reform of teacher education should be conceptually envisioned around the cultivation of post-formal practitioner thinkers. What coursework, what field experiences are best designed to produce such sophisticated teacher thinkers? Critical postmodern teacher education possesses an overt concern with the development of such thinking in every experience it provides. Field experiences are meta-analytical, the study of teaching technique is always viewed contextually, as a part of larger sociopolitical and pedagogical concerns. The general knowledge of pedagogy—including knowledge and skills related to teaching, knowledge of the general principles of instruction, knowledge and skills related to classroom management, and knowledge about the aims and purposes of education—is not viewed as a body of information simply to be transferred to prospective teachers. Such understandings are always questioned and reread as parts of larger discourses. When students do become aware of such information, they approach it skeptically. During field experiences, student teachers reflect on its relevance and applicability in their particular situations. Critical postmodern teacher education takes nothing as a given, as privileged information beyond reproach (Courteney 1988, 20; Daines 1987, 5).

In order to produce post-formal practitioners, critical postmodern professional education moves beyond top-down notions of educational reform and hierarchical structure. The teacher role is conceptualized as an autonomous one that is free from the tyranny of institutionally imposed curricula that allow little professional latitude. Robert Donmoyer helps us conceptualize this autonomous post-formal teacher role with his description of New Zealand's educational system. Despite the existence of a national testing system and a national curriculum, Donmoyer observed more autonomy at the school level and the classroom than in schools and classrooms in the United States where much lip service is paid to the concept of local control of education. New Zealand's educational system is grounded on the belief that teachers need much autonomy because they must accommodate the particularity of their individual classroom and because they need to enjoy a feeling of ownership of their own teaching. Thus, the national curriculum is viewed as a resource rather than a directive. Very few specific rules for teachers are to be found in New Zealand. Indeed, the ones that do exist are expressed as larger standards of behavior that are sufficiently general to permit much teacher prerogative. The comparison between teacher roles in New Zealand and the United States reveals the lack of autonomy teachers in this nation accept as a necessary aspect of school bureaucracy (Maher and Rathbone 1986, 226; Donmoyer 1990, 162).

Post-formal practitioner thinkers do not accede to these authoritarian definitions of the teacher role. As pedagogical iconoclasts, post-formal teachers transcend the restrictions of traditional roles, shatter stereotypes, encourage the development of critical consciousness, generate new interpretations, help create new knowledge, and shake up the comfortable hierarchy of schools. Refusing to give in to the modernist illusion of the bounded self free from social construction, post-formal educators analyze the production of their subjectivities as they search for a critical connected consciousness. They serve as impediments to the educational system's role as a cultural broker of passivity and resignation. In this situation, post-formal thinking becomes an act of courage and citizenship that empowers individuals to name and thus act upon their understanding of the way schools subvert their struggle for emancipation. In many "schools of excellence" of the last decade, students are treated as objects filled with officially validated ideas. They emerge from such schools into a culture where the mass media tends to perpetuate this process. Recognizing the tendency of the system to promote such realities, post-formal teachers act as a countervailing force (Shaker and Kridel 1989, 7; McLaren and Da Silva 1992, 11–12; Daines 1987, 5; Shor 1992, 28).

THINKING AS A DEMOCRATIC ACTIVITY: LEARNING TO BE ADMINISTERED

How can post-formal teachers act as a countervailing force? One of the most important ways involves challenging conceptually the administrative structures of schools. It is interesting that administration is taught only to people who serve at the head of the administrative structure and not to people who are to be administered. Ideas about democratic forms of management are not concepts that are typically discussed between principals and teachers or teachers and students. Without the awareness produced by such discussion, the social ambience of the school remains within an authoritarian frame. The ideological web formed by this authoritarianism produces a curriculum that teaches teachers and students how to think and act in the world. Both teachers and students are taught to conform, to adjust to their inequality and their particular rung of the status ladder, and to submit to authority. Teachers and students are induced to develop an authority dependence, a view of citizenship that is passive, a view of learning that means listening. The predisposition to question the authority structure of the school and the curriculum it teaches or to reject the image of the future that the structure presents to teachers and students is out-of-bounds. The politics of authoritarianism rubs democratic impulses the wrong way (Shor 1992, 26–27).

The authoritarianism that infects the technicist school emerges from an androcentrism that is comfortable with hierarchical relationships. Post-formal teachers ask if this androcentrism is compatible with more democratic forms of management—forms grounded on cooperation and independence. Indeed, teachers who have grown accustomed to such forms of management become uncomfortable when confronted with more feminine and democratic styles. Efforts of critically grounded administrators to employ inclusive management styles often are perceived as weakness by their teachers. In the same vein, emancipatory teachers who emphasize self-discipline and democratic attitudes toward their students are perceived as lenient. In fact, when teachers throw off authoritarian constructions of their role, they are astonished to find that some students perceive that they have been given permission to ignore assignments and misbehave. Young teachers at this point often revert back to authoritarian forms of classroom control, assuming that democratization simply doesn't work. In the culture of the authoritarian school, democratic management and teaching styles are often equated with low quality standards. Quality education in this context is, after all, something done *to* students.

When we observe the gender imbalance in educational administration, we are reminded of the patriarchal infrastructure of public schools in the United States. Despite the gains in awareness produced by the women's movement in the last quarter of the century, women are still inducted into a culture of passivity and acceptance of androcentric authority. Women who have drawn upon feminist theory to gain a new consciousness of patriarchy and its effects on their own consciousness construction often experience emotional conflict when they find themselves in the teacher role. It is in this situation that women teachers come to the discomforting realization that the democratic process and emancipatory thinking run head-on into the values promoted by the hierarchically structured technicist school. They begin to discover that the processes of emancipation that have played such an important role in their lives—the questioning of their belief system, their attempt to disembed themselves from the validated culture, and their efforts to transcend procedural forms of thinking—are sometimes considered inappropriate if not pathological behaviors in their schools (Maher and Rathbone 1986, 227; Shor 1992, 27–29; Torres 1992, 208).

TEACHER EDUCATION AS CRITICAL REFLECTION

Critical postmodern teacher education sees the cultivation of technical skills as merely a means toward larger goals—goals that involve forms of critical analysis and reflection that lead to action. Indeed, reflective inquiry is the core of the critical reconceptualization of teacher education. Drawing upon critical postmodern theory, post-formal teachers employ reflection as a means of making knowledge problematic. As they deconstruct the taken-for-granted practices, beliefs, and assumptions of teaching, such teachers break through the fog of expert knowledge that has often served to stifle progressive change in the schools. Critical postmodern teacher educators create situations where prospective teachers can explore and critique their tacit knowledge, their experiences in school, and their beliefs about teaching. The objective is not to induce teacher education students to deny the pertinence of these experiences, but simply to critically examine the beliefs in a way that leads to higher order thinking and practice (Goodman 1986, 32; Valli 1990, 49; Ross and Hannay 1986, 13; Ross 1988, 5).

As in most critical postmodern critiques, feminist theory takes on an extremely important role in post-formal teacher reflection. By focusing on female experience, teachers and students begin to recognize patterns of exception to the grand narratives of the role of education in the "American success story," to the generalizations made concerning intelligence and school success. As critical postmodern teacher educators illustrate the ways that women's inferior position as teachers and pupils has been a social construction rather than an innate condition, prospective teachers come to understand the nature of "difference" and the insight that emerges from such an appreciation. They see how single norms of school achievement may neglect and distort the skills and unique perspectives brought to the classroom by students who are in some way different. When teachers comprehend the parameters of behavior schools allow different kinds of students, they are empowered to better understand the ways that schooling shapes the future social and economic roles of students. For example, do race and social class help determine assessments of which children are merely "too frisky" or which children are "bad"? Such determinations may drastically influence the quality of a child's future.

As teachers come to reflect on the way middle-class white males have been viewed as the prototype universal human being, they begin to uncover various ways that individuals who fall outside this universe are deemed inferior. Such appreciations exert a powerful effect on the ways one approaches the teaching act. Teachers gain the ability to conceptualize different kinds of social success, academic skills, or forms of intelligence. Since technicist schools have formulated an exclusive measure of success based on an androcentric model of competitive performance, it becomes quite difficult for students who come from outside of the mainstream to excel in such institutions. As they reflect on such information, teachers begin to uncover the power of domination in educational settings. Everyday school events once ignored now begin to stand out like cancer cells highlighted by dye. Reflective teachers are shocked by the punitive attitudes of the curriculum toward students who speak nonstandard English, the irrelevance in the everyday classroom of the special talents possessed by black and Latino students, the racial and class imbalances in gifted and talented programs, the attention paid to boys as opposed to girls in classroom discussions, and the way levels of school funding differ based on the economic class of students in attendance (Maher and Rathbone 1986, 220, 230–31; Shor 1992, 26).

Thus, to critical postmodernist teacher education, reflection is a form of consciousness raising, an activity that directs teacher attention to the inseparability of thinking and politics. Drawing upon student observations in field experiences, teacher educators encourage questions about the conventional wisdom and taken-for-granted practices of the teacher work-place. Utilizing the ethnographic and semiotic techniques to which we referred in Chapter 9, less time is spent simply teaching in these field experiences. Unreflective practice teaching leads to an uncritical and indiscrete acceptance of weak and oppressive pedagogical practices. As critical researchers, prospective teachers bring their observations to sem-inars where they are questioned and deconstructed in light of social and pedagogical theory. In such a situation attention is focused on such themes as language, history, culture, and power. Questions concerning the moral and political implications of school structures and pedagogies are explored in light of the dominant perceptions of the role and responsibilities of an "effective teacher" (May and Zimpher 1986, 95–96; Noordhoff and Kleinfeld 1990, 174; Liston and Zeichner 1988, 14, 24–26).

Just as all forms of cognition possess political implications, all forms of teacher education are ideological. Though rarely stated explicitly, teacher education promotes specific political values in the visions it holds of good schools and good teachers. By promoting forms of reflection that do not take into account questions of domination and power, technicist teacher education programs ensure the perpetuation of inegalitarian school policies (Valli 1990, 53; Zeichner 1983, 3). Just because teacher educators pay homage to the goal of reflective practice and promote innovations such as action research, it does not necessarily mean that they embrace a critical postmodern approach to professional preparation. Indeed, when one ex-amines the discourse of reflection in teacher education, it becomes appar-ent that it often has fallen captive to the logic of technicalization. Reduced to a set of procedures, teacher reflection becomes little more than a skill to be learned as a part of a larger battery of competencies. (Did the teacher employ humor in the lesson? Was a personal example used to illustrate the information presented? Did the teacher *reflect* on the success or failure of the lesson?)

Reflection in a critical postmodern context is not viewed as an end in itself, but as a method of developing ethical judgments and emancipatory actions. Such reflection refuses to accept the social context in which teaching takes place as a given, a social condition impervious to change. Seeking ways of empowering the voiceless, critical postmodern reflection considers the ways that race, class, and gender biases lead to oppressive school policies. Understanding that an ethic of caring is important, post-formal forms of teacher reflection realize that it takes more than caring to change hegemonic social relations. Caring alone does not uncover the relationship between structural relations and school culture. Inequality exists and oppression is a reality; these sober truths must be confronted in any notion of reflection that attaches itself to democratic principles and the precepts of social justice. It is this type of reflection that leads to alternate educational actions that expand the frontiers of consciousness while appreciating and involving the dispossessed (Liston and Zeichner 1988, 23–26; May and Zimpher 1986, 96; Valli 1990, 49–50).

RESEARCH AND REFLECTION—THE MARROW OF POST-FORMAL TEACHER EDUCATION

Post-formal teacher education, unlike technical skills approaches, employs research and reflection as a core around which the curriculum of professional preparation revolves. Utilizing action research strategies as catalysts for critical reflection and post-formal practitioner thinking, critical postmodern teacher educators are dedicated to the development of novice teachers' ability to perceive classroom activities in a broad cultural and historical context. Understood in this manner, teachers preparation would involve preparing practitioners in a way that facilitated their ability to connect the postmodern condition and the vicissitudes of hyperreality to the consciousness construction of both their students and themselves. In order to facilitate such reflection critical postmodern professors of education involve their students in journal keeping, textual deconstruction, clinical interviewing, and reflective recall procedures where novice teachers view videotape recordings of their teaching and answer inquiries about their perceptions, thinking, intentions, assumptions, and conceptual schemes.

Along with such techniques these teacher education programs involve student teachers as full partners in the study of teacher thinking. Empowered in such a manner, teacher education students take responsibility for teaching themselves in the larger effort to learn about teaching methods. In addition to field experiences and professor-directed activities, prospective teachers explore various teaching approaches. Combining secondary library work with ethnographic interviews and videotaping of practicing teachers, students contribute to classroom research collections as they leave their data for the use of students in subsequent terms. Novice teachers obtain an appreciation of the social, political, and pedagogical dimensions of specific teaching methods, perceiving them as both students and teachers and reflecting on both forms of experience (Clark 1987, 13–14; Zeichner 1983, 6).

At the same time, teacher education students learn to apply deconstructive textual analysis in their attempt to understand and critically reflect upon the act of teaching. While they learn about semiotic techniques for teasing meaning from written texts, one of the most important forms of teacher inquiry leading to reflection involves the deconstruction of non-literary texts. Employing such strategies can empower teachers to make more critically grounded assessments of their own teaching and the teaching that surrounds them. Language arts and English teachers, for example, can use this form of research to understand why problems exist in so many classes where there is an attempt to teach writing. Deconstructing the assumptions behind certain techniques, teachers expose the fact that composition teachers often assess their students' writing by the standards of mainstream academic discourse. Deeming such standards to be obvious to everyone, teachers see no reason to teach them to their pupils. When students are confronted with such teacher assumptions, the researchers found that those who write poorly were labeled unintelligent, not simply ill-informed (Harned 1987, 12–14). In the same way, teacher education students deconstructing social studies classes find that students who perform poorly in this context are often not as much deficient in knowledge about the subject as they are in the discursive rules that underlie the classroom conversations and the evaluations of information covered in them.

As teachers become reflective researchers, they acquire the ability to adapt larger emancipatory ideas to specific teaching contexts. Contrary to Cartesian–Newtonian perspectives, qualitative educational researchers have found that what is known as good teaching is a highly subjective construct that varies with context. Even technical considerations such as what seems to be the correct amount of expectation for one class may be too demanding for another group and too easy for a third class. This is where research becomes extremely important as a pedagogical device. Teacher educators must provide novices the ability to read the semiotics of teaching, the ability to interpret the numerous layers of communications that shape the classroom, and to adjust their teaching strategies to address them. Doing so enables post-formal teachers to become far more familiar with student lives, with the knowledge they bring to the classroom, and the ways that this information can be connected to the goals of the classroom (Floden and Klinzing 1990, 18; Bowers and Flinders 1990, 225; Maher and Rathbone 1986, 228).

Paulo Freire and Ira Shor provide great insight into the attempt to explore student experience and integrate such knowledge into the curriculum. Such inquiry focuses on the spoken and written words of students in order that teachers might appreciate what they know, their goals, and the texture of their lives. I can teach effectively, Shor writes, only if I have researched my students' levels of thought, their skills, their feelings. Problems should be posed around the generative themes of the everyday life of students. This problem posing, Freire and Shor contend, takes place in the midst of academic study, as lessons become not facts to memorize but problems posed in the context of student experience. Subject matter is taught dialogically with students viewing their lives through the frames constructed by the knowledge of academic disciplines. Freire calls this reflective stance "an epistemological relationship to reality," a situation where one learns to critically examine personal experience, searching life for meaning and significance (Shor and Freire 1987, 8–9; Shor 1992, 33).

While teaching teachers on the Rosebud Sioux Reservation in South Dakota in a tribal college, I utilized reflective inquiry to help prospective teachers examine their personal experience in light of pedagogical concerns and their attempt to become professionals. As we examined the social and political context in which schools in general take place, we explored the specific context of the reservation in which my students had attended school and planned to teach. In the course of these studies my students examined their experiences as students and as community members, as well as the genesis of their desire to teach. Researching their own consciousness construction, they connected their life histories to the culture of the reservation and the lives of their own and their peers' experiences. The students began to uncover the ways social and political forces had shaped their identities and their lives as students.

In one particularly poignant class meeting after weeks of such explorations, all my students sat around a seminar table and cried together as they spoke of the peer rejection each of them had experienced. They talked in very personal terms about the cultural dislocation they had all realized. One student named the experience for the others as she described growing up with one foot in native and another foot in Anglo culture, not really understanding or belonging to either one. Because of the "civilizing" work of schools and religion, many of her connections to traditional native culture were broken, while at the same time life on the reservation was far removed from Anglo experience. Another student, a physically imposing Vietnam war veteran, struck a common chord when he described beatings he had received by his wife and her brothers when they got drunk. Attacking him with crowbars and tire tools, his wife and in-laws wanted to remind him that he was still an Indian, no better than them just because he was going to the "white" college. These prospective teachers could never approach teaching as simply a technical act; they could never view practitioner thinking outside of a cultural and political context.

THE POST-FORMAL EXTENSION OF FIELD EXPERIENCES

In the spirit of this reflective inquiry, critical postmodern teacher educators begin to reconceptualize the field experiences and student teaching component of professional preparation. Instead of simply teaching or tutoring in these experiences, critical postmodern teacher education students explore the culture of the teacher peer group and/or the youth cultures in the school and the social structures that sustain them. From a cognitive perspective such experiences help novice teachers gain a contextualized understanding, an ability to connect the effects of environment to the development of their consciousness as teachers. Pre–student teaching activities might involve ethnographic interviews of support personnel in the schools from guidance counselors to custodians in an attempt to gain a deep understanding of both explicit and implicit purposes of the school. Semiotic instruction would help student teachers uncover the hidden codes and signs that unconsciously move school events. The context in which student teachers apply their personal pedagogies takes center stage in the post-formal teacher education program. Analysis of the context and the development of strategies that address it become a primary cognitive activity in such programs (Britzman 1991, 241–42, Maher and Rathbone 1986, 229–30).

In technicist forms of student teaching, cooperating teachers are chosen on the basis of their teaching ability. The most desirable cooperating teachers are "master" educators who can show student teachers the "correct" way to teach. In such a situation the reflective aspects of the student teaching experience are overlooked, as technical concerns overwhelm the consciousness of all involved. Student teachers focus their attention on the mastery of information delivery and classroom management skills; broader concerns with the teacher's role such as knowledge production, curriculum development, and critical citizenship are irrelevant (Goodman 1986, 33; Liston and Zeichner 1988, 3–4). From a critical postmodern perspective, it becomes more important for student teachers to find cooperating teachers who are committed to the protection of the practicing teacher's right to experiment, to engage in practices unlike those used by the "master" teacher. Cooperating teachers who are supportive and who nurture and extend the ideas of young initiates are more valuable than cooperating teachers with great teaching skill. Care must be taken to create a stimulating learning environment in field experiences—one that is so tolerant and safe that chances can be taken. A post-formal student teaching experience cannot allow students to merely imitate teachers in the field. The chances it takes involve creating situations where students research the schools, in the process challenging their personal beliefs about the purpose of schools, teaching methods, the cognitive development of children, the definitions of school success, and their own motivations as teachers (Ferguson 1980, 307; Ross 1988, 8; May and Zimpher 1986, 96).

TEACHER EDUCATION AND THE FRAGILITY OF DEMOCRACY

Teacher education and especially its student teaching component often serve the hegemonic role of adapting novices to the existing forms of power that dominate the schools. The critical concept of learning how experience is named and rewarded and how consciousness is constructed in schools is not a part of technicist teacher education programs. The realization that democracy is fragile and must be zealously protected by schools and other social institutions is lost in the technical concern with teaching technique. The discourse of critical thinking and empowerment are diluted by technicist teacher educators who rarely question the content of critical thinking and empowerment for what purposes. Without a critical system of meaning and a vision of an egalitarian future, students in teacher education and students in general are merely adapted to the brutal competition of the existing school and society. While not dismissing the importance of teachers and students being able to "get by" or "make it" in the everyday world of the late twentieth century, it is essential that such individuals are exposed to alternatives, to visions of what can be. Without such visions we are doomed to the perpetuation of the structural inequalities and the cognitive passivity of the status quo. Democracy will struggle to survive in such circumstances (Giroux 1989, 182; Giroux and McLaren 1989, xiv-xxi; Simon 1989, 139).

Let us return for a moment to our discussion in Chapter 7 of cognitive stage theories of adult thinking. In the context of our present analysis of teacher education and democracy, we will reexamine the relationship of these theories to the realm of the political. Based on the early work of William Perry and the women's cognitive research of Belenky, Clinchy,

Goldberger, and Tarule, four levels of adult thinking were theorized. Level one, dualism/received knowledge, views knowledge as a compilation of isolated facts. The text becomes the authority, information is dualistic (either right or wrong), and interpretation is irrelevant. Level two, multiplicity/received knowledge, understands that conflicting interpretations and multiple perspectives are inevitable. Even though ambiguity is recognized, level-two thinkers don't know how to deal with it. Thus, they retreat to the position that knowledge is simply opinion. Level three, reflective skepticism/procedural knowledge, appreciates the notion that interpretations of information vary in quality and some means of assessing their worth is necessary. Thus, they develop a set of procedures, often the scientific method, to evaluate knowledge. Level four, commitment in relativism/constructed knowledge, accepts the idea that individuals must take a position and commit themselves to it though they can't be sure that it is correct. Personal knowledge is integrated with knowledge obtained from others, as thinkers on this level move beyond the procedural thinking of level three. At stage four, forms of meta-analysis begin to develop as thinkers ask who asks questions, why questions are asked, and the procedures by which questions are answered. Post-formal sociocognitive theory picks up at level four and attempts to socially and politically situate and thus sophisticate the types of thinking critical postmodern teachers cultivate (Kurfiss 1988, 9–10, 52–53; Belenky, Clinchy, Goldberger, and Tarule 1986, 35–43, 120–21; Bobbitt 1987, 62–65; Downing 1990, 7–10; Maher and Rathbone 1986, 224).

While resisting the scientistic tendency to transform these stages into a master narrative that is univeralized to all human experience, the stages are useful as heuristic devices. Used to help us understand the connections between thinking and politics, they become valuable in theorizing about critical postmodern forms of curriculum and instruction. Viewed in this manner we come to see more clearly the ways that pedagogy is a form of cultural politics When a democratic citizenry analyzes written and television/media texts only at levels one or two, serious political consequences result. They may not possess the ability to assess political arguments or to understand why particular positions are taken. Even at level three, when procedural thinking is applied to textual reading, the thinking strategies learned may be inadequate to read the messages transmitted at the level of intended coding and signing. Thus, the affective and subliminal impact of the communication's semiotic dimensions may remain unchallenged by the literal procedural reading. In a postmodern hyperreality with its proliferation of encoded communications, a post-formal ability to extract meaning from persuasive information forms such as political communiques, commercial and political advertising, and pictorial images becomes a survival skill. Critical theoretical notions of emancipation and ideological disembedding are contingent on such abilities; indeed, our postmodern notion of an educated person must eventually accommodate them.

The ethical and political demands of the attempt to preserve a democratic culture are on the line. All the critical pedagogical talk about extending democratic possibilities, combatting political tyranny, preventing assaults on human dignity and freedom, and promoting social justice is of little benefit if citizens are cognitively unable, for example, to deconstruct and expose the encoded intentions of George Bush's Willie Horton television advertisements. Educational visions that simply attempt to reveal fixed external truths or the great ideas of America (which typically include celebrations of white-male military and political victories) fail to engage students with living arguments and with practical forms of understanding that move us to acts of democratic courage. This ability to act democratically, to uncover power relations, to expose hegemonic intentions is a moral enterprise, a higher order cognitive maneuver, a courageous act of postmodern citizenship.

TEACHER EDUCATION AND SCHOOL CHANGE

These higher order maneuvers and courageous acts are noble dreams, but a world of schooling marked by bureaucratic irrationality and androcentric authoritarianism awaits the novices who emerge from our critical postmodern teacher education programs. When post-formal teacher educators simply teach their students to "do it differently," they fail to address the lived worlds they will encounter in the schools. Many times new teachers who enter the schools feel betrayed when they are unable to implement their community-based action research strategies, their whole language approaches, their reinterpretations of American history, and so on. Critical postmodern teacher educators owe their students exposure to the ways institutions operate, to the ways bureaucracies suffer goal displacement as they confuse form with substance. Along with methodological, foundational, and field experiences, critical postmodern preparation must provide institutional studies. Recognizing that beginning teachers enter prearranged institutional worlds, these studies assume that in order to be effective, teachers must understand how institutions often operate. Ways to work the system and methods of initiating democratic change given the constraints presented by organizations are central features of critical institutional studies.

A traditional debate within teacher education revolves around the tension between preparing teachers for schools as they presently exist or educating teachers for schools as they could become. Teacher education students often press their professors to prepare them in ways that will enable them to survive in the status quo. Entering colleges of education with a view of teaching as a technical act, students hunger for techniques that will allow them to fit in, to control student behavior, to allay the fears that interfere with their sleep. In no way should such concerns be dismissed as a part of a critical postmodern teacher education program—to do so would be to renounce our feminist democratic commitment to student experience. A healthy dialogue needs to be established among these concerns, the critical postmodern system of meaning, and institutional studies. Indeed, we want our students to survive in existing institutions, but such a concern cannot be allowed to negate the plethora of possibilities offered by the critical reconceptualization of teacher thinking in a post-formal context. A teacher who understands the subtleties of institutional policies and their effects on progressive innovation and the pursuit of justice has learned both a survival lesson and a lesson in practitioner thinking. The two discourses do not have to be in conflict (Goodman 1986, 34; Adler 1991, 77–78).

As teacher education confronts the issue of institutional change in the elementary and secondary schools, prospective teachers study not only the calcifying tendencies of school organization but the rigidifying features of their own consciousness construction. Data indicates that teacher education students often desire to teach in the suburban or rural environments in which they grew up. They typically want to teach children like themselves and find race, class, and gender concerns of multicultural teacher education to be marginal to their personal and professional lives. With such a mind-set they often fall into the belief that there is one preferred way of being which serves as a model for everyone—typically, this model is related to the white middle to upper-middle class. Thus, critical postmodern teacher education is charged with the task of eliciting self-reflection and promoting an awareness of the socially constructed nature of consciousness among such teacher education students. The behavior and knowledge of their own groups must be problem posed, rendered strange enough to evoke student exploration of the genesis of their social group's and thus their own ways of perceiving. As teacher education students study these behaviors and knowledges, they begin to understand the regulative functions of discursive conventions (Gomez 1991, 94–96; Harned 1987, 14). As they begin to learn the ways experience is discursively constituted, they become less likely to confuse cultural difference with inappropriateness or deficiency. This single recognition can lead to dramatic personal and institutional change, as it initiates the critical task of exposing what Peter McLaren and Tomaz Da Silva describe as "empires of consciousness" (McLaren and Da Silva 1992, 2).

Breaking away from these empires and their colonization of cognition, post-formal teacher education seeks to prepare teachers for participation in a pedagogy of consciousness. This critical postmodern consciousness is a connected consciousness that forges alliances and networks based on an ethic of solidarity (Torres 1992, 207; Daines 1987, 5). Networks of teachers and students and teachers and teachers are built upon the notion that reflection is best conceived as a communal activity. Critical networks of reflective practitioners and learners sustain and extend the learning of one another, all the time sophisticating their post-formal cognitive quest and their commitment to social and educational justice. These networks lead to communities of disclosure based on an expansion of political and educational participation that gradually extends into the larger community. Buoyed by the support of their reflective colleagues, post-formal teachers with their understanding of institutional dynamics become leaders in the movement for change in schools and society (Zeichner and Tabachnick 1991, 9). Empowered by their sociocognitive ability to get beyond the blinders of what is labeled common sense, to ask from where existing arrangements come, to expose the tacit ways that consciousness is shaped, and to separate difference from deficiency, post-formal teachers build the political alliances necessary to challenge oppressive school structures and to cure the cognitive illness.

Bibliography

Adler, S. 1991. "Forming a critical pedagogy in the social studies methods class: The use of imaginative literature." In B. Tabachnick and K. Zeichner (eds.), *Issues and Practices in Inquiry-Oriented Teacher Education.* New York: Falmer.

Agger, B. 1991. "Theorizing the decline of discourse or the decline of theoretical discourse?" In P. Wexler, *Critical Theory Now.* New York: Falmer.

Altrichter, H., and P. Posch. 1989. "Does the 'grounded theory' approach offer a guiding paradigm for teacher research?" *Cambridge Journal of Education* 19, no. 1, pp. 21–31.

Anderson, E. 1987. "Gender as a variable in teacher thinking." In R. Thomas (ed.), *Higher Order Thinking: Definition, Meaning and Instructional Approaches.* Washington, D.C.: Home Economics Education Association.

Arlin, P. 1975. "Cognitive development in adulthood: A fifth stage?" *Developmental Psychology* 11, no. 5, pp. 602–6.

Aronowitz, S. 1983. "The relativity of theory." *The Village Voice*, 27 December, p. 60.

Aronowitz, S., and H. Giroux. 1991. *Postmodern Education: Politics, Culture, and Social Criticism.* Minneapolis: University of Minnesota Press.

Ashburn, E. 1987. "Three crucial issues concerning the preparation of teachers for our classrooms: Definition, development, and determination of competence." In Erwin Flaxman (ed.), *Trends and Issues in Education, 1986.* Washington, D.C.: U.S. Department of Education.

Ashley, D. 1991. "Playing with the pieces: The fragmentation of social theory." In P. Wexler, *Critical Theory Now.* New York: Falmer.

Bakhtin, M. 1981. *The Dialogic Imagination.* Austin: University of Texas Press.

Bakhtin, M., and V. Voloshinov. 1986. *Marxism and the Philosophy of Language.* Trans. L. Matejka and T. Titunik. Cambridge, Mass.: Harvard University Press.

Baldwin, E. 1987. "Theory vs. ideology in the practice of teacher education." *Journal of Teacher Education* 38, pp. 16–19.

Barrett, G. 1985. "Thinking, knowledge, and writing: A critical examination of the learning process in schools." Paper presented to the International Writing Convention, University of East Anglia, Norwich, England.

Belenky, M., B. Clinchy, N. Goldberger, and J. Tarule. 1986. *Women's Ways of Knowing: The Development of Self, Voice, and Mind.* New York: Basic Books.

Benson, G. 1989. "Epistemology and science curriculum." *Journal of Curriculum Studies* 21, no. 4, pp. 329–44.

Besag, F. 1986. "Striving after the wind." *American Behavioral Scientist*, 30, no. 1, pp. 15–22.

Bloom, A. 1987. *The Closing of the American Mind.* New York: Simon and Schuster.

Bobbitt, N. 1987. "Reflective thinking: Meaning and implications for teaching." In Ruth G. Thomas, *Higher-Order Thinking: Definition, Meaning and Instructional Approaches.* Washington, D.C.: Home Economics Educational Association.

Bogdan, R., and S. Biklen. 1982. *Qualitative Research for Education: An Introduction to Theory and Methods.* Boston: Allyn and Bacon.

Bohm, D., and F. Peat. 1987. *Science, Order, and Creativity.* New York: Bantam Books.

Bowers, C., and D. Flinders. 1990. *Responsive Teaching: An Ecological Approach to Classroom Patterns of Language, Culture, and Thought.* New York: Teachers College Press.

Bozik, M. 1987. "Critical thinking through creative thinking." Paper presented to the Speech Communication Association, Boston, Mass.

Briggs, J. 1990. *Fire in the Crucible.* Los Angeles: Jeremy Tarcher.

Briggs, J., and F. Peat. 1984. *Looking Glass Universe: The Emerging Science of Wholeness.* New York: Touchstone.

————. 1989. *Turbulent Mirror.* New York: Harper and Row.

Britzman, D. 1991. *Practice Makes Practice: A Critical Study of Learning to Teach.* Albany, N.Y.: State University of New York Press.

Bronner, S. 1988. "Between art and utopia: Reconsidering the aesthetic theory of Herbert Marcuse." In R. Pippin, A. Feenberg, and C. Webel (eds.), *Marcuse: Critical Theory and the Promise of Utopia.* Westport, Conn.: Bergin and Garvey.

Brooks, M. 1984. "A constructivist approach to staff development." *Educational Leadership* 32, pp. 23–27.

Brown, S. 1982. "On humanistic alternatives in the practice of teacher education." *Journal of Research and Development in Education* 15, no. 4, pp. 1–12.

Bullough, R., and A. Gitlin. 1991. "Educative communities and the development of the reflective practitioner." In R. Tabachnick and K. Zeichner, *Issues and Practices in Inquiry-Oriented Teacher Education*. New York: Falmer.

Capra, F. 1982. *The Turning Point: Science, Society, and the Rising Culture*. New York: Simon and Schuster.

Carlson, D. 1991. "Alternative discourses in multicultural education: Towards a critical reconstruction of a curricular field." Paper presented to the Bergamo Conference on Curriculum Theory and Classroom Practice, Dayton, Ohio.

Carr, W., and S. Kemmis. 1986. *Becoming Critical*. Philadelphia: Falmer.

Cherryholmes, C. 1988. *Power and Criticism: Poststructural Investigations in Education*. New York: Teachers College Press.

Clark, C. 1987. *Asking the Right Questions about Teacher Preparation: Contributions of Research on Teacher Thinking*. Occasional Paper No. 110. East Lansing, Mich.: Michigan State University, Institute for Research on Teaching.

Codd, J. 1984. "Introduction." In J. Codd (ed.), *Philosophy, Common Sense, and Action in Educational Administration*. Victoria, Australia: Deakin University Press.

Combs, A., and M. Holland. 1990. *Synchronicity: Science, Myth, and the Trickster*. New York: Paragon House.

Connell, R. 1989. "Curriculum politics, hegemony, and strategies of social change." In H. Giroux and R. Simon, *Popular Culture: Schooling and Everyday Life*. Westport, Conn.: Bergin and Garvey.

Connelly, F., and M. Ben-Peretz. 1980. "Teachers' roles in the using and doing of research and curriculum development." *Journal of Curriculum Studies* 12, no. 2, pp. 95–107.

Courteney, R. 1988. *No One Way of Being: A Study of the Practical Knowledge of Elementary Arts Teachers*. Toronto: MGS Publications.

Cruickshank, D. 1987. *Reflective Teaching: The Preparation of Students of Teaching*. Reston, Va.: Association of Teacher Educators.

Culler, J. 1981. *The Pursuit of Signs: Semiotics, Literature, Deconstruction*. Ithaca, N.Y.: Cornell University Press.

———. 1982. *On Deconstruction: Theory and Criticism after Structuralism*. Ithaca, N.Y.: Cornell University Press.

Daines, J. 1987. "Can higher order thinking skills be taught? By what strategies?" In R. Thomas (ed.), *Higher Order Thinking: Definitions, Meaning and Instructional Approaches*. Washington, D.C.: Home Economics Education Association.

Da Silva, T., and P. McLaren. 1992. "Encounters at the margins: Paulo Freire and U.S. and Brasilian debates on education." In P. McLaren and T. Da Silva (eds.,), *Paulo Freire: A Critical Encounter—The Compassionate Fire of a Revolutionary Life*. London: Routledge.

de Lauretis, T. 1986. "Feminist studies/critical studies: Issues, terms, and contexts." In T. de Lauretis (ed.), *Feminist Studies/Critical Studies.* Bloomington, Ind.: Indiana University Press.

Delpit, L. 1988. "The silenced dialogue: Power and pedagogy in educating other people's children." *Harvard Educational Review* 58, pp. 280–98.

Derrida, J. 1976. *Of Grammatology.* Trans. G. Spivak. Baltimore: Johns Hopkins University Press.

_____. 1981. *Dissemination.* Trans. B. Johnson. Chicago: University of Chicago Press.

Dewey, J. 1916. *Democracy and Education.* New York: The Free Press.

Dobrin, R. 1987. "The nature of causality and reality: A reconciliation of the ideas of Einstein and Bohr in the light of Eastern thought." In D. Ryan, *Einstein and the Humanities.* Westport, Conn.: Greenwood Press.

Donmoyer, R. 1987. "Beyond Thorndike/beyond melodrama. *Curriculum Inquiry* 17, no. 4, pp. 353–63.

_____. 1990. "Curriculum, community, and culture: Reflections and pedagogical possibilities." In J. Sears and J. Marshall, *Teaching and Thinking about Curriculum: Critical Inquiries.* New York: Teachers College Press.

Downing, R. 1990. "Reflective judgment in debate: Or, the end of critical thinking as the goal of educational debate." Paper presented to the Western Forensic Association, San Francisco, Calif.

Doyle, W. 1977. "Paradigms for research on teacher effectiveness." *Review of Research in Education* 5, pp. 163–98.

D'Souza, D. 1991. *Illiberal Education: The Politics of Race and Sex on Campus.* New York: The Free Press.

Duke, D. 1979. "Environmental influences on classroom management." In D. Duke (ed.), *Classroom Management.* Seventy-Eight Yearbook of the National Society for the Study of Education. Chicago: University of Chicago Press.

_____. 1985. "What is the nature of educational excellence and should we try to measure it?" *Phi Delta Kappan* 66, no. 10, pp. 671–74.

Ebert, T. 1991. "The difference of postmodern feminism." *College English* 58, no. 8, pp. 886–904.

Eisner, E. 1984. "Can educational research inform educational practice?" *Phi Delta Kappan* 65, no. 7, pp. 447–52.

Elliot, J. 1989. "Studying the school curriculum through insider research." Paper presented to the International Conference on School-Based Innovations: Looking Forward to the 1990s, Hong Kong.

Fee, E. 1982. "Is feminism a threat to scientific objectivity?" *International Journal of Women's Studies,* 4, pp. 378–92.

Feinberg, W. 1989. "Foundationalism and recent critiques of education." *Educational Theory* 39, no. 2, pp. 133–38.

Ferguson, M. 1980. *The Aquarian Conspiracy: Personal and Social Transformation In Our Time.* Los Angeles, Calif.: J. P. Tarcher, Inc.

Fiske, D. 1986. "Specificity of method and knowledge in social science." In D. Fiske and R. Shweder, *Metatheory in Social Science: Pluralisms and Subjectivities.* Chicago: Ill.: University of Chicago Press.

Floden, R., and H. Klinzing. 1990. "What can research on teacher thinking contribute to teacher preparation? A second opinion." *Educational Researcher* 19, no. 5, pp. 15–20.

Fosnot, C. 1988. "The dance of education." Paper presented to the Annual Conference of the Association for Educational Communication and Technology, New Orleans, La.

Foucault, M. 1980. *Power/Knowledge: Selected Interviews and Other Writers.* C. Gordon (ed.). New York: Pantheon.

Freire, P. 1972. "Research methods." Paper presented to a seminar, Studies in Adult Education, Dar-es-Salaam, Tanzania.

———. 1985. *The Politics of Education: Culture, Power, and Liberation.* Westport, Conn.: Bergin and Garvey.

Frye, C. 1987. "Einstein and African religion and philosophy: The hermetic parallel." In Ryan, D., *Einstein and the Humanities.* Westport, Conn.: Greenwood Press.

Gardner, H. 1983. *Frames of Mind: The Theory of Multiple Intelligences.* New York: Basic Books.

Garman, N., and H. Hazi. 1988. "Teachers ask: Is there life after Madeline Hunter?" *Phi Delta Kappan* 69, pp. 670–72.

Garrison, J. 1988. "Democracy, scientific knowledge, and teacher empowerment." *Teachers College Record* 89, no. 4, pp. 487–504.

Gergen, K. 1991. *The Saturated Self: Dilemmas of Identity in Contemporary Life.* New York: Basic Books.

Giddens, A. 1986. *Central Problems in Social Theory: Action, Structure, and Contradictions in Social Analysis.* Berkeley: University of California Press.

Gilbert, P. 1989. "Personally (and passively) yours: Girls, literacy, and education." *Oxford Review of Education* 15, no. 3, pp. 257–65.

Gilligan, C. 1981. *In a Different Voice: Psychological Theory and Women's Development.* Cambridge, Mass.: Harvard University Press.

Giroux, H. 1981. *Ideology, Culture, and the Process of Schooling.* Philadelphia: Temple University Press.

———. 1983. *Theory and Resistance in Education.* Westport, Conn.: Bergin and Garvey.

———. 1988a. *Schooling and the Struggle for Public Life.* Minneapolis: University of Minnesota Press.

———. 1988b. *Teachers as Intellectuals: Toward a Critical Pedagogy of Learning.* Westport, Conn.: Bergin and Garvey.

———. 1989. "Educational reform and teacher empowerment." In H. Holtz, et al. (eds.), *Education and the American Dream.* Westport, Conn.: Bergin and Garvey.

_____ . 1991. "Introduction: Modernism, postmodernism and feminism: Re-thinking the boundaries of educational discourse." In H. Giroux, *Postmodernism, Feminism, and Cultural Politics: Redrawing Educational Boundaries*. Albany, N.Y.: State University of New York Press.

_____ . 1992. *Border Crossings: Cultural Workers and the Politics of Education*. New York: Routledge.

Giroux, H., and S. Aronowitz. 1985. *Education under Siege*. Westport, Conn.: Bergin and Garvey.

Giroux, H., and P. McLaren. 1988. "Teacher education and the politics of democratic reform." In H. Giroux, *Teachers as Intellectuals: Toward a Critical Pedagogy of Learning*. Westport, Conn.: Bergin and Garvey.

_____ . 1989. "Introduction: schooling, cultural politics, and the struggle for democracy." In H. Giroux and P. McLaren, *Critical Pedagogy, the State, and Cultural Struggle*. Albany, N.Y.: State University of New York Press.

_____ . 1991. "Language, schooling, and subjectivity: Beyond a pedagogy of reproduction and resistance." In K. Borman, P. Swami, and L. Wagstaff (eds.), *Contemporary Issues in U.S. Education*. Norwood, N.J.: Ablex Publishing.

Giroux, H., and R. Simon. 1989. "Popular culture as a pedagogy of pleasure and meaning." In H. Giroux and R. Simon, *Popular Culture: Schooling and Everyday Life*. Westport, Conn.: Bergin and Garvey.

Glickman, C. 1985. "Development as the aim of instructional supervision." Paper presented to the Association for Supervision and Curriculum Development, Chicago.

Gomez, M. 1991. "Teaching a language of opportunity in language arts methods course: Teaching for David, Albert, and Darlene." In B. Tabachnich and K. Zeichner (eds.), *Issues and Practices in Inquiry-Oriented Teacher Education*. New York: Falmer.

Goodman, J. 1986. "Constructing a practical philosophy of teaching: A study of preservice teachers' professional perspectives." Paper presented to the American Educational Research Association, San Francisco, Calif.

Gordon, E., F. Miller, and D. Rollock. 1990. "Coping with communicentric bias in knowledge production in the social sciences." *Educational Researcher* 19, no. 3, pp. 14–19.

Gould, S. 1981. *The Mismeasure of Man*. New York: W. W. Norton.

Greene, M. 1988. *The Dialectic of Freedom*. New York: Teachers College Press.

Greene, M. 1986. "Reflection and passion in teaching." *Journal of Curriculum and Supervision* 2, no. 9, pp. 68–87.

Grimmett, P., G. Erickson, A. MacKinnon, and T. Riecken. 1990. "Reflective Practice in Teacher Education." In R. Clift, W. Houston, and M. Pugach, *Encouraging Reflective Practice in Education: An Analysis of Issues and Programs*. New York: Teachers College Press.

Grumet, M. 1992. "The curriculum: What are the basics and are we teaching them?" In J. Kincheloe and S. Steinberg, *Thirteen Questions: Reframing Education's Conversation*. New York: Peter Lang.

Grumet, M. 1988. *Bitter Milk: Women and Teaching*. Amherst, Mass.: University of Massachusetts Press.

Harned, J. 1987. "Post-structuralism and the teaching of composition." *Freshman English Notes* 15, no. 2, pp. 10–16.

Haroutunian-Gordon, S. 1988. "Teaching in an 'ill-structured' situation: The case of Socrates." *Educational Theory*, 38, no. 2, pp. 225–37.

Harris, K. 1984. "Philosophers of education: Detached spectators or political practitioners." In J. Codd, *Philosophy, Common Sense, and Action in Educational Administration*. Victoria, Australia: Deakin University Press.

Harrison, B. 1985. *Making the Connections: Essays in Feminist Social Ethics*. Boston: Beacon Press.

Harvey, D. 1989. *The Conditions of Postmodernity*. Cambridge, Mass.: Basil Blackwell.

Hebridge, D. 1989. *Hiding in the Light*. New York: Routledge.

Held, D. 1980. *Introduction to Critical Theory: Horkheimer to Habermas*. Berkeley, Calif.: University of California Press.

Hultgren, F. 1987. "Critical Thinking: Phenomenological and Critical Foundation." In Ruth G. Thomas, *Higher-Order Thinking: Definition, Meaning and Instructional Approaches*. Washington, D.C.: Home Economics Education Association.

Hunter, M. 1987. "Beyond rereading Dewey . . . what's next? A response to Gibboney." *Educational Leadership*, 35, pp. 51–53.

Hutcheon, L. 1988. *A Poetics of Postmodernism*. New York: Routledge.

Jaggar, A. 1983. *Feminist Politics and Human Nature*. Totowa, N.J.: Rowman and Allanheld.

Jaynes, J. 1976. *The Origin of Consciousness in the Breakdown of the Bicameral Mind*. Boston: Houghton Mifflin.

Jones, N., and M. Cooper. 1987. "Teacher effectiveness and education: A case of incompatibility." Paper presented to the American Educational Research Association, Washington, D.C.

Kamii, C. 1981. "Teacher's autonomy and scientific training." *Young Children* 31, pp. 5–14.

Kaufman, B. 1978. "Piaget, Marx, and the political ideology of schooling." *Journal of Curriculum Studies* 10, no. 1, pp. 19–44.

Kaye, H. 1991. *The Powers of the Past: Reflections on the Crisis and the Promise of History*. Minneapolis: University of Minnesota Press.

Kegan, R. 1982. *The Evolving Self: Problem and Process in Human Development*. Cambridge, Mass.: Harvard University Press.

Kellner, D. 1991. "Reading images critically: Toward a postmodern pedagogy." In H. Giroux (ed.), *Postmodernism, Feminism, and Cultural Politics:*

Redrawing Educational Boundaries. Albany, N.Y.: State University of
New York Press.

Kimball, R. 1990. *Tenured Radicals: How Politics Has Corrupted Our Higher
Education.* New York: Harper and Row.

Kincheloe, J. et al. 1987. "From Jaynesian consciousness to critical consciousness." Paper presented to the Louisiana Philosophy of Education Society, New Orleans.

————. 1991. *Teachers as Researchers: Qualitative Paths to Empowerment.*
New York: Falmer.

Kincheloe, J., and W. Pinar. 1991. "Introduction." In J. Kincheloe, and W. Pinar,
*Curriculum as Social Psychoanalysis: Essays on the Significance of
Place.* Albany, New York: State University of New York Press.

Kincheloe, J., S. Steinberg, and D. Tippins. 1992. *The Stigma of Genius: Einstein and Beyond Modern Education.* Wakefield, N.H.: Hollowbrook.

Koetting, J. 1988. "Educational connoisseurship and educational criticism:
Pushing beyond information and effectiveness." Paper presented to the
Association for Educational Communications and Technology, New
Orleans, La.

Kramer, D. 1983. "Post-formal operations? A need for further conceptualization." *Human Development* 26, pp. 91–105.

Kristeva, J. 1987. *In the Beginning Was Love.* New York: Columbia University
Press.

Kroath, F. 1989. "How do teachers change their practical theories?" *Cambridge
Journal of Education* 19, no. 1, pp. 59–69.

Kuhn, T. 1962. *The Structure of Scientific Revolutions.* Chicago: University of
Chicago Press.

Kurfiss, J. 1988. *Critical Thinking: Theory, Research, Practice, and Possibilities.* Washington, D.C.: Association for the Study of Higher Education.

Lampert, M., and C. Clark. 1990. "Expert knowledge and expert thinking in
teaching: A response to Floden and Klinzing." *Educational Researcher*
19, no. 5, pp. 21–23, 42.

Langman, L. 1991. "From pathos to panic: American character meets the future.
In P. Wexler, *Critical Theory Now.* New York: Falmer.

Lankshear, C. 1992. "Functional literacy from a Freirean point of view." In P.
McLaren and P. Leonard (eds.), *Paulo Freire: A Critical Encounter—
The Compassionate Fire of a Revolutionary Life.* London: Routledge.

Lash, S. 1990. *Sociology of Postmodernism.* New York: Routledge.

Laster, J. 1987. "Problem solving: Definition and meaning." In R. Thomas,
*Higher Order Thinking: Definition, Meaning, and Instructional Ap-
proaches.* Washington, D.C.: Home Economics Education Association.

Lavine, T. 1984. *From Socrates to Sartre: The Philosophic Quest.* New York:
Bantam Books.

Lawler, J. 1975. "Dialectical philosophy and developmental psychology: Hegel
and Piaget on contradiction." *Human Development* 18, pp. 1–17.

Leshan, L., and H. Margeneu. 1982. *Einstein's Space and Van Gogh's Sky: Physical Reality and Beyond*. New York: Macmillian Publishing Company.

Lesko, N. 1988. *Symbolizing Society: Stories, Rites, and Structure in a Catholic High School*. New York: Falmer.

Lincoln, Y. and Guba, E. 1985. *Naturalistic Inquiry*. Beverly Hills, Calif.: Sage Publications.

Liston, D., and K. Zeichner. 1988. "Critical pedagogy and teacher education." Paper presented to the American Educational Research Association, New Orleans, La.

Longstreet, W. 1982. "Action research: A paradigm." *The Educational Forum* 46, no. 2, pp. 136–49.

Lowe, D. 1982. *History of Bourgeois Perception*. Chicago: University of Chicago Press.

Luke, T. 1991. "Touring hyperreality: Critical theory confronts informational society." In P. Wexler, *Critical Theory Now*. New York: Falmer.

Lyotard, J. 1984. *The Postmodern Condition*. Minneapolis: University of Minnesota Press.

McKernan, J. 1988. "Teacher as researcher: Paradigm and praxis." *Contemporary Education* 59, no. 3, pp. 154–58.

McLaren, P. Forthcoming. "Postmodernism/post-colonialism/pedagogy." *Education and Society*.

———. 1989. *Life in Schools*. New York: Longman.

———. 1991a. "Decentering culture: Postmodernism, resistance, and critical pedagogy." In Nancy B. Wyner, *Current Perspectives on the Culture of Schools*. Boston, Mass.: Brookline Books.

———. 1991b. "Schooling and the postmodern body: Critical pedagogy and the politics of enfleshment." In H. Giroux (ed.), *Postmodernism, Feminism, and Cultural Politics: Redrawing Educational Boundaries*. Albany, N.Y.: State University of New York Press.

———. 1992. "Collisions with otherness: 'Traveling' theory, post-colonial criticism, and the politics of ethnographic practice—the mission of the wounded ethnographer." *Qualitative Studies in Education* 5, no. 1, pp. 1–15.

McLaren, P., and T. Da Silva. 1992. "Encounters at the margins: Paulo Freire and U.S. and Brasilian debates on education." In P. McLaren and T. Da Silva (eds.), *Paulo Freire: A Critical Encounter—the Compassionate Fire of a Revolutionary Life*. London: Routledge.

Madaus, G. 1985. "Test scores as administrative mechanisms in educational policy." *Phi Delta Kappan* 66, no. 9, pp. 611–17.

Maeroff, G. 1988. "A blueprint for empowering teachers." *Phi Delta Kappan* 69, no. 7, pp. 472–77.

Maher, F., and C. Rathbone. 1986. "Teacher education and feminist theory: Some implications for practice." *American Journal of Education* 94, no. 2, pp. 214–35.

Mahoney, M., and W. Lyddon. 1988. "Recent developments in cognitive approaches to counseling and psychotherapy." *The Counseling Psychologist* 16, no. 2, pp. 190–234.

Mandell, S. 1987. "A search for form: Einstein and the poetry of Louis Zukofsky and William Carlos Williams." In Ryan (ed.), *Einstein and the Humanities*. Westport, Conn.: Greenwood Press.

Marcuse, H. 1955. *Eros and Civilization*. Boston: Beacon Press.

Mardle, G. 1984. "Power, tradition, and change: Educational implications of the thought of Antonio Gramsci." In J. Codd (ed.), *Philosophy, Common Sense, and Action in Educational Administration*. Victoria, Australia: Deakin University Press.

May, W., and N. Zimpher. 1986. "An examination of three theoretical perspectives on supervision: Perceptions of preservice field supervision." *Journal of Curriculum and Supervision* 1, no. 2, pp. 83–99.

Mies, M. 1982. "Toward a methodology for feminist research." In G. Bowles and R. Klein, *Theories of Women's Studies*. Boston: Routledge and Kegan Paul.

Moore, M. 1989. "Problem finding and teacher experience." Paper presented to the Annual Meeting of the Eastern Educational Research Association Meeting, Savannah, Ga.

Morrow, R. 1991. "Critical theory, Gramsci and cultural studies: From structuralism to post-structuralism." In P. Wexler, *Critical Theory Now*. New York: Falmer.

Munby, H., and T. Russell. 1989. "Educating the reflective teacher: An essay review of two books by Donald Schon." *Journal of Curriculum Studies* 21, no. 1, pp. 71–80.

Munday, L., and J. Davis. 1974. *Varieties of Accomplishment after College: Perspectives on the Meaning of Academic Talent*. Iowa City, Ia: ACT Publications.

Myers, L. 1987. "The deep structure of culture: Relevance of traditional African culture in contemporary life." *Journal of Black Studies* 18, no. 1, pp. 72–85.

Nixon, J. 1981. "Postscript." In J. Nixon (ed.), *A Teachers' Guide to Action Research*. London: Grant McIntyre.

Noffke, S., and M. Brennan. 1988. "Action research and reflective student teaching at UW—Madison: Issues and examples." Paper presented to the Association of Teacher Educators, San Diego, Calif.

———. 1991. "Student teachers use action research: Issues and examples." In B. Tabachnick and K. Zeichner, *Issues and Practices in Inquiry-Oriented Teacher Education*. New York: Falmer.

Noordhoff, K., and J. Kleinfeld. 1990. "Shaping the rhetoric of reflection for multicultural settings." In R. Clift, W. Houston, and M. Pugach, *Encouraging Reflective Practice in Education: An Analysis of Issues and Programs*. New York: Teachers College Press.

Nyang, S., and A. Vandi. 1980. "Pan Africanism in world history." In M. Asante and A. Vandi, *Contemporary Black Thought: Alternative Analyses in Social and Behavioral Science*. Beverly Hills, Calif.: Sage Publications.

Oldroyd, D., and T. Tiller. 1987. "Change from within: An Account of school-based collaborative action research in an English secondary school." *Journal of Education for Teaching* 12, no. 3, pp. 13–27.

Oliver, D., and K. Gershman. 1989. *Education, Modernity, and Fractured Meaning: Toward a Process Theory of Teaching and Learning*. Albany, N.Y.: State University of New York Press.

O'Loughlin, M. N.d. "Rethinking science education: Beyond Piagetian constructivism toward a sociocultural model of teaching and learning." *Journal of Research in Science Teaching*. Forthcoming.

Orteza Y Miranda. 1988. "Broadening the focus of research in education." *Journal of Research and Development in Education* 22, no. 1, pp. 23–28.

Peters, W., and B. Amburgey. 1982. "Teacher intellectual disposition and cognitive classroom verbal reactions." *Journal of Educational Research* 76, no. 2, pp. 94–99.

Piaget, J., and R. Garcia. 1989. *Psychogenesis and the History of Science*. Trans. Helga Feider. New York: Columbia University Press.

Pinar, W. 1975. "The analysis of educational experience." In W. Pinar (ed.), *Curriculum Theorizing: The Reconceptualists*. Berkeley, Calif.: McCutchun Publishing Company.

Pinar, W., and M. Grumet. 1988. "Socratic *Caesura* and the theory-practice relationship." In W. Pinar (ed.), *Contemporary Curriculum Discourses*. Scottsdale, Ariz.: Gorsuch Scarisbruck.

Ponzio, R. 1985. "Can we change content without changing context?" *Teacher Education Quarterly* 12, no. 3, pp. 39–43.

Popkewitz, T. 1981. "The study of schooling: Paradigms and field-based methodologies in education research and evaluation." In T. Popkewitz and B. Tabachnick (eds.), *The Study of Schooling*. New York: Praeger.

———. 1987. "Organization and power: Teacher education reforms." *Social Education* 39, pp. 496–500.

Poplin, M. 1988. "Holistic/constructivist principles of the teaching/learning process: Implications for the field of learning disabilities." *Journal of Learning Disabilities* 21, no. 7, pp. 401–16.

Porter, A. 1988. "Indicators: Objective data or political tool?" *Phi Delta Kappan* 69, no. 7, pp. 503–8.

Posner, G. 1987. "Epistemological and psychological aspects of conceptual change: The case of learning special relativity." In D. Ryan, *Einstein and the Humanities*. Westport, Conn.: Greenwood Press.

Poster, M. 1989. *Critical Theory and Poststructuralism: In Search of a Context*. Ithaca, N.Y.: Cornell University Press.

Postman, N. 1985. "Critical thinking in an electronic era." *Phi Kappa Phi Journal* 65, pp. 4–8, 17.

Pumroy, D. 1984. "Why is it taking so long for behavior modification to be used in the schools/or am I being too impatient?" Paper presented to the National Association of School Psychologists, Philadelphia, Pa.

Reinharz, S. 1982. "Experiential analysis: A contribution to feminist research." In G. Bowles and R. Klein (eds.), *Theories of Women's Studies*. Boston: Routledge and Kegan Paul.

Reinharz, S. 1979. *On Becoming a Social Scientist*. San Francisco, Calif.: Jossey-Bass.

Resnick, R. 1980. "Misconceptions about Einstein." *Journal of Chemical Education* 57, no. 12, pp. 857–62.

Reynolds, R. 1987. "Einstein and psychology: The genetic epistemology of relativistic physics." In D. Ryan, *Einstein and the Humanities*. Westport, Conn.: Greenwood Press.

Richards, C. 1988. "Indicators and three types of educational monitoring systems: Implications for design." *Phi Delta Kappan* 69, no. 7, pp. 495–99.

Riegel, K. 1973. "Dialectic operations: The final period of cognitive development. *Human Development* 16, pp. 346–70.

Rifkin, J. 1989. *Entropy: Into the Greenhouse World*. New York: Bantam Books.

Rifkin, J. 1987. *Time Wars: The Primary Conflict in Human History*. New York: Simon and Schuster.

Ross, D. 1984. "A practical model for conducting action research in public school settings." *Contemporary Education* 55, no. 2, pp. 113–17.

Ross, E. 1988. "Teacher values and the construction of curriculum." Paper presented to the American Educational Research Association, New Orleans.

Ross, E., and L. Hannay. 1986. "Toward a critical theory of reflective inquiry." *Journal of Teacher Education*, pp. 9–15.

Ruddick, J. 1989. "Critical thinking and practitioner research: Have they a place in initial teacher training?" Paper presented to the American Educational Research Association, San Francisco.

Scholes, R. 1982. *Semiotics and Interpretation*. New Haven, Conn.: Yale University Press.

Schon, D. 1987. *Educating the Reflective Practitioner*. San Francisco, Calif.: Jossey-Bass Publishers.

Schon, D. 1983. *The Reflective Practitioner: How Professionals Think in Action*. New York: Basic Books.

Shaker, P., and C. Kridel. 1989. "The return to experience: A reconceptualist call." *Journal of Teacher Education*, pp. 2–8.

Shannon, P. 1989. *Broken Promises: Reading Instruction in Twentieth-Century America*. Westport, Conn.: Bergin and Garvey.

Shapiro, H. 1982. "Functionalism, ideology, and the theory of schooling: A review of studies in the history of American education." *Paedogogica Historica* 22, no. 1–2, pp. 157–72.

Shapiro, M. 1992. *Reading the Postmodern Polity: Political Theory as Textual Practice*. Minneapolis: University of Minnesota Press.

Shor, I. 1992. "Education is politics: Paulo Freire's critical pedagogy." In P. McLaren and P. Leonard (eds.), *Paulo Freire: A Critical Encounter— The Compassionate Fire of a Revolutionary Life*. London: Routledge.

Shor, I., and P. Freire. 1987. *A Pedagogy for Liberation*. Westport, Conn.: Bergin and Garvey.

Siegel, F. 1986. "Is Archie Bunker fit to rule? Or: How Immanuel Kant became one of the founding fathers." *Telos* 69, pp. 3–29.

Simon, R. 1989. "Empowerment as a pedagogy of possibility." In H. Holtz, et al. (eds.), *Education and the American Dream*. Westport, Conn.: Bergin and Garvey.

Slaughter, R. 1989. "Cultural reconstruction in the postmodern world." *Journal of Curriculum Studies* 3, pp. 255–70.

Spring, J. 1991. *American Education: An Introduction to Social and Political Aspects*. New York: Longman.

Talbot, M. 1991. *The Holographic Universe*. New York: Harper Collins.

Talbot, M. 1986. *Beyond the Quantum*. New York: Bantam Books.

Torney-Purta, J. 1985. "Linking faculties of education with classroom teachers through collaborative research." *The Journal of Educational Thought* 19, no. 1, pp. 71–77.

Torres, C. 1992. "From the 'pedagogy of the oppressed' to 'a luta continua': The political pedagogy of Paulo Freire." In P. McLaren and P. Leonard, *Paulo Freire: A Critical Encounter—The Compassionate Fire of a Revolutionary Life*. London: Routledge.

Tripp, D. 1988. "Teacher journals in collaborative classroom research." Paper presented to the American Educational Research Association, New Orleans, La.

Valli, L. 1990. "Moral approaches to reflective practice." In R. Clift, W. Houston, and M. Pugach, *Encouraging Reflective Practice in Education: An Analysis of Issues and Programs*. New York: Teachers College Press.

Van Hesteran, F. 1986. "Counseling research in a different key: The promise of human science perspective." *Canadian Journal of Counselling* 20, no. 4, pp. 200–34.

Walkerdine, V. 1984. "Developmental psychology and the child-centered pedagogy: The insertion of Piaget into early education." J. Henriques, W. Hollway, C. Urwin, C. Venn, and V. Walkerdine, *Changing the Subject*. New York: Methuen.

Weedon, C. 1987. *Feminist Practice and Poststructuralist Theory*. London: Blackwell.

Weisberg, J. 1987. "Sex and drugs and Heidegger." *Washington Monthly* 19, pp. 49–53.

Welch, S. 1985. *Communities of Resistance and Solidarity*. Maryknoll, N.Y.: Orbis Books.

———— 1991. "An ethic of solidarity and difference." In H. Giroux (ed.), *Postmodernism, Feminism, and Cultural Politics: Redrawing Educational Boundaries.* Albany, N.Y.: State University of New York Press.

Wertsch, J. 1991. *Voices of the Mind: A Sociocultural Approach to Mediated Action.* Cambridge, Mass.: Harvard University Press.

White, H. 1978. *Tropics of Discourse.* Baltimore: Johns Hopkins University Press.

Whitson, J. 1986. "Interpreting the freedom of speech: Some first amendment education cases." In J. Delly (ed.), *Semiotics: 1985.*

Wilson, S. 1977. "The use of ethnographic techniques in educational research." *Review of Educational Research* 47, no. 1, pp. 245–65.

Wirth, A. 1983. *Productive Work—In Industry and Schools.* Lanham, Md.: University Press of America.

Young, R. 1990. *A Critical Theory of Education: Habermas and Our Children's Future.* New York: Teachers College Press.

Zavarzadeh, M., and D. Morton. 1991. *Theory, (Post)modernity, Opposition: An 'Other' Introduction to Literary and Cultural Theory.* Washington, D.C.: Maisonneuve Press.

Zeichner, K. 1983. "Alternative paradigms of teacher education." *Journal of Teacher Education* 34, no. 3, pp. 3–9.

Zeichner, K., and B. Tabachnick. 1991. "Reflections on reflective teaching." In B. Tabachnick and K. Zeichner (eds.), *Issues and Practices in Inquiry-Oriented Teacher Education.* New York: Falmer.

Zeuli, J., and M. Bachmann. 1986. *Implementation of Teacher Thinking Research as Curriculum Deliberation.* Occasional Paper No. 107. East Lansing, Mich.: Michigan State University, Institute for Research on Teaching.

Ziglar, E., and M. Finn-Stevenson. 1987. *Children: Development and Social Issues.* Lexington, Mass.: D. C. Heath.

Name Index

Alexander, Lamar, 92
Apple, Michael, 128
Aronowitz, Stanley, 93, 98

Bacon, Francis, 3, 44
Bahktin, Mikhail, 54, 96, 111
Bateson, Gregory, 152
Belenky, Mary Field, 76, 227
Benjamin, Walter, 74
Bennett, William, 22, 53, 70, 92
Bloom, Allan, 3, 54, 60, 70, 92, 208
Bohm, David, 28, 101, 102, 148,
    152, 157, 167–68
Bohr, Niels, 28
Brennan, Marie, 180
Bullough, Robert, 10
Bush, George, 9, 31, 48, 55, 57, 92,
    104, 105, 178, 179, 229
Byrne, David, 85

Carlson, Dennis, 52
Clark, Christopher, 19
Clinchy, Blythe McVicker, 76, 227

Da Silva, Tomaz, 231
Da Vinci, Leonardo, 168

Dean, James, 86, 91
Delpit, Lisa, 64
Demme, Jonathan, 86
Derrida, Jacques, 61, 63, 90, 91, 97,
    98, 112, 113, 129, 165
Descartes, René, 2, 3, 44, 114
Dewey, John, 4, 35, 54, 84, 163,
    164–65, 179, 184, 189, 190
Donmoyer, Robert, 218
D'Souza, Dinesh, 53, 60, 208
Du Bois, Barbara, 153
Duchamp, Marcel, 160
Duke, Daniel, 12, 13
Duke, David, 70, 93

Eastwood, Clint, 57, 58, 79
Ebert, Teresa, 85
Eco, Umberto, 94, 209
Einstein, Albert, 28, 101, 148, 166,
    168, 171

Ferguson, Marilyn, 103, 144
Finn, Chester, 208
Foucault, Michel, 39, 97, 111, 159,
    169, 183

Freire, Paulo, 4, 42, 64, 65, 72, 74, 120, 177, 180, 198, 207, 208, 225
Freud, Sigmund, 166

Garbut, John, 68
Gardner, Howard, 41, 60
Garrison, James, 17, 35
Gesell, Arnold, 24
Gilligan, Carol, 52, 76, 140
Giroux, Henry, 11, 42, 79, 81, 93, 98, 208
Gitlin, Andrew, 10
Goldberger, Nancy Rule, 76, 228
Goodman, Jesse, 15, 80
Gould, Sstephen Jay, 96
Gouldner, Alvin, 114
Gramsci, Antonio, 64, 123, 158
Greene, Maxine, 4, 63, 74, 156
Groening, Matt, 63
Grumet, Madeleine, 20, 152, 154, 214

Hall, Edward, 153
Haroutunian-Gordon, Sophie, 213
Heidegger, Martin, 27
Heisenberg, Werner, 28, 166
Hermes, 146, 147, 148
Hofstadter, Richard, 53
Horkheimer, Max, 79, 117
Horton, Willie, 229
Hunter, Madeline, 21, 45
Huxley, Aldous, 93

Jaynes, Julian, 132, 134, 135, 136
Jung, Carl, 158, 166, 171

Kaye, Harvey, 74
Kellner, Douglas, 90
Kierkegaard, Soren, 155
Kimball, Roger, 53, 60
Klee, Paul, 148
Knapp, Robert, 68
Kohlberg, Lawrence, 52, 76, 78, 79
Kristeva, Julia, 104

Kuhn, Thomas, 28

Lewin, Kurt, 21
Lifton, Robert Jay, 95
Liston, Daniel, 43–44
Lyotard, Jean-François, 6, 48

McLaren, Peter, 13, 36, 42, 46, 81, 86, 88, 92, 124, 147, 154, 171, 179–80, 186, 190, 208, 231
McLuhan, Marshall, 90, 199
Marcuse, Herbert, 62, 63
Marx, Karl, 60
Merleau-Ponty, Maurice, 215
Morrison, Toni, 27
Mozart, Wolfgang, 166, 168

Newton, Isaac, 2, 3, 28, 44
Nietzsche, Friedrich, 80
Noffke, Susan, 180

O'Keeffe, Georgia, 160
O'Loughlin, Michael, 65

Perry, William, 141, 181, 227
Piaget, Jean, 5, 21, 22, 41, 60, 78, 107, 108, 110, 113, 116, 117, 126, 129, 131, 139, 140, 141, 142, 154, 164
Pinar, William, 20, 69, 146, 164, 215
Posner, George, 121
Postman, Neil, 91
Prigogine, Ilya, 101, 102
Proteus, 96

Reagan, Ronald, 9, 31, 48, 55, 57, 58, 104, 105, 178, 179
Rousseau, Jean Jacques, 24
Russell, Bertrand, 139

Saussure, Ferdinand de, 85
Schon, Donald, 22
Shor, Ira, 180, 225

Simpson, Bart, 63
Simpson, Lisa, 63
Skinner, B. F., 21, 22

Tarule, Jill Mattuck, 76, 228
Taylor, Fredrick W., 7, 8, 10, 21
Thorndike, Edward, 7, 9, 10
Tyler, Ralph, 10

Walker, Alice, 27
Wallace, George, 102

Weedon, Chris, 95
Welch, Sharon, 67, 74
White, Hayden, 119
Williams, William Carlos, 160
Woolf, Virginia, 149

Young, Robert, 138

Zeichner, Kenneth, 43–44, 195

Subject Index

Accommodation (Piaget), 41, 110, 116–20; anticipatory accommodation, 120, 189, 193, 215; conditions surrounding student accommodation, 121; critical accommodation as emancipatory risk, 120; and critical postmodern teaching, 121–22, 212; impediments to, 122; and intelligence, 118; and irony, 119–20; and new contexts, 164; the particularity of individual classrooms, 218; and power, 169, 212; and questioning, 121; radical potential of, 117, 216; and research, 186; and teacher intuition, 216; and theory, 216; the unexpected, 215

Adult thinking, 22, 140; cognitive stages (Perry), 141–43, 228; commitment in relativity/constructed knowledge, 142, 228; dualism/received knowledge, 141–42, 228; multiciplicity/received knowledge, 142; reflective skepti-cism/procedural knowledge, 142, 228

American politics, 56–58

Antimodernists, 5

Assimilation (Piaget), 41, 110, 116–20, 164

Beginning of the End, 71

Behavioral objectives, 9, 22

Behavioral psychology, 7, 22, 46, 118, 195, 200, 214

Cheyenne, 103

Chinese, 7

CIA, 90

Class, 12, 13, 48–49, 68, 69, 70, 73, 75, 76, 85, 86, 102, 109, 118, 126, 127, 149, 159, 182, 187, 189, 198, 203, 221, 222, 223, 230

Cognitive illness: cure of, 122, 124, 139; educational manifestation of postmodern condition, 28, 55; and literalness of the visual, 190; magnified by hyperreality, 190; postmodern challenge to, 80; restriction of social imagination, 29; strangles reform, 186

Common school crusade, 7

Concrete thinking: and adult cognition, 142; measured by standardized tests, 18

Consciousness, 6, 13, 29, 37; connected consciousness, 131–38, 183, 193, 202, 203, 214, 230, 231; construction of, 31–32, 35, 37, 38, 50–51, 57, 59, 69, 71, 73, 87, 88, 89, 90, 92, 94, 95, 97, 108, 109, 110, 111, 112, 119, 122–23, 131, 139, 140, 146, 153, 157, 159, 165, 166, 167, 177, 180, 188, 189, 190, 192, 198, 199, 203, 206, 207, 208, 212, 215, 220, 225, 226, 230, 231; critical form, 99, 109, 117, 216, 218; expansion of, 66, 72, 97, 223; Freirean stages of, 65, 72; and history, 122–23; individuals unaware of how consciousness is constructed, 123; pedagogy of, 231; and place, 165; postmodern, 87, 88, 94, 95, 97, 222, 223; reconstructing self, 124, 189; semiotic of introspection, 191; shaped by media, 92, 95; student consciousness shaped to ignore ethics and morals, 112

Conservatives, 53–54, 56–58, 60, 68, 70, 73

Constructivism, 22, 36–38, 65, 107–12, 116–17, 120, 121, 122, 123, 124, 125, 126

Critical Constructivism: the accommodation of new definitions of intelligence, 118; action research as extension of, 191–92; and the analysis of discursive formations in the classroom, 112, 113; cognition cannot be separated from historical context, 122–23, 191; and complexity of learning situations, 116; and connected consciousness, 137, 193; and creation of knowledge, 121, 192; criteria for adequate constructions, 111; exposure of developmentalism as a socio-historical construction, 127; forces reconceptualization of social justice, 46; form of world making, 109; individuals operate as different cognitive stages simultaneously, 127; interrelationship between behavior and context, 126; knowledge is negotiable, 61, 147; leads to emacipatory construction of consciousness, 71, 118; learning from comparisons of different contexts, 120; many paths to sophisticated thinking, 115; mind creates rather than reflects, 110; the movement from constructivism to, 36, 65, 78, 109; negation of pre-arranged thinking, 118; and origins of constructions, 113, 122; and passion, 116; producing cognitive dissonance, 121; questioning laboratory research, 115; recognizing social construction of frames of reference, 122; rejects Cartesian truth, 111; rejects dualistic epistemology, 114; responsibility for meaning making rests with humans, 112; and the social construction of knowledge, 48–49, 109, 110; and the social construction of mind, 127; and the social construction of self, 88, 109, 115; as socio-cognitive theory, 110; teacher education, 37–38, 115; ultimate expression is social action, 64–65, 119; value of personal experience, 113

Critical system of meaning, 5, 22, 26, 27, 38, 71–72, 94, 97, 118, 125, 143, 144, 150, 151, 159,

160, 177, 179, 188–89, 190, 191, 205, 217, 227, 230

Critical theory, 22, 41, 78–79, 85, 97–99, 109; action research as the logical educational extension, 182–85; concepts of negation, 117; grounded on a recognition of oppression, 182; reconceptualized form, 97–99

Critical thinking: challenge to tacit political dimensions of the mainstream, 42; as a cognitive skill to be mastered, 25; critical thinking, 26, 27, 179; and emancipation, 26; and empowerment, 26–27; erasing the boundaries between feeling and logic, 26; measurement of, 141; often operates within the boundaries of developmentalism, 128, 141; and social transformation, 25; and subjugated knowledge, 71–75; technicist efforts to cultivate it, 23; uncritical critical thinking, 25, 26, 124

Cult of expertise, 9, 11, 20, 35, 49, 71, 177, 181, 183, 185, 198, 201, 220

Cultural capital, 46, 183, 199

Culture of conformity, 11, 219

Culture of passivity, 14, 154, 181, 204, 218, 219, 220

Currere, 146

Curriculum as Social Psychoanalysis: Essays on the Significance of Place (Kincheloe and Pinar), 69

Curriculum theory, 26–27, 66, 68, 69, 91, 110, 118, 208

Democracy: and accommodation, 118; action research and democratic thinking, 175–78; and androcentrism, 219; and authoritarianism, 219; and forms

of management, 219; fragility of, 27–29, 209; and hyperreality, 97–99, 210; and knowledge, 183, 209; never static, 54; and postformal teachers, 219–20; and power, 49, 97, 99; prodemocracy movement in education, 198; role of learning in a, 23; teacher education, 36, 196, 202, 210; threats to, 80

Deskilling, 8–9, 27, 83; and bureaucracy, 131; and industrial revolution, 206; and modernism, 178, 179

Difference, 65–71, 97, 118, 136, 155–56, 191, 221, 231

Dissemination (Derrida), 112

Dissipative structures, 101

Dreaming, 66

Educational modernism: blinds us to "primitive" goals of education, 138; cognitive essentialism, 125–28; cognitive stagnation of, 99–101; crisis in, 31; crumbling of paradigm, 28; culture of manipulation, 55, 77, 114; deskilling of teaching, 8–9, 131, 178, 179; discomfort with play, 147; etymology, 7; exclusionary conception of intelligence, 126; fragmentation of knowledge, 12, 23, 24, 25, 55, 122; fragmentation of reality, 20, 29, 30, 157, 164; instructional models, 8, 21; lack of imagination, 141; logocentrism, 61, 71, 77, 126, 153; maintenance of status quo, 9, 15–16, 45; and marginalized students, 9; and measurability, 129, 165; political neutrality, 21, 42, 44, 45, 48, 53, 54, 72, 180, 182; procedural knowing, 153, 193, 204, 220; quantitative measure of thinking,

60; rape of natural world, 30; separation of schools from society, 29; silence on moral and ethical matters, 21, 44, 151, 205; social classification as school purpose, 189; standardization of schooling, 10, 11, 15, 18, 21, 23–24, 70, 116, 164; and student teachers, 15; and teacher certainty, 18–19; teachers as knowledge consumers, 18; and time, 29; and trivial, 129

Educational reform: adapts teachers to the status quo, 35, 56; crisis in modernism, 30–31; epistemological assumptions of, 149; formulated outside of social context, 29–30; post-formal reform revolves around the development of teacher thinkers, 217–19; right-wing reforms, 177; romantic maturationists, 24–25, 38; top-down implementation of, 176, 178, 218; will not work without teacher empowerment, 178

Efficiency, and the development of twentieth-century schooling, 8

Epistemology: academia based on fatalistic forms of, 211; Afrocentric ways of knowing, 155–56; and the attempt to accommodate, 123; beginning with the understandings of the oppressed, 161; and certainty, 142; conflict between indigenous and European, 155; connected knowing, 78–79; and consciousness construction, 110–12; and constructivism, 107; critical postmodern, 33, 70, 74, 208–9; and deconstruction, 112; expanding awareness of, 67, 68, 100, 121, 141, 177, 180, 186; feminist, 75–79, 153–55, 156; historical epistemologists understand the etymology of knowl-

edge, 158–59; of hyperreality, 92; knower and known, 107, 114; logical autonomy, 78–79; modernist dualistic form of, 114; modernists locate truth in external reality, 110; Native American ways of knowing, 155; one-dimensionality, 68; one-truth epistemology, 3–5, 23, 55, 137; and political, 44–47; postepistemology, 112; realist, 208; recognizes context, 130; and research, 180, 181; standpoint, 74; and subjugated knowledge, 73, 161; and subversion of post-formal realm, 155; and technicist teacher education, 20; tendency of modernism to seek simple answers, 128; and transcendental signified, 112

Equilibration (Piaget), 116–20

Evaluation, 130; formal (Piagetian) procedures, 143; hidden assumptions of, 184; and post-formal notion of relationship, 152, 202; and self-reflection, 202

Explicate order, 101, 102, 103, 148–49

Factoids, 8

The family: decline of, 87; and electronic communication, 87

Feminist theory: challenge to central concepts of academic disciplines, 78; challenge to Piagetian logocentrism, 126, 153; and cooperation, 76; and critical thinking, 26; and critique of objective thinking, 154; and critique of patriarchal thinking, 75–78; and diverse models of cognition, 140, 203, 207; and ethic of caring, 59, 76, 78, 79, 140, 208, 223; expands definition of thinking, 126; and liberalism, 36, 79;

and life, 78; and multi-cultural-
ism, 207; and oppression of
women, 221; and the particular,
214; and passionate scholarship,
153, 155, 160, 203, 214; privileging of males as norm, 221; quest
for connected consciousness,
131–32, 140, 172, 178, 203; and
role of emotion in learning and
knowing, 160, 203; and self as instrument of understanding, 155;
and teacher awareness of patriarchy, 220; and teacher education,
204, 207; value of relationship,
76, 79, 132, 140

501 Jeans, as an example of
advertisers' use of symbols, 91

Formal thinking, 22, 65; and abstraction, 140, 154; and adult thinking, 140, 142; and creativity,
168; and discrete cognitive
stages, 139–44; and disembedded
thought, 117, 154; disinterestedness, 143; emphasis on logico-
mathematical ability, 141, 154;
and explicate order, 148, 149;
and generalizations, 120, 214;
and logocentrism, 126, 154, 167;
and problem solving, 129, 140,
141, 143, 160; procedural thinking, 119, 141, 142, 178; separates
teaching and ethics, 119; student
perceptions do not matter, 139;
tendency to deemphasize accommodation, 117

*Frames of Mind: The Theory of Mul-
tiple Intelligences* (Gardner), 60

Functionalism, 9–10

Fundamentalist Christians, 5, 50–
51, 158, 179

Gender, 13, 37, 38, 44, 48, 52, 53,
56, 59, 69, 70, 73, 75–78, 85, 89,
92, 102, 109, 112, 113, 126, 127,
140, 149, 154, 159, 178, 182,
198, 203, 204, 219, 220, 221,
223, 230

Get Off My Cloud, as an example of
meaning depending on context,
162

Higher order cognition, 6, 23, 50,
51, 70, 75, 117, 125, 130, 138,
140, 143, 149–50, 155, 158, 169,
173, 185, 188, 216, 221

High-tech jobs, 83

Hopi, 7

How-to: academically contextualized notion of, 211; coequal to
knowing what, 212; deemed impractical, 12; devaluation of, 211

Identity: breakdown of Cartesian
self, 95, 96; construction of, 13,
87–88, 90, 94–97, 123–24, 144,
182, 205; death of the subject,
96; and disembedding of personal knowledge, 120; divided
self, 104; formation of emotional
investments, 87; individual's
story of self-production as grand
narrative, 119; and language, 95;
as pastiche, 87; postmodern
multiphrenia, 95, 96, 97, 205;
and power, 128; protean self, 95–
97; self-reflection, 94, 120

Implicate order, 101–2, 148–49

Individualism: and consciousness,
198; critical reconstruction of,
88; middle-class notion of, 88;
and motivation of students, 88;
and postmodernism, 88, 127

Indo-European languages, devaluation of relationship, 6

Industrial revolution, 206

Information producers: seduce public into collaboration, 86, 87; sep-

arated from information consumers, 86

Jaynesian connected consciousness: the analog "I," 132; the analog "you," 135–36; can only be described metaphorically, 132; conciliation, 133; critical conciliation, 136–37; critical excerption, 134–35; critical narratization, 136; critical spatialization, 133–34; critical volition, 137–38; excerption, 132; the metaphor "me," 133; the metaphor "us," 135–36; narratization, 133; and post-formal thinking, 137–38, 183; post-Jaynesian connected consciousness, 183; spatialization, 132

Knowledge of academic disciplines, 62

Liberalism, 43, 52–53, 68, 70, 73, 79
Liberation theology, 72
Ludic postmodernism: critical appropriation of, 90; as opposed to critical postmodernism, 85

Masculinity, 57, 89, 90
Marlboro advertisements, Douglas Kellner's use of, 90
Miller Lite Beer, advertisers' game plan for, 89
Modernism: androcentrism, 189; birth of, 1–3, 77; Cartesian dualism, 28, 114; cause-effect logic, 6, 7, 28, 30, 120, 166–73, 186; certainty, 6, 8, 22, 34, 62, 104, 111, 114, 128–29, 131, 144, 147, 171, 179, 180, 213; and community of consensus, 67, 70; devaluing of emotion, 52, 78, 153, 154; disdain of spiritual, 172; effi-

ciency and, 7–8, 68; and explicate order, 101, 102, 103; and formal thinking, 120; fragmented thinking of, 5, 20, 29, 102, 122, 157, 163, 172; impedes accommodation, 122; justice, 79; language as neutral medium of conversation, 6, 43, 113; liberalism's valuing of process, 52, 79; methods of physical science, 45; and misogyny, 77; negation of caring, 78; pedagogical expressions of, 5; and personal knowledge, 78; positivism, 44, 45, 189, 214; and prediction, 120; and progress, 99, 100; rationalism, 52, 77, 79, 81, 114, 149–50; realism, 114; reductionism, 42, 60, 103, 113–16, 128–31, 149, 163, 165, 168, 217; scientific knowledge, 17, 29, 77, 164; shaping of twentieth-century pedagogy, 9–24, 28; static notion of self, 124; and survival of species, 75–78; technical rationality, 149–50; thinking as mirror of external events, 110; thinking shaped by rigid constructs, 217; and time, 13, 68, 168, 172; unable to study mind, 28; view of knowledge, 3, 32; the world as a mechanical system, 2, 103
Multiculturalism, 68, 70, 161, 202–3, 206, 207

Name of the Rose (Eco), 209
Native Americans, 66, 225
The Neanderthal Man, 71
Nude Descending a Staircase (Du-Champ), 160

The Origin of Consciousness in the Breakdown of the Bicameral Mind (Jaynes), 132

Paradigm shift, 28–32, 122

Place, 13, 69, 70, 84, 85, 124, 127; brings the particular into focus, 164; linking particular with general, 215

Pleasure, 86, 93, 94

Politics of thinking: ability to expose hidden assumptions, 36; action research, 178; alignment with the disempowered, 38, 39, 74; cognitive passivity and political freedom, 40–43; commodification of thinking, 55; discursive practices, 39, 138; and emotionality, 58; focus on educational outcomes exaggerates importance of cognitive processes, 188; and gender, 75–78, 119; the ideological consequences of cognitive style, 26, 40–43, 45, 119, 187, 190; and intelligence, 36, 41, 47, 60, 68, 69, 70, 73, 74, 96, 169–71; invisibility of the political, 49, 50, 51, 53, 187–89; mobilization of consent, 58; modernist separation of political from cognitive, 168; overcoming political naivete, 43–44, 54; and postmodernism, 27, 39, 69, 96, 97; power dimensions of thinking act, 26, 35, 38, 39, 90, 96, 97, 169–71; privileging of abstraction, 75, 77, 119; and reading of media, 90, 190; reclaiming subjugated voices, 59, 68, 69, 71–75, 178; right-wing reform, 179; seduction of neutrality, 26, 38, 45, 72; seeing beyond the surface of reality, 190; and social practice, 27–51; and teacher education, 198–99; teacher unawareness, 39, 169; value of diversity, 59–62, 74, 118

Popular culture, 38, 41, 42, 57, 92, 93–95, 124

Post-formal thinking: abandoning of certainty, 50, 104–5, 130, 131, 142; adolescents, 140; asking unique questions, 149–51, and the body, 154, 155, 214; cognitive cubism, 160, 161; cognitive revolution, 172, 179, 183; and connected consciousness, 131–38; connecting logic and emotion, 153–56, 160; contextualizing, 79, 161–63, 188, 189, 192–93; creation of one's own knowledge, 145, 192, 208, 209; and critical system of meaning, 143–50; deconstruction, 54, 61, 66, 165–67, 171, 224; deep structures, 102, 148–49; and difference, 66, 136, 191, 221; and discourse analysis, 190; disengagement from social forces, 23; distinguishing between knowledge and habit, 164–65; draws upon ethical impulses, 44; elasticity of, 145, 172; eludes specific definition, 27, 145; and empathy, 160–62, 193; and etymology, 142, 158–59, 172; expands boundaries of sophisticated thinking, 125–26, 140, 203; exposes hidden assumptions, 149; facts as parts of larger processes, 157–58; and fundamentalism, 50–51; and genealogy, 159; high complexity teachers and adaptability, 130; holographic mind and holographic reality, 157–58, 160, 172; and ideology, 129, 146, 206; and the implicate order, 102, 148, 149, 152, 157, 158, 160, 162, 168, 172, 193; and intelligence, 29; interaction of particularity and generalization, 163–64, 214–15; and interpretation, 50, 51, 79–80, 143; and isolation of events, 162; knowing involves transform-

ing reality, 60, 64–65, 156; levels
of connection between mind and
ecosystem, 171–73; and making
of history, 65; meta-awareness,
138–39, 150; metaphoric cognition, 151–53; moves beyond abstract reasoning, 65, 78–79;
moves beyond problem solving,
129, 141, 143, 150, 151; negation
of cognitive essentialism, 128–
31; non-linear holism, 167–68;
no text is beyond questioning,
139; and origins of knowledge,
141, 143, 158–60; and parody,
147; and the play of the imagination, 146–48; post-conventional,
139; reconsideration of cognitive
stage theory, 139–44; rejects objectivity, 143; revealing patterns
of life-forces, 171–73; role of
power in shaping representations
of the world, 168–71; and role of
reader, 166; as science fiction
writers of education, 171; science
viewed as text, 166; self-reflection, 22, 29, 130, 131, 139, 146,
202; and significance, 189; and
synchronocity, 171, 172; texts
viewed as code and symbol systems, 50, 79–81, 165–67; thinking about thinking, 146–48, 177,
185, 188, 192, 208; transcendence of egocentrism, 131–38;
transcendence of psychologizing,
143; uncovers cultural fictions,
64; vaccine against cognitive illness, 29
Postmodern condition: and advertising, 57; arises from world created
by modernism, 6; change of
change, 31, 100; climate of deceit, 90, 122, 139; cognitive illness, 28; commodification
process, 55; culture of consumerism, 89; crisis of motivation, 55,

88; hyperreality, 84–93, 95, 96,
97–99, 102, 121, 122, 183, 190,
198, 201, 210, 223, 225; image,
84, 88–93, 95; loss of community, 84, 88; and media, 42, 81,
83, 84, 88, 90, 91, 92, 93, 95, 99,
190, 219; and personal isolation,
83; postmodern manipulation,
90, 92, 93, 105; shaped by ethic
of manipulation, 56, 93, 97, 137;
and the sign, 88–93, 181; social
amnesia, 89; social vertigo, 84–
87; surrender of meaning, 85; undermines Piaget's stable
structures, 117
Postmodern critique: admits new evidence, 5; and aesthetics, 62–63;
alternate forms of teacher thinking, 7, 22, 80; anti-Cartesian tradition, 60, 114; and cognition,
27, 74; and the cognitive illness,
28–32, 122, 124, 129, 231; and
deconstruction, 85, 90, 91, 97,
98, 100, 112–13, 124; and difference, 67, 68, 69, 118, 155–56,
231; freedom from tyranny of
meanings, 80; grounded in critical theory, 85, 97–99, 109;
grounded in feminism, 79, 155,
156; humility of, 62, 76, 104,
131; and irony, 119; language
and, 7, 85, 111, 123, 190–91; localism, 70, 100–101; meaning reflects ideology, 129; multiple
perspectives, 62, 67, 112, 137,
140, 159–61; overcoming egocentrism, 131; and partiarchy, 75–
78; poststructuralism, 123, 129,
205; production of knowledge,
34; progressive social change
and, 5; public expression of empathy, 29, 160–61; and the reconceptualization of school purpose,
178; redefining life, 172; rejects
universal reason of formalism,

104; removal of social knowledge from its pedestal, 61; rescue of "primitive," 156; and risk of emancipation, 80; and self, 70, 94–97, 111, 127, 131, 139, 192; simultaneity, 6, 160, 168; social imagination, 93–95; solidarity, 67, 68, 72, 178, 198; takes us beyond nihilism of modern world, 6, 81, 96; teacher knowledge, 32–36, 48–49; textual analysis used to uncover power, 85, 112
Postmodern physics, 101–4
Power: acts like superego, 169; and advertising, 86; and affect, 86; complex manifestation of, 128; and the construction of experience, 43, 48, 95, 188; and democracy, 99; and discursive practices, 17, 48, 92, 95, 112, 113; and human will (volition), 137; ignored in most cognitive theory, 143; informational technology, 86, 92; inhibits critical accommodation, 169; irrelevant in measurement of intelligence, 170–71; and knowledge, 48–49, 52, 169, 212; and language, 85, 95, 109, 206; masking of, 64, 99; plays an exaggerated role in the construction of consciousness, 191; pleasure and social control, 86, 93, 94; and post-formal thinking, 169–71; in postmodern hyperreality, 86, 92, 95, 97, 98, 99; produces myths of inferiority, 49; reason is a social construction, 144; and self-production, 128; sharing of, 43, 53; status quo protected by ideological innocence, 187; and teacher research, 185; and teaching, 12, 112; and tracking, 13, 49; uncovered by semiotic analysis, 98–99; validation of, 49

Praxis, 80, 85, 98, 119, 189, 198, 203

Quantum physics, 6

Race, 12, 13, 27, 37, 38, 49, 53, 66, 69, 70, 73, 76, 85, 86, 102, 109, 118, 126, 127, 149, 159, 161, 182, 189, 198, 203, 221, 223, 230
Radical love, 59
Reading education, 8, 23–24, 53, 130
Research as a cognitive act: action research as a way of life, 193; analysis of the assumed, 190; analytical orientation, 192; anticipatory accommodation, 193; aware of metaphors that shape meaning, 180; becoming knowledge producers, 192; cognitive sophistication through research, 192–93; consciousness raising, 177; cultivates empathy, 193; extends epistemological analysis, 180; extends teacher's ability to perceive and act, 180; interpretation, 192; knowledge not something to be discovered, 180; learning to teach ourselves, 193; negates reliance on procedural thinking, 193; seeing what's not there, 189–91; self-reflection, 180, 191, 192; transcending modernist thinking, 175; why we see what we see, 188
Rosebud Sioux Reservation, 225

Scientific management: of educational workplace, 177; pedagogy and, 7, 13; and proponents of human capital development, 55; and standardization, 20
Scientific method, 4, 22, 129, 168, 179, 183, 215

Sexual preference, 69, 89, 198
Solidarity, 67, 68, 72, 178, 198, 231
Something Wild, and image of the rebel, 86
"Stop Making Sense," 85
Students: construction of consciousness, 51, 124, 138, 159, 184, 225, 230; and difference, 67; establishing a critical dialogue with, 208; grounding curriculum on questions asked by, 151; and information which disrupts world views, 118, 121; as partners in the study of teacher thinking, 223; and popular culture, 94; post-formal curriculum constructed around lives of, 181, 202, 207; post-formal reinterpretation of student lives, 145, 224; relation between knowledge and experience of, 152, 206, 207; as researchers, 201; stories of, 207, 210; the struggle to gain sense of self, 59; teaching themselves in pedagogy, 223
Subjugated knowledge, 71–75, 97, 199

Talking Heads, 85
Teacher education: and achievement of students, 64; and action research, 197, 223–26; alienation from traditional academic culture, 15; analysis of student constructions of reality, 38; apprenticeships, 196; and autobiography, 210; banking view of, 11; behavioral form of, 10–11, 12; concern with affective domain, 203; and conformity, 21; and confrontation with myths that oppress, 210; conservative students, 14; critical postmodern form, 33, 34, 37–38, 47, 92, 109, 119, 201–2, 207, 208, 209, 210–

11, 220–23; as critical reflection, 220–23; and democracy, 36, 92, 202, 207, 210, 227–29; and developmental psychology, 127; emphasis of novice survival, 14; and epistemological analysis, 47, 108; and expertise, 199–203; failure of reform of, 203–5; fitting prospective teachers to school, 180, 196–97, 205; and generic theory, 204, 205; grounded in practical knowledge of teachers, 216; hegemonic adapting of teachers to school, 227, 230; ideological studies, 197–98; individualist ethic, 11, 13; and information studies, 92, 210; and linguistic analysis, 206; and media analysis, 91–92; and methodological recipes, 14, 115; methods courses, 34, 207, 208, 217, 223; modernist devaluation of theory, 183; must understand consciousness construction, 109, 210; paradigms of, 195–97; and pluralism, 203; political dimension of, 198–99, 204; post-formal form of, 197–98, 199–203, 209–10, 211; power, 38, 39, 64, 92, 197; praxis, 203; and procedural thinking, 204; and the production of knowledge, 205–11; rationalism and, 10, 19; and reflective practice, 205, 220–26; research, 33, 37, 45–46, 180, 211; and school change, 229–31; and the separation of cognition from context, 23, 33; and social theory, 203; socio-cognitive mapping, 119; student teaching, 37, 218, 226–27; teacher-proof curricula, 20; teachers as self-directed learners, 210; technical teacher education, 10–16, 20–21, 28, 35, 36, 161, 199, 204, 205, 227; thinking-in-action, 33, 201–2, 216, 217; top-down power flow, 20

Teacher knowledge: critical grounding of practical form of, 215–17; development of, 32, 33, 34; kinetic form of, 183; postmodern respect for, 104; teachers producing their own, 34–35, 145, 192, 207, 208, 209; validation of, 39, 183

Teachers-as-researchers, 22, 33, 37; action research as an oppositional activity, 179–82; assume role of knowledge producers, 181, 183, 184; autobiography, 155, 185; biography, 185; controlling research design, 177; criteria of critical research, 175; and critical theory, 182–85; educational change ultimate goal of, 184; emancipatory communities of researchers, 176, 178; and epistemological analysis, 177, 211, 225; ethnography, 34, 91, 119, 181, 211, 222, 223, 226; expose ideological restrictions, 189; expose tyranny of teaching workplaces, 180; as genealogists, 159; helps overcome perception of teachers as low-level workers, 176; historiography, 118, 155, 181, 211; improving thinking by researching, 192–93; incompatible with vanguardism, 176; interpretation of school life, 184, 212; and knowledge, 130, 181–82, 183, 184, 186; phenomenology, 37, 119, 181; purpose is three dimensional, 189; reinterpreting texts, 180; semiotics, 34, 37, 91, 98–99, 119, 155, 181, 189–91, 211, 215, 222, 224, 226, 228; study the meaning of learning experiences to students, 190; and teacher empowerment, 178–79;

theater, 155; uncovering sociocognitive maps of students, 119, 225; uncritical appropriation of, 185–87; and value neutrality, 187–89

Teacher thinking: alternate forms of, 7; and ambiguity, 130; art of improvisation, 201–32; and autonomy as professionals, 26, 34, 71; aware of power, 201; cognitive growth vis-à-vis cognitive manipulation, 55–58; committed to world making, 201; constricted view of, 10; critical accommodation, 41; and the cultivation of situated participation, 202; decontextualization of, 14, 21, 46, 100; discursive nature of knowledge, 138; and empirical research, 19; engagement with symbols of a culture, 54; execution of expert conceptualizations, 71, 176; and feminist theory, 16, 160; generalization not helpful in classroom, 163; high complexity teacher, 130; holographic view of students, 160, 161; hyper-rationality, 25, 44; inquiry oriented, 201, 202; knowledge producers construct curriculum around student lives, 181; learning by comparing different contexts, 41, 71–75; and media decoding, 90; negotiation of role, 31–32; overview of forms of teacher thinking, 200–201; post-formal, 22, 23, 27, 29, 44, 50, 54, 61, 66, 79–81, 125, 201–2; postmodern uncertainty, 33, 104, 161; post-Piagetian form, 22, 41, 125; and power, 201; self-analysis, 109, 130, 161, 176, 178, 202, 218; shaped by social context, 34, 38, 41; situated practitioner cognition, 200; teachers as intellectuals, 11; technicist form of, 19, 40; transcending traditional scientific ways of seeing, 1

Teaching: and accountability, 21; centrality of interpretation, 113; child-centered pedagogy, 127; conventional forms often rewarded, 188; and decoding, 90; and deconstruction, 90, 91; and difference, 67, 71, 74, 118; and discursive rules of the classroom, 223, 224; examination of cognitive structures which impede change, 118; and fragmentation of knowledge for memorization, 23, 24; and indoctrination, 42, 43, 118, 209; as information delivery, 187, 226; and learning to be administered, 219–20; measurement of good teaching, 12; media education, 91; and metaphorical spaces, 74; monitoring of student accommodation, 121; as neo-white man's burden, 199; post-formal teacher, 145; and the postmodern condition, 83, 90, 91; the postmodern curriculum, 91; and power, 12, 90, 112; problems are not standardized, 216; rewards for reflecting dominant ideology, 41; science of, 23–24, 32, 33; silence on social forces which shape, 12–13; and student experience, 66, 121, 138; teacher empowerment, 17, 31–35; that reveals victims of oppression, 72, 74; of thinking, 115, 118, 145; uncertain nature of, 213; understanding student consciousness, 138, 145, 191, 224; as virtuoso performance, 32–33; of writing, 224

Theory of relativity, 148
Tibetan Buddhism, 147
Time, 13, 29, 68–69, 168, 172

Vocational education, 13, 49

Watson-Glaser Critical Thinking Appraisal (WGCTA), 141
Women crusaders of the nineteenth century, 156
Women's ways of knowing, 22, 26, 59, 75–78, 79, 126, 131–32, 140, 153, 154, 155, 156, 160, 203, 208, 214, 223
Workers, 8, 51, 55–56, 83, 94, 199

About the Author

JOE L. KINCHELOE is Professor of Education at Florida International University. He is the author of six books on education, specifically related to a radical approach to teaching, and of numerous articles on the subject.